High_Scapes

Alps

edited by Pino Scaglione

Content from the first edition of
The ALPS Biennial, Alpine Landscape and Mountains Biennial,
Trento/Rovereto 20-21 June 2008

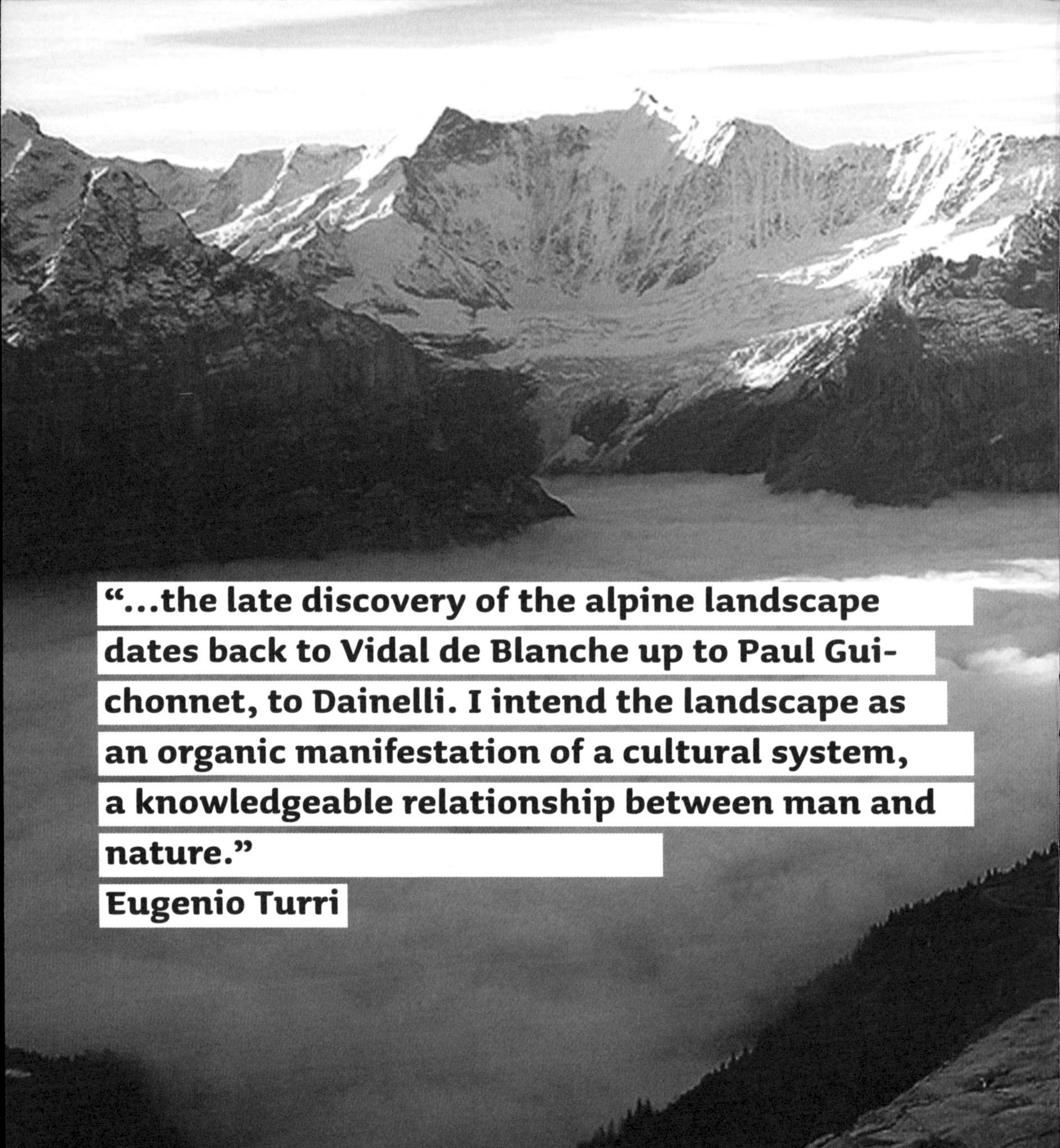

"...the late discovery of the alpine landscape dates back to Vidal de Blanche up to Paul Guichonnet, to Dainelli. I intend the landscape as an organic manifestation of a cultural system, a knowledgeable relationship between man and nature."

Eugenio Turri

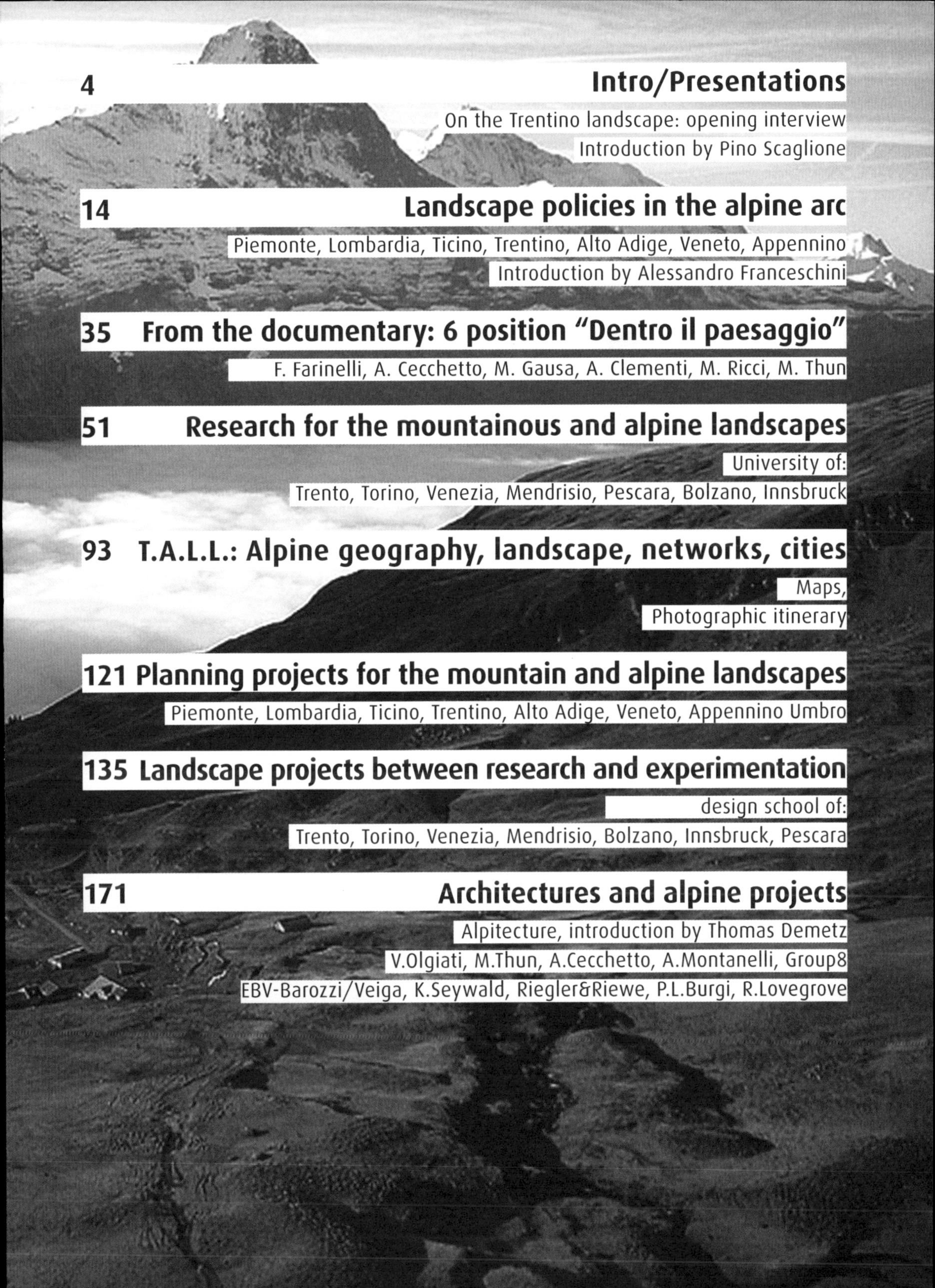

Presentations

Lorenzo Dellai

With interest and satisfaction: I want to interpret this first edition of the Alps Biennial in such terms. Interest for the reason that the Alpine Landscape and Mountains Biennial which decides to position evident topics linked to our daily lives in the midst of the argument - such are the landscape, cities, European alpine arc's architecture -, that helps each and every one of us understand how to confront delicate issues, decisive for the quality of life and the environment, however closely associated to the economic development, agriculture, as well as the cultural sphere. Satisfaction because it is our land, Trentino, that places itself as a crossroad in this moment of conflict, entrusted to more languages and suggestions accurately condensed in this volume. The exhibitions and seminars hosted by the borough of Trento and Rovereto have been the occasions to reflect about the landscape from many perspectives that have given the chance to think of the new changes in our territory as the plug for a common and shared experience from many regions as well as the nations of the alpine arc. Trentino has also set the landscape in the center of planifying activity of our territory with the recent approval of the new Urbanism Plan of Trentino. Landscape is not obviously intended with aesthetic value – that from the end of the nineteenth century has rendered our land notable – but above all, as a box of shared values by a community that build the identity of a population. In a time where globalization may render cultural and traditional heritage trivial, Trentino has decided to invest its own energy and attention to the acknowledgment of its own collective identity, history and cultural heritage. In the belief that the challenges that time quickly imposes can be handled only alongside the attention for technological innovation as well as research, we will then know how to keep our feet firmly welded to our roots, or rather our landscape.

President of Autonomous Province of Trento

Davide Bassi

New research on alpine landscape starting from the University of Trento. ALPS, the biennial exhibition on Alpine Landscape Project Sustainability, is a new initiative which, through the coordination of the Faculty of Engineering of our University, brings together several prestigious universities of the Italian and European Alpine area and stimulates, by means of seminars and meetings, scientific contact and exchange among them. In the last few years the landscape has been object of more and more up-to-date and transversal research activities in different university study courses with focus on the many transformations which the landscape has undergone. These are treated also in the European Landscape Convention undersigned by all countries, Italy included. The University of Trento has recently joined Uniscape, the European network of universities for the implementation of this convention and for the deepening and supporting of research and teaching on the fundamental issue of human and territorial resources. Thanks to this biennial initiative, the related prize for studies, research and projects on landscape, all seminars and workshops and all the results of these activities, the University of Trento intends to become more and more an attentive and expert partner for those institutions and research centres which want to deepen and use our knowledge and competence as an occasion for the relaunching of advanced policies necessary to protect the landscape and increase its value. For a better and more sustainable future of environment and settlements.

Rector of the University of Trento

Marco Tubino

From time now, landscape has also grown in the scientific interest of research performed by the Departments of the College of Engineering of the University of Trento. Alongside the traditional effort to read the changes in the territory as well as the peculiarity of the alpine environmental system (from ecologic, hydraulic, geomorphologic perspectives), in Trento the fields that are in charge of the landscape project have more constantly been taking space and consideration. The teaching staff, researchers and students of the degree course in engineering construction/architecture, for some years now, have in fact been working actively to confront the studies of the landscape, often characterized from the interpretation of theoretic and philosophic nature, a planning approach defined by the convergence of such fields of study that from the urbanism, to the architectural composition, infrastructural engineering and ecology have the construction of the open space as its objective. Traditional intervention on the landscape of engineerical type cannot be viewed only from the functional perspective. Today in fact, more than ever, it occurs that the various competences which professionals apply to the landscape work to give handwork – above all, those visible also at a large scale - the shape and significance that makes human operation in the landscape a well placed event in the conditions of the surroundings and positively accepted by the local communities. In this way, the Alpine Landscape and Mountains Biennal has been an important occasion – and these acts are the evidence – of harmonious convergence that the fields and educational experiences can have. Of particular interest is the part that this volume dedicates to the academic research projects and the effort of didactic experimentation of the various universities located on the alpine arc. An occasion to share experiences and results with the goal of constituting the "network" in which the landscape is probably the most evident metaphor.

Dean of Faculty of Engineering, University of Trento

Guglielmo Valduga

In June 2008 Rovereto hosted the opening day and the exhibition of the first edition of the Alpine Landscape Biennial: ALPS.
The "quercia" city has then so been nominated to be a "landscape" city. This is also the philosophy that guides the new program in which the term "landscape" is meant as a group of locations that communicate among themselves at different scales; locations that are responsible for the bond with society, economy, history; and that find their most profound significance in the relationship with men that contemplate, travel and transform them. Therefore, Rovereto "the landscape city", regardful of the evolution of research and an innovative outlook that regards this delicate and primary common good, conserved in our alpine landscapes as well as history and urban dimension of the city itself. Besides the actual issues – from historical, collective, artistic and social assets – correlated to the quality of the environment, conveyed in its wholeness, can find argumentative areas and elaboration in the museum network that qualify the city.
The aspiration is that Rovereto will remain and be certified as the landscape city in Trentino as well as beyond, more appealing not only to researchers but tourism that will open new and enduring possibilities.

Mayor of Rovereto

Trento for the alpine landscape

Non very many years ago, the word landscape had an eminently aesthetic definition. It was enough to think of an expression as common as "postcard scenery", that almost identified the landscape with the view, panorama, of a far off place populated by old farmers and patient shepherds. Secondly, landscape was considered a natural element: therefore not the result of human labor, rather a motionless scenic painting with nature that in some cases was portrayed in a benevolent or malignant way. Today fortunately the concept of landscape evokes more complex definitions: landscape is a shared good by the community, it is the mirror reflection of its identity, it is the seismograph that records the state of health of a geographic area and those who inhabit it. Landscape defines who we are, what are values are, what are the results of our choices. Unmistakably, landscape is the judgment of the quality of relationship between man and the environment, between development and natural resources. All this being so, it is clear that the landscape deserves more attention than what has been granted up till now from our mercantile and utilitarian civility. Ascertain that the return to nature tout court is impossible, to cultivate the idea of an intact and almost mythical mountain is futile, there is nothing left but to govern the present searching a new balance, the most advanced possible, between nature and settlements. In my opinion, Alps-Biennial of alpine landscape and mountains commits this research of possible and operable solutions. That if taken care of, are not "lower" compromises, but simply courses capable of coalescing a high cultural profile to concreteness. To this purpose, I think that one of the most important merits of Alps is that of favoring the confrontation – and therefore the emulation – between projects and already experimented suggestion in the reality of the alpine arc. In other terms, Alps contributes to diffuse the knowledge of virtuous examples, experimented and adopted solutions that will be taken and adapted according to the context. In fact, often the alpine cities, like Trento, have found themselves assuming service functions, becoming a reference point for the surrounding territory. This has exposed them to a series of risks: the subversion of the primal urban system, above all, with the cementation of new areas. No less dangerous has the invasion of the so-called "city users", outliers that travel by automobile rendering roads and parking lots completely insufficient. The landscape cannot become unaffected by these factors: a disharmonic growth can result fatal not only for the landscape, but the dwelling and urban identity itself. Precisely to avoid the risk of excessively expanding the outskirts, Trento has, for example, chosen a plan that does not aim towards expanding but the redevelopment of internal spaces of the city, abandoned buildings, factories and brownfields that have seized production and that because of this should have been regained for new purposes and new urban quality. To avoid consuming other territory, a resource that is not abundant in the mountains, the new urban segments of future Trento will therefore originate not because of explosion, but implosion, through the overcoming and adjustment of lapsed functions of the ever changing demands of the citizens.

In the alpine city, the quality of landscape is dually linked to urbanism quality that cannot be disregarded from the capacity of interpreting the historical stratification as future circumstances. As it is, the topics to develop are numerous, solutions to be individuated, corrections to be introduced so that an alpine city can define its landscape's vocation better.

It is therefore a golden opportunity for Trento, along for Rovereto, to become a workshop for the topics of the landscape's construction (and not just conservation) both for those who have scientific interest for the matter as well as for administrators and citizens interested in the future of our city. Above all, in my opinion, this volume, rich in ideas, will give a wonderful contribution to the debate often paralyzed by the conflicting integral opposition. I think that this is the Alps' bet: to pull through controversy from going from drawing petitions to the concreteness of solutions. Not only will the cultural debate obtain advantages but our landscape as well.

Alessandro Andreatta, mayor of Trento

Trentino: province of landscapes
Interview with Mauro Gilmozzi

Trentino has just approved the new town planning law and the PUP (Provincial Town Planning Scheme). What role does the landscape have within this context?
The PUP represents a plan for the future of Trentino, namely the situation towards which the provincial area planning system intends to work in order to realise the medium-long term expectations of the community. In this context, as compared to environmental and socioeconomic issues at European or even global level, the PUP represents a strategic framework for the definition of action at area level aimed at coordinated and shared development.
This strategic aspect of the new plan revolves above all around the issue of the landscape, understood not merely as an aesthetic aspect - a "picture postcard" – but rather as an expression of the identity of this province and an element reinforcing the competitiveness of the area. The landscape is something with which we identify, not only in terms of the elements conserved, but also in relation to its transformation and the sharing of common values, recalling that the values which count are those that evolve over time, allowing dialogue with the world and generating opportunities and innovation. Identity is not a trademark, but rather a dynamic context which is chosen and created over time; in this context the landscape described in the PUP relates to a network of relationships relating to our historical and cultural background.
The landscape also has to do with the appeal of the area and the "framework of conditions" which are so significant, also in terms of global economics, for the competitiveness of those working in this area, determining its growth and development.
In this context planning of the landscape is an important and innovative challenge of the new PUP, precisely because it proposes an approach intended to overcome the dichotomy between what is "offered" by the area and limitations in terms of "not doing". The approved plan puts quality, the excellence of the area, the environment and the landscape at the centre of development strategies.

What concrete action has been taken in Trentino in order to interpret and apply the European convention on the landscape?
Trentino is an area in which local identities have been the driving force for models of development, much more so than in other regions, even in alpine areas. What is more, Trentino, together with Alto Adige, is a province that has limited the decline and abandoning of mountain areas in an exemplary manner. One of the reasons for Trentino's capacity to hold onto these areas lies precisely in the fact that the development model, within which each part of the area has found its own reasons for remaining and growing, is strongly linked to the resources present in the area: in Trentino there is a sense of ownership - private/collective - of the area and in relation to the correct use of its resources.

The experts who have assisted in the work to revise the PUP believe that there are social and economic reasons for this, but that it is also related to cultural roots, in that area identity is embodied in a sense of common ownership of the landscape.
While the concept of "landscape" as perceived by the population - and hence intrinsically linked to the identity of the area and the community - is a particularly innovative element of the convention, this concept is given substance and application in the new PUP, counting on the fact that there is a strong local ability to interpret the landscape and ensure it becomes a driving force for enhancement.

The approved PUP sees the interweaving of action to safeguard and enhance the landscape. Can you summarise the most significant features?
The landscape charter represents a summary of the new approach, protection and exploitation representing two sides of the same coin. In essence, through the development of this charter, interpretation of the landscape and its fundamental elements is incorporated into area planning and the area is regulated bearing in mind the safeguarding of representative landscapes and the enhancement of what makes up the identifying framework of the community. In this way the coherence of any intervention to transform the area - the so-called "if" - is already verified in preparing the plan, not merely postponing safeguarding to control of "how" building takes place. In line with this approach, the new system for management of the area provides for unification of the organs responsible for the control of planning tools and building works through the town-planning law, with an awareness that verification of the effects on the area must initially be carried out on the basis of tools - such as the landscape charter - which are intended precisely to highlight the specific characteristics and relationship of elements distinguishing the area.

As councillor for town planning, one of your measures has been the introduction of regulations tending to limit building in important agricultural areas, hence safeguarding the agrarian landscape. Can you explain the origin of this need?
Agricultural areas represent just 10% of the province and the 1987 PUP, despite relatively strict regulations, nevertheless did not succeed in limiting erosion of these areas and their transformation into residential areas.
When we began work on the new plan, the need to defend the agricultural role and landscape of these areas and at the same time to ensure their permanence in quantitative terms through compensation was shown to be inescapable, not just following requests from representative associa-

tions but also as an appeal to safeguard resources for future generations, Agricultural areas are thus targeted for cultivation, with the specific objective of safeguarding products with a protected designation of origin, which already significantly characterise Trentino agriculture, ensuring conservation of the landscape, protecting it both from urban development and on the other hand from abandon and afforestation.
The town planning law regulates methods for ensuring compensation for transformed agricultural land and establishes a steering group of departments to check on admissible and functional building work for farms in relation to the agricultural and town-planning profile.

To sum up: in your opinion, what characterises the Trentino landscape within the alpine context?
In the much wider and varied context of the Alps, Trentino is characterised by a landscape which makes its way down from the peaks, seeing the development of pasture, woods, lakes, watercourses, countryside and historic centres.
However at the same time Trentino is marked by a strong identity deriving both from the uniqueness of certain assets, the relationship between developed and intact areas and urban development, which still takes on very recognisable forms of identity from valley to valley.
The Dolomites, perhaps among the most beautiful mountains in the world and not by chance a possible UNESCO natural world heritage site, act as a background to the different Trentino valleys; woods cover more than half the area, in which nature parks, areas of community interest, biotopes and lakes are almost a demonstration of a widespread and high level of naturalness; each watercourse Is classified, also in terms of environmental values, within a specific plan; important crops, olive groves, vineyards and apple orchards are carefully highlighted and safeguarded and lastly the historic towns, different in each valley, are planned with the same care.
All this demonstrates that the Trentino landscape is still marked by its quality and intact nature, characteristics which we have been so well aware of that since the 1960s we have conceived, adopted and managed town planning tools at times general, at times specific, but always innovative.

Interview with Mauro Gilmozzi
Provincial Councillor for Town Planning at the Autonomous Province of Trento
by Pino Scaglione

Introduction
ALPS: a biennal for the alpine landscape

The wide context of the alpine territory, thus strongly marked by the presence of landscapes of exceptional value – and at the same time from a group of urban systems and urban centers that outline settings in progress of a widespread and diffused alpine city network – places the subject of and urgent reflection of the relation among settlement, networks and landscapes, above all to become in tune with the European policies in a delicate, as much as significant, sector of the community strategies.

Beginning from some EU official documents, in the course of elaboration of the research launched in the College of Engineering of Trento – in collaborations with universities and other public and private structures – about contemporary and actual topics of the landscape policies, objective of the Biennial Seminar and the initiative linked to it, is to aim to contribute in the Trentino/South Tyrol context – and pervasively in a confrontation with the regions of the whole Italian-European Alpine Arc – to define new, advanced and oriented methods of operation in this important field of territorial resources, which configures to be the landscape. In the case of the alpine system, and that of the mountains more widely in areas and geographic context, thus significantly distinguished from the presence of optimum locations, as much of a strong drive to civilization, as well as settlment models, sometimes exasperating, set against the necessity of innovation as for the protection and valorization. Traditional planning instruments, territorial and urban plans and programs of classic settings and conceptions, have difficulty in comprehending, governing and proposing adequate policies for the landscape in new, more certified and effective acceptance and the architectural models are also often inadequate and obsolete. In many new and original ways of research recently developed in Europe, a new shared direction is emerging that pushes towards solutions and processing of new methods of operation and culture, not only of the diffused sustainability, but one that can be founded based "on the recognition of landscape values in all the planning and government deeds of the urban and territorial changes in coherence, precisely, with the European Convention of the Landscape which is now fully operating (Clementi).

It is convenient and urgent to propose a work seminar in Trento and Rovereto, therefore in the Trentino area, today representing a model to recognize and redefine, – in a time which these issues have been discussed recently in Italy and that in Europe positive experimentation has been performed – to understand and to be aware of that created and how to improve movement for the future. This specifically means to reach a significant confrontation and elaboration with the more advanced production, at a wide geographic and cultural scale, particularly for what concerns policies and strategies of operation, adequate settlment models and quality architecture. Referring in the first place

to the exceptionality of the landscape of the "green heart" of Europe, which is the alpine system and of those parts – that are composing elements – that are outside of preservation areas, degraded, in disuse and neglected, as well as those that overflow with touristic activity, mobility along the infrastructure, as far as to include those parts, here present, of ordinary landscape or that pertain to the dynamics and contradictions of contemporary human settlement. From here on, the necessity, the opportunity – also considered the course of redefinition of the arrangements that the new PUP of Trentino is carrying on – of an appointment with pre-established regularity – every two years – that will be assumed and considered as an appointment of true "biennial of the European alpine landscape" (today existing only in Barcelona, mostly for the architecture of the landscape in general) nominating Trento, Rovereto and other cities, thus Trentino, a sort of "Davos of the landscape", which also binds the institution of a European Award for the most original research in the topic of the alpine landscape and mountains, this last one in collaboration with the Urbanism Department, Environment and Public Labor of the Province, University of Trento, municipalities of Trento, Rovereto, Riva del Garda and BorgoValsugana (in the first edition, awaiting to extend the rose in the next editions).
The activities of this first cycle were developed in June 2008, with a two-day seminar as well as an exhibition of alpine architecture of quality and a video projection. After the Economy festival, in order to continue, means understanding the landscape as a real and large economic, cultural and environmental resource of the Trentino territory and of the Alps. In the years following this first edition, further enterprise is expected in public occasions (an annual exhibition regarding the topic, workshops, seminars, books, research, etc.) and other places beyond Trento and Rovereto, like an itinerant biennial, followed by the ALPS Award as an occasion for other events. In this opportunity, the expected program, coordinated by the College of Engineering and of the University, in accordance with the Autonomous Province of Trento and other interested institutions, that from time to time will be able to join other structures of research and other interested institutions in the matter, both Italian and foreign, as results by the numerous supporters of this first edition. The documentary film "Alps- inside the landscape", filmed for the occasion, re-launches the topics of the Trentino and alpine landscape, but in general the actuality and centrality of this matter and issues linked to it, through images and contributions by the researchers. The ALPS newspaper has anticipated content and topics of the seminar, and with a collection of results of the whole program, this international volume comes to life, with the DVD of the documentary film attached, "Inside the landscape".

Pino Scaglione, University of Trento, Director of Biennale Alps

Landscape policies in the alpine arc

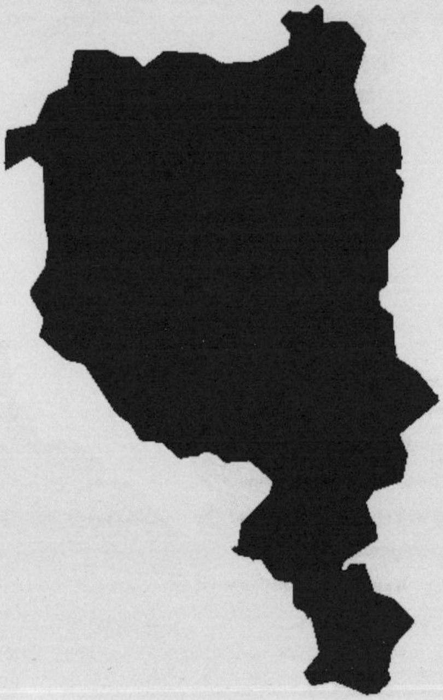

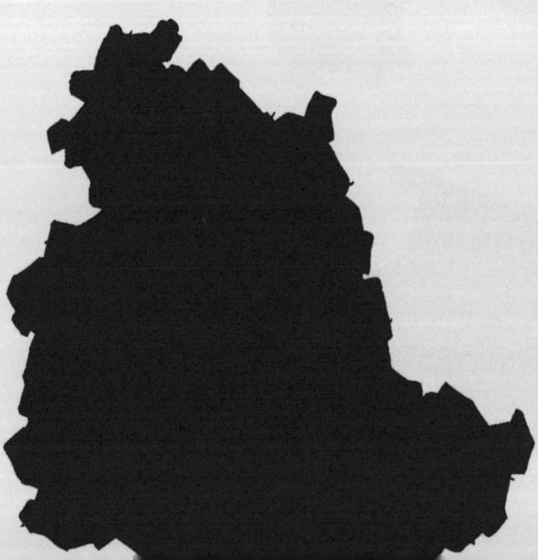

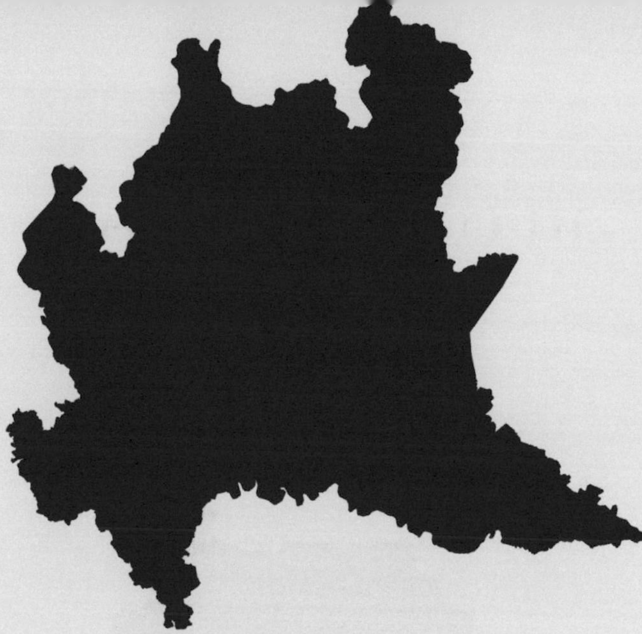

Landscape as a vast area

"Italy – wrote Giò Ponti the architect in his volume "Love Architecture" – was made half by God and half by architects". The volume was given to the press agency by the end of the 1950's, surely, the famous founder of the Domus magazine, would have never imagined that in the following decades the "bel paese" would immediately deconstruct its landscape due to its own "architecture" scarcely attentive to the Genius Loci and the peculiarities of our environmental system. A lack of attention and sensibility combined with the planning instruments and protection, have taken our peninsula to a stage of serious landscape compromise. The legislation has begun, in time relatively recent to reflect upon these alterations. Particularly, since the European Landscape Convention (signed in 2000 but ratified some years later from the members of the EU), the planning and normative regulations on the territory have started to favor, the most consolidated as well as less effective actions of protection in single parts of the territory, policies of landscape planning formed by integrated projects and redevelopment. Since eight years that the Convention was signed, the time has come to balance out how it has transformed the landscape planning at a vast scale, with particular reference to the alpine regions. In fact, this programming document along with the most recent "Urban Code" and the not yet sufficiently implemented "Rutelli Code" has represented a moment of a cultural turning point in the planning still to be deciphered and systematized today.
To understand how much the planifying approach of vast areas has changed, it is necessary to remember, alongside with these new instruments of planning, the paradigmatic change in the European environment and the birth of a new principle to which the planifying at a regional scale has its maximum legitimation, or to be more precise that of "subsidiarity". The principle was established in the Treaty of Maastricht (that regulate the affairs between the European Union and the Member State): "In areas which do not fall within its exclusive competence, - says the article - the Community shall take action, in accordance with the principle of subsidiarity, only if and in so far as the objectives of the proposed action cannot be sufficiently achieved by the Member States and can therefore, by reason of the scale or effects of the proposed action, be better achieved by the Community." From this point of view it appears evident how two topics of the urbanism policies make part of the planifying of provincial and regional areas: those that comply with the environmental systems (the protection and use of the natural and cultural resources, the landscape, the protection of the ground and water and the operations performed to prevent risks); and those that regard the great equipment of the territory viewed as the settlment system. The vast area is however the ideal context in which the local community, craftsmen of their own landscape, express itself. The landscape, as noted, is the fruit of labor

of a society on their own natural environment. And at the same time, the community itself is the fruit of a cultural script operated by the landscape on its inhabitants. The relation between landscape and consumer is mediated by the perception – term introduced by the Convention – that articulates the visual and social image of a part of the territory. This image is, in many cases, an image at an over municipal scale, because the expressive dimensions of the landscape rarely coincide with political limits of the organism of our administrative system. The regions and provinces that interface with the alpine space have not been considered without activating planifying policies aware of the new insights and instruments. The gathering of projects and experiences on vast areas which we propose in this section of the volume is just a brief selection of the efforts that the single administrations have accomplished to give sense to the precepts of the new petitions of the European norms and to pursue, at the same time, reclamation and redevelopment of those landscape fragments that constitute that unicum known by everyone, which is the alpine region.

An "alpine" setting

The following pages propose a small sample of the experiences in act of the landscape planifying at a regional scale in the Alps. This sequence has the objective of providing a unitary vision in the alpine range – at least in the Italian boundary – of the labor performed in recent years by the Regions and Provinces that have accomplished numerous and virtuous project efforts as well as conservation of the landscape, however, without the demand to use up the activity of the individual administrations but with the need to summarize in limited space the complex work of the management of the territory.

Piedmont Region: landscape as sustainability

The base concepts of the Regional Landscape Plan of Piedmont are those of quality of landscape and environment, viewed as base elements to launch a substantial development sustainable at a regional scale. The plan not only aims towards conserving the elements of the landscape's heritage (intended as the interaction of natural and anthropic elements), but the improvement of the quality of life in the territory as well, reinforcing the fascination and competitiveness in the global setting.

Lombardy Region: landscape as an opportunity

In Lombardy, the Regional Landscape Territory Plan is currently updating, approved in the 1950's, with strong anticipation of the attention to the planned landscape. This update is not just the consequence of the will to receive guidelines from the Urban Code, but above all the

opportunity to implement an integrated approach to the landscape, pursuing the involvement of various actors that are the real protagonist of the collective construction of the landscape.

Veneto Region: landscape as a quality

With the Piave Strategic Project of the Veneto Region, the objective is to coordinate and acknowledge, with a single planifying instrument, the territories that relate to the Dolomite landscape. This deals with the summation of specific areas, endowed with identities also very different among themselves, but associated by the will of promoting different cultural and natural values within an overall sketch of the landscape. The particular location of this area, in addition, positioned in boundary with the autonomous regions of northern Italy and with the transnational boundary, has requested a need to coordinate with the neighboring administrative systems.

The Province of Trento: landscape as an interpretation

In 2008, the second revision of the Provincial Urbanism Plan, the result of the improvement of the Giuseppe Samonà Plan (1967) and that of Franco Mancuso (1987). It deals with a plan, that at the same time, has the value of a landscape plan. For this reason, the interpretation of the landscape has a fundamental role in the construction of settings that result so well-endowed with incisive planning and straightforward tutelary action. The goal is to reach landscape not in a purely conservative sense, but as an occasion for a joint project.

Province of Bolzano: landscape as a resource

The province of Bolzano plans, along with the communal traditional instrument of planning (Puc), the Landscape Plans adapted at communal scale in tight synergy between central provincial administrations and local communities. This deals with a group of small effective instruments for the landscape management, seen first and foremost, as the projecting expression of the community settled in a particular place. Landscape is perceived, first of all, as a resource which the community has to primarily refer and look after according to principles of responsibility and interrupting naturally the precepts that form the European Landscape Convention.

Friuli Region: landscape as a value

Friuli Venezia Giulia has also elaborated a regional territorial plan. The primary objectives are those that surpass conservational logics limited to single parts of territory (or even single subjects), but to consider the landscape as a structural element of government policies of the territory. In this sense, fragmented preservation has been substituted by a safeguard generated by a conceptual and planned coincidence between territory and landscape that will constitute the "value" of the territory. Maximum conservation, in this way, is acknowledged in the areas not yet urbanized, while on the remaining parts of the territory the redevelopment actions of the systems and structures are scheduled where necessary.

Liguria Region: landscape as a system

Among the actions placed in range of the Liguria Region about the topic of redevelopment of the landscape, in review it could be the executed work to individuate a system of the green areas that cross al the regional territory. This system integrates the complex morphological environment system of the existing region taking the value of the green areas viewed, from one side, as elements to increase the quality of life, the green areas as an added value, and on the other side, as the occasion of economic and touristic advertisement of the territory, the green areas as an element that strengthens competitiveness.

Ticino: landscape as equilibrium

In 2007 the Swiss region of Ticino has adopted the Managing Plan different from the previous, launched 18 years before, it distinguishes itself by and approach that is released by the usual dynamic of the tutelary properties to consider valorization, redevelopment, promotive actions of the landscape. Not just attention to the environment's rich nature, but to all the aspects of the landscape, from those of the valley to those of the mountains, from the outskirts to the inner city, in concordance to the precepts of the European Landscape Convention and the most advanced planning and cultural sensibility.

An invitation to the reading

From this gathering of plans and projects in a vast area, it appears evident as if the encouragement has been the same for each administration (Urban Code, European Landscape Convention, Subsidiarity Principle), the results of the single regions and provinces have been characterized by a genuine action, mediated by the dominant culture of the single locations and instinctively linked to the particularity of the territorial context where they operated. It is exactly the discussion and understanding of the individual approaches that is the encouragement and reference for modern landscape planning, linked to the most advanced cultural petitions and projected in a future plan dimension, that is nothing but the essence of the landscape itself.

Alessandro Franceschini, Faculty of Engineering, University of Trento

PIEMONTE

Regional Landscape Plan

The Piedmont Region launched in 2005 a new phase of planning of the entire regional territory, that particularly involves the formation of the Landscape Regional Plan (PPR), under the Cultural and Landscape Heritage Code (D.Lgs. 42/2005) and the European Landscape Convention (Council of Europe, 2000). The present affair concludes the phase of the studies for the plan executed by the Polytechnic University of Turin and other collaborations and the "technical proposal" by which the region intends to develop the collaboration with other institutions and other social shares, beginning from the province. In the table of the territorial planning process launched by the region, the PPR represents the main instrument to establish, in the quality of the landscape and the environment, the sustainable development of the entire regional territory. The central objective is therefore the conservation and redevelopment of the landscape, natural and cultural heritage, not just in the improvement of life of the population and their cultural identity, but as well as the reinforcement of the attractiveness of the region and competitiveness in the network of relations that expand at a global scale. Above all the PPR aims such goals in coherence with the Territorial Plan:
a) promote substantially the significance of the regional territory as well as its values and problems, with particular attention to the "structural" factors, of great stability and existence, that condition the transformation processes;
b) outlining a strategic reference plan, by which to obtain maximum social consent and by which to guide the multi-sectored governance policies of the regional territory as well as its links with the international context;
c) building a normative device coherent with the prospects of the legislative reform at a regional and national level, in which to account the local authorities to adequately preside over the values of the territory and improve the efficiency of the public policies.
In order to join the landscape and environmental, urban and infrastructural, economic and social diversities of the territory, as much as possible, the PPR articulates the awareness and evaluations, the objectives and the strategic indications and normative directions, in 76 "fields of landscape" distinctly known throughout the regional territory. The articulation of the landscape in the areas is individuated by evaluation sheets of the natural and historic-cultural factors that characterizes each field. Such files constitute a dossier attached to the present affair. One of the files of the dossier is presented in appendix 1. The evaluation sheets for each area must follow in the phase of the executive editing of the PPR, an in-depth evaluation that define the nature, critical points and the potential of the landscape at the unit scale of the landscape, making the application of the skills and strategic prospect of the operation possible. An example of the in-depth evaluation with the relative technical notes as a guide for the reading and drafting is attached to appendix 2. The cognitive framework, organized by four fundamental axes, has been collected for the fundamental aspects into one single representation: the "structural rendering", elaborated for the scale rendering of 1:100.000 and this same one available in IT support and reproduced at a scale of 1:250.000.

From the documents of the Piedmont Landscape Regional Plan

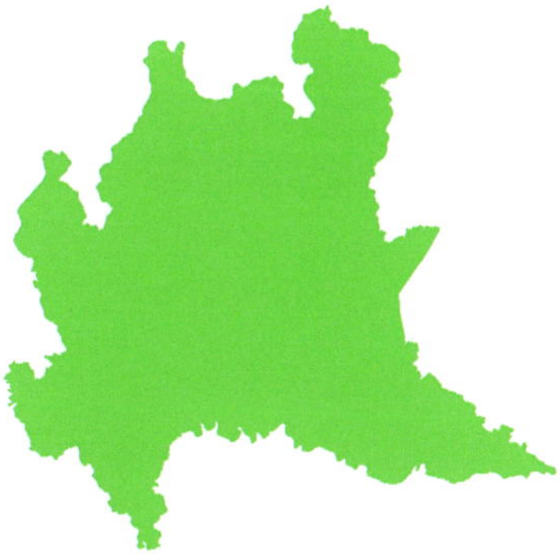

LOMBARDIA

Loto/Landscape opportunity/ Landscape and transformations

The European Landscape Convention (October 2000 - ratified by Italy in 2006) focuses our attention on the principle that the whole territory is landscape. Town and countryside, natural panorama and suburbs should be the object of a careful landscape policy to improve their natural, social, cultural, habitative characterization.

The landscape quality is connected with the quality of the places where we live and with the life quality; the different landscapes of European territories are a legacy, they are a social, cultural, environmental and economic richness that we have to safeguarde, to manage carefully, to plan in order to propose new landscape where it needs.

Ten years ago, Regione Lombardia decided to involve its whole territory and all territorial public bodies in the landscape planning. The Lombardia Regional landscape plan (PTPR) , that defined the new regional landscape age, was definitly approved in the 2001 and has been updated from the 2008. The regional landscape approach is dynamic and integrated, it wants to involve all municipalities and counties that are asked to promote a propositive role of landscape planning into their spatial strategies and policies.

The Regione Lombardia landscape policy intends:

- safeguarding the characterizations that define the regional different landscape identities and that allow to recongnize them; it can be done by a carefull check of transformation processes in order to preserve historical, traditional and natural values
- improving the landscape and architectural quality of projects in order to improve territorial tranformation and to create new qualified landcape
- upgrading population awareness on landscape values and characterization, also promoting more opportunities to enjoy it.

The PTPR general regulation explain that all the territorial and urban plans have to consider local landscape characterization and the regional landscape raccomandation and they also have to specify regional rules with regard to the territory they are planning. In this way the different plans can increase the Regional Landscape Act in order to improve the regional landscape knowledge, safeguarding and upgrading.

Having a territorial planning more responsible and aware is important but it isn't enough. If we want to have better results we have to consider that landscape attention would also have to regard all the project and designe choices and many policies that act on landscape configuration.

The landscape management isn't easy in in dynamical territories and many experts and public administration are not ready to use landscape information and data as operative tools into development choices and decision process. This awareness steered Regione Lombardia to propose LOTO project idea.

The aim of the transnational project LOTO (Landscape Opportunities for Territorial Organization) co-funded by the E.U. - Interreg IIIB CADSES Programme, was to identify a landscape interpretative reading methodology which could serve as a shared operating framework to steer and verify decisions regarding spatial change, restoration or enhancement.

On the base of the principles expressed in the European Spatial Development Perspective, LOTO is founded on the awareness that the different landscapes of European territories are a legacy to be safeguarded and

on the COE principle that all the whole territory is landscape and should be the object of a careful landscape policy. The project goals were inspired by the awareness that, too often, spatial transformation plans and choices don't take into full account questions regarding the enhancement and landscape management of the area involved. In fact there appears to be widespresd difficulty in tackling the processes of economic and social change which often upset the light balance and interrelationships that characterise both traditional and more recently-formed landscape. The currrent policies and instruments still seem to be often tied to a traditional approach oriented above all at safeguarding the outstanding landscapes and at a passive protection of them. This is not enough to safeguard, enhance and upgrade landscapes. But the whole territory is landscape as well, the territory is continuously changing and consequently landscape transformations cannot be avoided but they can be wisely directed, that is, well oriented and consistently managed. This means formulating clear landscape policies aimed at putting measures to design considering landscape context and opportunities of improving landscape quality by local landscape features enhancement and upgrading damaged landscape. The devlopment of landscape opportunities can be a possible starting point for new sustainable development strategies. The project's approach is geared to overcome a sectoral vision in favour of an integrated and olistic vision of the landscape which interprets its evolution as a unitary system in which the ecological and natural components interact with the social, cultural, human, socio-cultural and economic ones. However, integrating this landscape approach into spatial planning requires drawing up simple and effective, not dispersive, landscape interpretation methodologies; therefore an effort must be made to produce effective summaries and clear, transparent forms of collation and presentation of landscape interpretation results to involve inhabitants and going beyond an exchange between just experts.
Any land transformation process, like any new intervention, however tend to change landscape, either reinforcing or weakening its relations and basic elements, offering new references or enhancing the existing ones. Physical transformations, both in the past and nowadays, are more or less "consciously" the results of various attitudes towards the sites condition in which they occur: they may either interact with natural characters, landscape architecture characters, historic-cultural characters or they may overlap them.
Gaining awareness of this means questioning how to make the relations between plan and project and the underlying idea of landscape, clear and mutually shared; it also means trying to identify specific moments and modes of communication useful for discussing on the present landscape characters and the landscape characters we would be obtained. To this end, LOTO project intends to help to provide tools to govern the landscape's evolution, using the landscape as a frame of reference for any territorial project in order to focus spatial development instruments on it in a complementary way.
The methodological approach definition had to follows some requirements:
- to examine the outcome of previous experiences;
- to try to integrate the various approaches to landscape while considering the view described in the European Convention;
- to point up the primaly use of available data in order to be able to apply it extensively;
- to test the work hypothesis on real situations either solving and managing specific local territorial problems or in defining land enhancement policies.
The project was split into three phases, which took place one after the other with interaction between them:
- A preliminary stage explored and highlighted potential contributions from other experiences, and sought a better understanding of skills, approaches and spatial interpretation and planning methods currently used in various countries.
- An intermediate stage focused on defining the key points of a methodology proposal in line with the above-

described requisites, aimed at testing its possible developments in the experimental solution of real situations.
- A final stage to bring together the results in relation to the project's core objective: the shared document "Guidelines for a landscape reading and interpretation aimed at steering the choices of territorial transformations".
The writing of the guidelines document followed the project life from the first step to the end, every part of the LOTO work offered some contribution to it. Regione Lombardia and IReR, that were responsible for guidelines framework definition and the final document editing, took attention to it, so the final document is a shared result.
The methodological path would give effectiveness, within the processes of defining spatial transformation, to an open, frank discussion about:
- What kind of landscape we have and how we perceive it ?
- What kind of landscape will it became?
- What kind of landscape do we want?
The methodolgical path defines a clear distinction between the interpretation of the current state and a study of the trends and development forecasts, so as to identify the possible threats and opportunities regarding a given landscape. The time when the various territorial parties compared and therefore shared the interpretative framework was seen as the fundamental moment for defining the conditions for a landscape policy.
The Methodological Framework is organized into five cognitive and operational Activity Cores:
A. Characterization/qualification;
B. Future evolution trends and transformation demands;
C. Interpretative synthesis – landscape threats and opportunities;
D. Cognitive framework sharing;
E. Definition of premises for landscape policies and operational choices.
The methodological path is a flexible and circular process in order to better respond to the many use requirements. It may start at any point with respect to the aims, it must be open and suitable to the real needs resulting from the policies definition. It can change the scale and the extension of the study area according to the problem or the specific theme. It is most important that the various activities in the methodological process must be easily recognized, maintaining their autonomy and having clear purposes, tools, cognitive sources and processing. This is particularly useful for building up clear information, going over and checking the sites' reading/interpretation activities, putting in the process new data and requirements, monitoring results, but it is also useful for transferring knowledge. Clear and exact communication is basic to shared and participative planning and management. The high numbere of partner was an importnt richness of the project, it allowed a wide debate on each part of the research and on the different problems, also taking in account the results from pilot actions.
A wide work that allowed to refine the methodological procedure and explore its different operating levels, to clarify the conditions in order to define the key questions for a landscape interpretation checklist, that is an operational tool for carrying out studies on landscape as a whole rather than on its specific elements. A tool that uses a simple and synthetic language, a chance to compare different knowledge and not only some expert ones.

Anna Rossi, Land and Urban Development- coord. of LOTO project

TICINO

The landscape project as an occasion of equilibrium between urban and mountainous areas

For the internal context, the risk of the Ticino as a two-speed region was represented by the Concentrated setting, while the opportunity of equilibrium is represented by the Cohesion setting.

Landscape
The central element of the heritage area is the landscape, which the role of a resource in function of the quality of life and tourism has been acknowledged.

Definition
According to the European Landscape Convention, ratified by Switzerland in 2000, the term landscape designates a determined part of territory, as how it is perceived by the inhabitants of the place or from the visitors, in which the aspect and feature derive from the actions of natural and/or cultural (or rather human) factors. This definition takes into account the idea that the landscapes evolve with time by the effect of natural forces and human actions. It underlines equally the idea that the landscapes form a whole, in which the natural and cultural elements are considered concurrently.
The landscape policies have also passed from an aspect characterized by conservation and protection of the landscape emergencies to a more active approach, which introduces the concepts of development and promotion of the landscape.
Il PD 90 focused on the conservation of the natural landscape; the urban landscape of the valley, where most of the population lives and works did not receive the same attention.

Evolution of the landscape
The area of the settlements increases prominently in the valleys; the agricultural area decreases due to unproductive, forest and settlement areas; forest areas decrease in the plains and increase in the mountains.
The considerable and quick alterations that interest the valley; in some areas the diffused and extensive urbanization causes the loss of characteristic elements of the landscape. The areas of the hinterlands and mountains transform more slowly; the growth of the forest in open areas tends to form a homogeneous landscape where the forest draws close to the limits of the inhabited areas. If it is not governed, this evolution hides the risk of trivialization and homogenization of the valley's landscape and a loss of variety of the mountain landscape. The territory of the canton presents such qualities whereby a targeted policy of the landscape could consent the emergence of opportunities that however cannot be adopted only through the conservation and protection policy, but have the need of concrete and active measures of development, that can increase usability.

Integrated policy of the landscape
The 5th of October 2005 the Council of State adopted an integrated policy of the landscape, carried out through projects at a district and coordinated scale among the various interested sectors. The general principles are:

-subsidiarity, that promotes the active role of the local organizations;
-flexibility, that consents the application of instruments and incentives in function of the local and regional actuality;
-the development of opportunity rather than constraints;
-the concern to all the territory.
A confrontation with the landscape policies in other cantons, in Lombardy and Alto Adige has evidenced that almost all of the planning instruments press the necessity to work at an appropriate scale, mostly by districts. To accomplish solid results, it must be done by surpassing the constraints and propose a safeguard to seek through vast participative ways. In addition it is necessary to place close attention to the new landscapes that are generated by the achievement of important work, by which to become opportunity and not consequences.

Local landscape project
The local landscape projects should instead regard those enterprises that, while maintaining an interdisciplinary approach, concern a more accurate area, of which the recovery of the terraced vineyards in Bassa Vallemaggia, the protection and management of the marshy landscape of Lucomagno, the recovery and development of the center of Corzutt a Montecarasso, the recovery of the chestnut woods in Malcantone. These operations limited to single objects are not considered local landscape projects, like the restoration of cultural heritage, the development of a biotope or the recover of a single chestnut woods: this type of operation is entrusted to the relative sector policies.
A clear example of an integrated project is the Linescio Terraced Village Project, subject to the platform of the Association for the Protection of the Artistic and Architectural Heritage of Vallemaggia (APAV) and Pro Linescio. Values intertwine behind the development of a significant landscape, like the rediscovery of the rural culture of Valle Rovana, the safeguard of biotopes, the recovery of agricultural areas, the promotion of tourism. The work of coordination between the various services and research of the financing has allowed to give the organizers a solid and positive answer in a short time.

Relation between the urban and mountain areas
To promote the socio-economic affairs between the urban and mountain areas it is, first of all, necessary to assure that the division of the areas and criteria for the centrality defined by the Management Plan [65] serve also as reference for the other sector policies, in particular, for the aggregation and the new regional policy.

From the Management Plan of Ticino – 2007

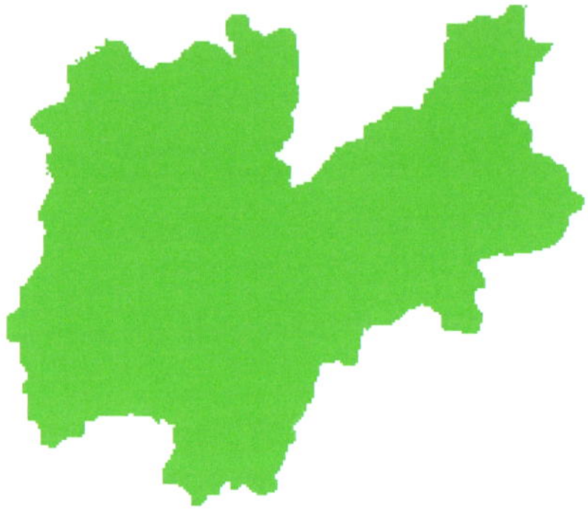

TRENTINO

Interpreting the landscape

The first provincial planning scheme (PUP) for Trentino was drawn up in 1967 by Giuseppe Samonà and was made possible thanks to the legislative autonomy of Trentino. It became a rare example of excellence in the context of Italian town and regional planning. Despite Trentino's limited geographical extension (around 6000 sq. km), there was a distinct lack of equilibrium, with excessive domination of the city of Trento and progressive abandonment of the valleys.

The 1967 PUP was also innovative because it anticipated not only the need for equilibrium within the area, based on the concept of the "extended city" but also issues that would then become problems, such as safeguarding of the landscape. The subsequent 1971 law on landscape protection made it possible, not without the inevitable contradictions, to keep more radical transformation under control. After twenty years, the second PUP paid even greater attention to the environment. It reviewed all the areas already subject to landscape protection, cataloguing all the assets making up the landscape, both natural and cultural. Safeguarding of the landscape continued to be entrusted to eleven commissions, one for each district (corresponding with the main valleys in Trentino), plus a central provincial commission with jurisdiction for action on a wider scale. The judgments of the commissions, made up of technical staff and politicians, were based on the "Criteria for Landscape Protection", contained in the 1987 PUP.

This widespread control of thousands of construction projects each year (up to 15,000), while not ensuring high architectural quality, at least made it possible to avoid deterioration.

One should also recall the 1978 law on historic centres, which catalogued around 100,000 sites present in roughly 1500 historic centres, providing indications regarding admissible restoration, renewal and renovation work. Today, 20 years after the second PUP and 40 years after the first, the new PUP is ready, further analysing methods for studying the landscape, in order to allow more targeted protection.

The new " Landscape Charter" is the result of careful interpretation of the landscape in order to preserve its identity, this being one of the general objectives of the third PUP. The starting point is thus different as compared to the previous scheme, in which protection of the landscape was delegated to individual decisions regarding construction projects, as already stated, without integrating planning of the landscape and town planning. Linking the landscape to planning schemes is increasingly more urgent, given that the spaces available within the province are limited, in some cases very limited, while evolutionary trends common to the rest of Italy have been consolidated, leading to the linking of towns and villages and scattered building around the countryside, thus destroying the traditional configuration of the area, made up of small rural villages.

The Landscape Charter first subdivides the area into basic systems deriving from the state of the land to which the planning scheme relates.

Subsequently the basic landscape systems are brought together into five large overall systems making up the Trentino identity: alpine areas, forested areas, traditional settlements. These systems are indeed present throughout Trentino, although their presence, extent, distribution and identity vary from area to area and from one environment to another.

Each system can also be broken down into a multiplicity of sub-systems representing its complexity, wealth, variety and diversity.

The combination of the overall systems gives rise to landscape units which can be identified thanks to physical borders such as passes and ridges, which are clearly visible in the area. To conserve the identity of the landscape, given the relationship between open land and built-up areas, the Landscape Charter dedicates particular attention to areas alongside towns which are currently still free of development, as they are the object of apparently unstoppable expansion in terms of building. In more delicate cases two limits have been introduced. One, represented by a red line, identifies a front of particular significance in terms of historic or natural interest, while the other is indicated by a black line and instead marks the point of no return, namely the point beyond which transformation and settlement of any kind would irreversibly distort the traditional landscape, turning it into a landscape where towns are no longer separated from one another but rather joined and confused, a landscape which disregards the characteristics of the area, with construction along roads and the abandoning of historic centres. Thanks to this combination of analysis and indications, the Landscape Charter will be a fundamental tool for town planning, offering a choice between different options and making it possible to have a clear view of the consequences: disappearance of agricultural areas, compromising of the river system and loss of the traditional landscape, or vice-versa enhancement and consolidation of the environmental values that represent one of Trentino's few resources, a resource which is not however renewable. The Landscape Charter is accompanied and supplemented by planning guidelines based on more than 30 years' experience of safeguarding the landscape. These guidelines are both methodological, suggesting methods of interpretation coherent with the PUP at subordinate levels, guaranteeing continuity and coherence, and operational, providing indications developing from interpretation of the transformation that has taken place.

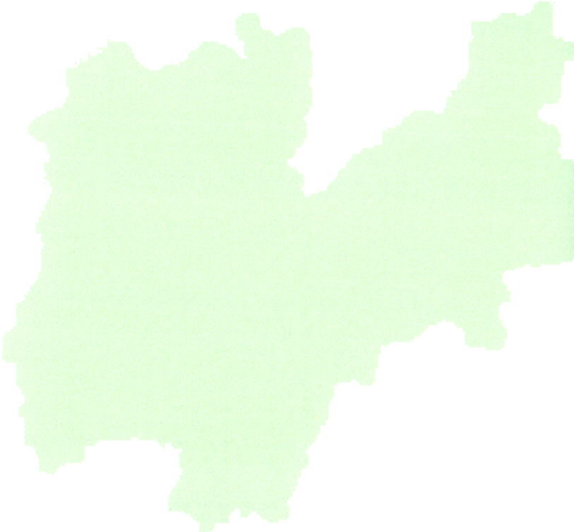

The indications are specific and subdivided into components and problems regarding each system:

A Traditional settlements integrated landscape system

Subjects: compact and scattered historic centres (perimeter - categories – overall picture - urban junctions – landscape surveys – planning of external areas – views – indexes, type and orientation), recent settlements (upgrading - readjustment) future settlements (sizing - location – spatial organisation - architecture). Planning guidelines in relation to the Landscape Charter: town planning equilibrium, quality of towns, environmental sustainability, harmony of the landscape.

B Rural areas integrated landscape system

Subjects: relationship between built-up and free areas, role of the area, quantity, characteristics (type, predominance, trends, nature of terrain, relationship with towns, area role, volumes, use, new volumes, perimeters, zones). Planning guidelines in relation to the Landscape Charter: integrity, continuity, tradition, equilibrium.

C Forested areas integrated landscape system

Subjects: relationship with towns, water, seasonal constructions, other infrastructures, pasture.

Planning guidelines in relation to the Landscape Charter: integrity, continuity.

D Alpine land integrated landscape system

Subjects: integrity, unitariness. Planning guidelines in relation to the Landscape Charter: integrity, continuity .

E River areas integrated landscape system.

Subjects: characteristics (point, line, surface), integrity, altitude, course, zoning, intervention to restore ecosystems.

Planning guidelines in relation to the Landscape Charter: integrity, continuity, homogeneity.

Enrico Ferrari, Department of Urban and Landscape Planning, Autonomous Province of Trento

ALTO ADIGE

Towards the quality of the operations

The landscape – our great resource

Our landscape – what is it made of? Are we thinking of the Dolomites, of the shepherd's huts, the vine tilled lands of Santa Maddalena, the lake of Caldaro? Yes, they are undoubtedly part of our landscape. But also the Brenner motorway, productive settlements, urban areas, the valley floor with its apple monocultures covered by anti-hail nets, they are also part of it.
We are the users of this landscape, and our contribution is mainly characterized by the behavior of a mere user, we just think about our urbanization, tourist and industrial needs.
We are talking of the landscape as a resource for our identity. But on which elements does - what we define - the identity of our region nourish itself?
Do the stereotypes we print on our tourist's brochures prevail, or is it instead, and rather probably, the whole of it all?
We are convinced that an environmentally integrated approach in terms of the conception of a strategic accomplishment is needed. We are also sure that the same society is bound to safeguard nature and the development of the various landscape structures, such responsibility is due not only to a specific authority or a minority group in charge.

The conception of environmental conservation

The foreseen integrative strategy is the basis for the single steps to be taken for the attainment of predefined objectives and measures. In the present context the challenge is to control by law in the necessary limits, and to safeguard nature by contract as much as possible.
At an administrative level, the main tool - together with the well-known town planning tools (PUC), is the landscape plan drafted by the competent provincial office in close collaboration with the interested municipality. The landscape plan is at the moment a rather traditionally conceived tool, if you consider that its main objective is identified in the imposition of safeguard commitments for entire portions of the territory or for single objects. It also foresees that the commitment regulations have to be acknowledged at a town planning level.
The landscape plan has been a valid and stable tool in the latest decades, as much as the categories to be safeguarded contemplated by the same.
Besides the administrative plans, active are promotional tools for the safeguard of the environmental heritage, for the adoption of ecocompatible agricultural practices, and for the awarding of prizes for the care and maintenance of the landscape.

Projections into the future

The Environmental Department has taken an active part for years in the public discussion on the quality of building intervention on the territory.
The provincial Council, by instituting in December 2005 the provincial Committee for culture, building and landscape, has taken an important step for the promotion of a modern architecture in terms of quality, tuned in with the features of the site.
The committee is made by three architects who do not live and work in South Tyrol, and who, thanks to their artwork in an Alpine context, were granted international acknowledgment.

The committee has an exclusively advisory function and it shares in awakening and orienting public opinion towards a building culture particularly attentive towards both site and landscape.
It seems that the time has arrived to go from what has been until now voluntary advice, to an institutionalized procedure, and to take the definite step from a conservative safeguard to an actual planning, and to the development of the environment by encouraging a close collaboration among the provincial offices and the municipalities.
A discussion of a broader extent will be needed, too, able to involve the population, the administration and those who are in charge, in order to establish specific agreements on criteria oriented towards a "good" architecture compatible with the landscape.
The Autonomous Province of Bolzano will commit itself to pursue the said objectives.

Peter Kasal, Nature and Landscape Division, Autonomous Province of Bolzano

LOMBARDIA

A project for Pedemontana

A motorway in widespread and dense urbanization

The Pedemontana Lombardy motorway crosses one of the most urbanized territories of Europe. A extraordinarily dynamic territory with its thick networks of small, medium and large companies and its articulate social structure, but also very congested in its infrastructural network, fragile from an ecologic-environmental point of view due to the high levels of air pollution (equal and superior to those of Milan), the high level of impermeableness of the ground, the scarce open spaces and the deterioration of them. The degraded landscape is the clear symbolic and material expression of the living conditions, always more precarious, with the difficulty that the single infrastructural building operations and the use of the open spaces have in construction a quality landscape that renders common good.

In the Pedemontana conurbation the infrastructural and landscape-environmental emergency seem to intertwine and express the two faces of the same matter: the development seems always less accessible to the quantitative growth (the number of companies, employees, buildings, kilometers of infrastructure), but always more accessible to the qualification of each of these elements and the accession of those paradigms of sustainability placed in the center of the winning candidature of Milan at the EXPO.

An unsuccessful plan integrated by infrastructure and open spaces. In a similar territory there are other good reasons to consider the project of the individual infrastructural in a collective reflection of the entire multimodal networks jointed to a large redevelopment project of the open spaces. Such has not been for many and different reasons now linked to the will of the actors- than have even been given legitimately other priorities -, now to the governance models – that have never brought the voice of the environment upon the table of the deciders -, now to prevail with incisive sector-based technical cultures (of the road engineers) and/or of opposing abstract rhetorical planning (of an urban planning that claims to be all-comprehensive).

Consequently, the transversal motorway operation is defined in a table in which the transversal railway planning remains uncertain (also linked to the opening of the tunnel of Gottardo), the very consistent investments of the motorway network place themselves beside those very limited ones of the railway system, the residual open space in the dense grid of the conurbation and close to the new infrastructure, is not the center of an integrating policy and planning, but sometimes still seems to await new sprawled construction. Despite all that being easy to observe how the different quality of the urbanized landscape and the improved living condition in the other large European conurbations originates not just from the motorway density per kilometer but as well as the presence of a differentiated network of infrastructure of mobility, from the beauty of the great infrastructures, conceived as a part of the city, the renewed quality of the open spaces and from time to time reconsidered as urban parks, new woodland, as undisturbed agricultural areas, or better yet simply as parkland and woodland of deceleration and silence in noisy and congested territories, rather than as deteriorated spaces awaiting repair. All this has generated some critical points of the preliminary project approved by the CIPE, flaws that by now are given facts.

Omitting those relative to the lack of integration between the motorway and iron operations and those between the production of the infrastructure and examination and the limitations of the possible induced building (through an area plan), this points out just the most macroscopic ones relative to the placing of some junctions and service areas in woodland areas, the landscape in some sensible areas and above all the great part of the road network actions complementary to the center of few residual open spaces; all the situations that had possible alternative solutions and that therefore could be avoided through integrated planning (for finality, technical skills and involved authorities) and from a more prudent way those environmental reasons and those long term ones that do not have the will of expression upon the table of actions.

Restarting from compensations

The master plan for the environmental compensations prepared by the Polytechnic University of Milan, desired by the new Management of Pedemontana and the expression of a new sensibility towards these topics of the Lombardy Region and the provinces and municipalities involved, arrives downstream from all of that. It does not move away from the integrated planning but instead it pursues – as it usually happens – in making urbanism an amending procedure, precisely to "compensate" the damage. Nonetheless, this arduously tries to go back and as much as possible towards an integrated project, towards large and non-sectoral public policies for the Pedemontano territory. Above all, it does it with well reasoned and fair choices:

-distinguish the environmental mitigations (necessary but to be defined with the infrastructure project) from the environmental compensations: the first ones are accurate and have to do with the break down of localized inconveniences and restraints, the second ones belong to the system and confront, above all, with the ground consumption and the pollution of the induced area;

-assert that the resources for the environmental compensation (3,5% of the work cost equal to 100 million Euros) are effectively destined to environmental compensation (to therefore create meadows, forests, bicycle and pedestrian paths and not for new roads and parking lots or for financing the pavement repair of a square or the roof of a public building, etc.);

-point out that these have to respond both to a general system design and to careful observation of the characteristics of the possible areas of operations and the local planning emerging in time;

-insist that the environmental and forest compensation (which its organization is associated with the deforested areas) should not overlap (that is, additional), but instead at the same time should be considered in one territory and landscape project;

-expand to the maximum the effects both by low unit cost operations as well as start up projects that wish to launch an evolutionary process of some of the spaces rather than distinguish a definite structure, that seek synergy with the other possible financial resources in a more complex design of environmental and landscape redevelopment, a structural diagram.

From these principles it achieves a very simple structural design that explains three purposes of the master plan:

1)the reinforcement of the strong North-South environmental systems crossed by Pedemontana;

2)the construction of the fundamental connection and the junctions of a transversal green corridor;

3)the interconnection and transversal circulation between large North-South environmental systems through the regional green corridor.

Arturo Lanzani, Professor of Geography of Landscape and Urban Planning of the Polytechnic University of Milan, in charge of the Work Group and Author of The Master Plan of the Pedemontana Project

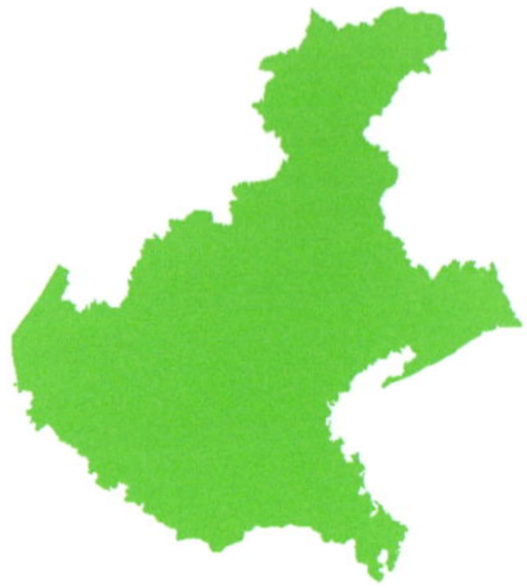

VENETO/ALPI ORIENTALI
Alpine terraced landscapes

Terraced landscapes, one of the oldest signs of sedentary colonisation in our planet, are a typical feature of the Alpine area and the processes affecting it acquire an emblematic value for the entire mountain area. Research studies carried out in the context of the Alpter project 'Terraced landscapes in the Alpine arc (funded by the EU community initiative Interreg III B "Alpine Space" programme) made it possible to identify and classify their variety, but above all to recognise a number of constants relative to both characteristic features of terraced areas as well as to the transformation processes that have affected them.
Terraced areas have experienced periods of development as well as of decline, often followed by a sudden collapse which led to their gradual abandonment. There are numerous reasons underlying this decline or collapse making it extremely difficult to define strategies for local restoration and for the promotion of the remains of these important structures. An attempt was made to respond to these renovation objectives by means of various projects launched in experimental form in a series of terraced sites distributed throughout the Alpine arc involved in the ALPTER project.
These pilot projects are interesting in terms of what each single project offers, as well as representing an important occasion for comparing different planning experiences. This "cross-referencing" opportunity allows us to hypothesise integrated policies and actions favouring the recovery and renovation of these complex structures. This approach to the development of transformation proposals considers the single project in terms of the wider context and not just as a specific recovery programme. The project focus shifts from the single terrace to the terraced slopes, to terraced settlements, thus becoming a territorial project whose structural base is terracing. The challenge lies in overcoming regrets for the loss of an unrepeatable past by looking for ways to leave nostalgia behind and involve local communities in recovery projects that make it possible to build new landscapes, new cultural, environmental and settlement frameworks, transforming the old traditional landscapes into a new value. The pilot projects launched in different Alpine contexts tackle an important shared issue: how can we ensure that terraced areas, environments that are notoriously difficult, costly and hard to manage, comply with contemporary living and working requirements and styles? The recognition of several important territorial values, like safeguarding from hydrogeological risk and reinforcement of the biodiversity features of sites and of the sustainability components of territorial arrangements, may be indispensible but they are not adequate to the task of promoting the launch of a recovery and renovation process of these landscapes. The project itineraries launched in the various case studies also dealt with other questions such as the involvement of local communities in renovation programmes, pointing out the strong identity value of these landscapes; the need to combine different intervention instruments to help revitalise these sites, from the physical project to financial policies and legal provisions; the possibility of introducing new technologies, innovating the way terracing is used and attempting to promote their energy-producing potential, with possible partial consequences for the landscape image.
These actions, based on the wide range of cognitive studies launched by the Alpter project partners in the study area, aim to renovate and promote landscaping resources in accordance with the objectives established by the European Landscape Convention.

Enrico Fontanari and Domenico Patassini, University IUAV- Venice

UMBRIA

Umbria, italian landscape paradigm
New Regional Landscape Plan

The Region of Umbria's New Landscape Plan assumes the notion of a trans-scalar approach as the key to operations of interpreting the landscape and proposed strategies of intervention. The trans-scalar concept is innate to the visible forms and meaning of the landscape itself, whose qualities result from the overlapping of the small and large scale. On a case-by-case basis, these contexts combine the territorial 'rooms' to which they belong: geomorphological formations (i.e. large valleys, alternating with the corrugations of hills and mountains); forms of settlement; the detailed material and chromatic qualities of individual elements (i.e. building typologies, built forms and material patterns with different grains).

The trans-scalar qualities of the landscape must be matched by a model of governance founded on the inter-dependence between different institutional levels, called on to share frameworks of understanding, value judgements and responsibilities regarding the conservation and active management of transformations. Thus, in alternative to our traditional "top down" model, which unidirectionally transmits a system of regulations and rules from the state to the local level, we propose the use of a "progressively circular" model, aimed at developing and favouring a shared vision by the State, the Regional, Provincial and Municipal Governments.

This does not, however, mean that we propose that the State or Regional Governments abdicate their responsibilities over landscape policies. On the contrary, we must focus on their explicit reinforcement within a more complex system of multilevel governance founded on the shared assumption of responsibilities and effective conviction of the various institutional actors involved in transforming the landscape.

In particular, we are speaking about the organisation of adequate interactive contexts by the various subjects governing the territory, in order to promote shared strategies of development founded on a comprehensive vision of the landscape, of its values to be conserved and the new qualities to be pursued. This requires a strong level of inter-dependence between the instruments of governance at the regional, provincial and municipal scale, and thus between the Landscape Plan, the Regional Spatial Plan, the Spatial Coordination Plans and the Municipal Master Plans.

This structure, which focuses on reducing the existing asymmetries between processes of interpreting landscape values and attributing responsibilities to the institutional system, regards the notion of context as a decisive anchor as much for policies of planning as those of management.

Assuming the landscape as a collective work, in which each of us bears a share of the responsibility for the future we were concerned with identifying the different scales of environments of reference (contexts). It is with respect to these contexts that we must organise awareness and, at the same time, identify the most suitable forms of cooperation between the various institutional subjects, as part of the prospect of focusing their respective strategies on shared objectives of landscape quality. The agreement between the Ministry and the Regional Government must function as a guarantee regarding the responsibilities of decision-making, which must resist any exception that tends to invest other actors with improper functions.

Alberto Clementi, New Landscape Plan Coordination of the Umbria Region
Dean of The Architetcural School of Pescara

6 positions within the landscape

from the documentary
“Dentro il paesaggio, le Alpi”

Franco Farinelli

1

"Personally I do not believe that it is correct to speak of just natural landscape because the distinction between nature and culture in modernism has never existed. Bruno Latour explains today that we have never been modern exactly because the distinction that we have produced between nature and culture has never really worked. Exactly for the landscape, exactly in the case of the landscape, the impossibility to think in just natural and naturalistic terms is still more evident, because actually the landscape includes in itself the presence of an observer who is natural until a certain point...

In my opinion, the landscape breaks down all that which is excluded in the cartographic image of the world or map. And since the cartographic image of the world, the map, corresponds substantially to the space, and since the space today stands aloof (because the network exists), landscape becomes pretentious in the other senses of the world, to impose itself, to re-establish its own preponderance."

Alberto Cecchetto

2

“

Defining the landscape is an arduous task, and perhaps today, a bit inopportune. When I started to occupy myself with the project, twenty-five years ago, I remember that in the university it was not permitted to use the word landscape. If I used this term in the research I would not receive a single lira. I was forced to speak of “context” and “building's surroundings”. Landscape was perceived exactly as a romanticistic connotation, post-nineteenth century: landscape paintings, John Ruskin, watercolor paintings, the panoramas. Instead, today the word landscape is overused. It has become a sort of s “passepartout” for letting through a bit of everything...

Architecture without architects, like the rural one, is a substantially ethical one. It knew how to work at best with the materials, reaching, thanks to thousands of years of experimentation, constructive perfection of ethical sort: every material was used up to its maximum potentiality.
I have studied rural architecture not because I am nostalgic, not in the least, seeing that I am a contemporary designer, but as Giuseppe Pagano used to say at the class of 1934 when he presented the first exhibition of Italian rural architecture, within rural architecture lies the code, the DNA, of contemporary architecture. Thus implying an idea of purity and bond with the place

”

Manuel Gausa

3

"

Here is a topic of great exploration today: recycling the touristic zones that we have, introducing the landscape as "relational space". Constructing a new touristic zone that alongside the urban datum reserves importance to what is natural. It is important to construct in the landscape in the most "sensible", "interactive" and "combined" way – moving away from the old logic of the detached house. Landscape requires, above all, architecture to be sensible., but at the same time creative. But not in a "disguised" or "integrated" way in a classic meaning: nor sacred, nor ostentatious...

Today landscape proposes a certain scalar ambiguity. This scale skipping is a multiscalar game that also responds to the necessity to inquire flexible mechanisms of spatial organization and formulation capable of propitiating and generating intersected devices, of encounter and synthesis between the various elements of the project that the landscape itself includes and embodies.
It is the idea of the landscape destined to produce and urge periodic logics, but significant between the local and global dimensions. It is the idea of the landscape that includes territory, cities, infrastructure, habitats and systems, and it transforms them into categories of a modifiable project. Compressing trajectories, models and evolutionary processes in base devices of the formulation of a new "operative" mode to designate the landscape and the project to the various scales. This is a possible line of work for the present and the future.

"

Alberto Clementi

4

"

I think we should change the approach. Not just the constraints (yes, even constraints, since the market pressure is strong), but projects, continuous reinterpretations and resource investments. But above all, the landscape should be included in the sector policies, in road building, wind farms and garbage storage systems.
In conclusion, landscape should be included in all the – infinite - policies that this country has and should not be called out within the landscape projects that take up the time that they find...

What relation that will establish itself between the great objects that will be placed on the territory and those values and quality of landscape that we would want not just to conserve but recreate, is the actual modern topic, a contemporary one, that wants to repossess the landscape. Unfortunately our procedures are terribly unprogressive: it is not just the Environmental Impact Assessment that can help us. It is necessary to reason differently: or rather insert the landscape inside the "concept", inside the initial idea of the projects of large installations that are literally transfigurating the meaning of our landscape. There is nothing wrong if we do, the only thing that is wrong is if transformation occurs unawarely because there is no landscape in these projects.

"

Mosè Ricci

5

“

The landscape is our wealth. It is the highest value that we can lay out on the international market. It is our cultural identity. Italy is the “bel paese” par excellence. But if we continue to build and erode our patrimony, our economy may fall into crisis. And this is the risk: landscape defined in very simple terms...

If the territory requested stability and persistence from architecture(after all, architecture fights against time), and demanded project as an author’s “authoritive” decision, the landscape requests undefined time, to age with architecture, to change continuously by it and to request project to be a polyarchical being, thought and shared by many, and to contribute to the construction of a portrait, not of an author but of a society...

The landscape is a portrait. This definition of the landscape artist, Joao Nunez, has always fascinated me. Because within it is the idea of Dorian Grey, or rather the idea of a landscape that ages with its population or, on the contrary, that should not age, but withstand the changes that the economy of modern society brings to find new strength and development from this transition. The territory is no longer able to describe reality and our condition: instead, landscape which at the same time it is what I am able to observe in a physical inhabited space, in a physical natural space, but at the same time it is what I have “inside” my eye, my culture, my point of view, the way I see it, represents our identity.

”

Matteo Thun

6

"Landscape and identity are, in my case, the same thing. Or rather the sloped floor of a person who lives in the middle of the mountains, it is an enriching element. I must confess that compared to my friends of the Po Valley I feel a bit privileged by the capacity to manage the third dimension: the x,y and z. Or rather something I have experienced since I was young...

At the same time, landscape and architecture are the same thing to me. Architecture is plenty in the alpine arc. As an architect I should say "no" to all the new construction plans in the Alps. For what reason? Because the "third dimension" gives an evident perspective of the "fifth façade", or rather the roof. In the mountain the roof has a primary function unlike the plain where instead this role is interpreted from the façade. So in the alpine arc the perception strongly suffers from the construction. In case it is intended to construct, it is necessary to use silk gloves, after perfectly understanding the soul of the place. And this is nothing but the landscape itself that expresses itself through the dolomite rock, wood and other various materials of the place...

I think that the motorways, railways (with tunnels and turns) are important. But they are operations that cut across and change the landscape: in this case it is necessary to work distinguishing the concepts of "natura naturans" and of "natura naturata": from one side it is God who commands and you cannot oppose. On the other side courage is needed to affirm one's self. For example, a bridge that crosses a valley in the mountains must be planned without following the concept of mimesis."

JVC
Vinten
Vinten

"Inside the landscape" The documentary film for alps

Program

The video has been thought as an extension of a "story" through images and aimed to illustrate with film techniques some of the changes arising in the alpine landscape, referring to emerging elements of the issues that regard the interpretation of the phenomenons of transformation and change in the landscape.
Above all, referring to four great issues of possible intervention from the public organization and as topics of innovative research: neglected and abandoned landscape, overcrowded and overused landscape (winter tourism, hiking, etc.), new landscape of the infrastructural and mobility networks, ordinary and urban landscape.
The topics have been declined assuming the different contexts that from time to time are capable of declining the notion of landscape and aimed strategies: from historic places to valley communities, to rural and intensive agricultural areas, of the grapevines and orchards above all, the caverns of porphyry, mountainous and valley areas, unused space, and those intermediate one between the dense cities and surrounding territory.

Format

The video, programmed to be about 35 minutes, intends to highlight the identifying characteristics of the alpine and mountain landscape, and in this first observation, and with the help of "witnesses" and researchers, evidence the problems that must be confronted where the pressure of change risks causing harmful processes and improper alterations or where the excess of conservation causes to remain or introduce imported and faulty/traditional models. This is even more prominent in the alpine contexts. For every reference topic and all the other emerging ones, a series of particular and significant contexts have been selected and privileged for their capacity of evoking the problems that must be confronted for the purpose of conservation or the sustainable transformation of the identifying values. The landscapes in doubt have been carried through with various and in-depth formalities (from the top, bottom and the inside) as an opportunity of reflection by various interlocutors (see note below) capable of surfacing the topics and problems. The film is in Italian with subtitles in English. It has also been though to evoke the direction taken by the individuated interlocutors' vision. From autumn it will be projected in universities and schools of Trentino, as well as festivals and other public occasions. final editing tends to render the experiences from the landscape as a "background" up till the landscapes in movement and with diverse modes of progress and collective use.

Note

The film originates from an idea and hypothesis by Pino Scaglione, discussed and confronted with Alessandro Franceschini who has edited the drafting, and then with Carlo e Luca Dal Bosco/Filmwork that have produced it, directed by Andrea Andreotti, with the support from: Autonomous Region of Trentino Alto Adige, Autonomous Province of Trento, Autonomous Province of Bolzano, Brennero Motorway, University of Trento, Commune of Riva del Garda, Commune of Borgo Valsugana, Architects Association of Trento

Alpine art and landscapes
Artesella

Art among the Alps
Arte Sella is an international exhibition of contemporary art which began in 1986, that is developed in the open, in the woods of Val di Sella (Borgo Valsugana, TN). From 1996, the project di Artesella has been developed along a path in the woods on the southern slope of Mount Armentera: it has outlined an ideal route named Artenatura along which the visitor can observe the works of arte and enjoy the particularity of the place. The idea of the exhibition is to display works of art, but above all, as a creative process: the works of art are followed each day in their development and the presence of the artist must express the respectful relationship with nature by which they elicit creativity and inspiration.
The works are generally three-dimensional and made with stones, leaves, branches and tree trunks. When the exhibition closes, many of the works are left to become part of the nature's cycle of life; others are taken to art galleries and exhibitions in Italy or abroad. In the past few years the activity of Artesella has been developed in Malga Costa, where exhibitions, theatrical performances and events have rendered this place as a cultural area.
Along the usual activity in the last few years, a network of contacts and collaborations with famous musicians, actors and other cultural celebrities have been developed. Always more often, Artesella represents an occasion of creative growth and experimentation favored from the cultural and artistic context of the course of contemporary art and as well as extraordinary contextualization in a natural environment, rich and pure, where nature's language expresses itself to those who know and want to listen. Artesella also presented itself as the reality that stimulates the cultural vivacity of the place, thanks to the initiative taken by the internationally known performers. It has produced collaboration and entrusting the musical direction to Mario Brunello, who has previously thought up, interpreted and encouraged to make Artesella possible as well as the experimentation to create cultural initiatives. The purpose is experimentation, the reflection of a possible relationship among creativity, music and nature. The belief that supports the action is that the influence of the place will convey the various peculiarities and artistic sensibility into a single and coherent "creative product".

Research for the mountainous and alpine landscapes

Experiences and proposals
from design schools

Studies and research on the occasion of ALPS

"Every now and then I go to see the beautiful photograph taken from nine hundred and ten kilometers above our heads from the Lanstat satellite and I watch it in the silence of my bedroom. With a good magnifying glass I scan the cities and rivers, mountains, lakes, communication routes; particularly the lagoon between Brenta and Piave with Chioggia, Pellestrina, il Lido, Venice, the islands, the Grand Canal, Ponte della Ferrovia, Marghera, Canale dei Petroli...but how crowded are the bedrooms of the men between Venice, Padua and Treviso!
They all seem like a single metropolis. And then Colli Euganei, Berici, Vicenza, Verona, Lake Garda; the joyful hills of Mincio al Tagliamento.
The cities, viewed from so far away have a thick reddish color. It also considers "centurazioni romane" in the countryside northeast of Padua and intuits Claudia Augusta, which heading towards Norico crossed the Alps and Postumia that went into Illirico..."
"...this layer of sedimentary rock from where red marble comes from is found along our Pre-Alps and sometimes emerges over our pastures like a cliff, forming that natural phenomenon that geologist call "the marble passageways of Malm".
The opening phrase is a small tribute to a writer: Mario Rigoni Stern. A great narrator who has surely described our mountains like no other, who has outlined landscapes through his writing in the most effective way like no other iconographic instrument, narrating about men within so many and different mountainous landscapes, events and single images. Rigoni Stern makes me think of the transformations of the landscape without nostalgia, but with the clarity of one who lives the present intensively, turning back sometimes but more often looking ahead. And the ALPS Biennial, I believe, can be considered in harmony with this cultural approach. We have thought that Trentino, the Alps, the mountains and landscape of this great setting that separates and unites two different parts of Europe, merit a specific initiative, measured and thought out, for the peculiarities of these places where images, projects and research bring forth these significant characteristics, geographical conditions, settlements, contradictions and the urge for transformation. Along with many other universities of the alpine arc, we have obtained this intuition by carrying out an ambitions plan of research that, under the initials: AAA, Active Atlas of the Alps (Atlante Attivo delle Alpi), can restore a clear image of this central and great "green heart" of Europe and at the same time launch a series of coherent projects and strategic hypothesis capable of establishing a reference point for the active policies of the individual states and regions.
And for this reason we have rapidly prepared this first ALPS Biennial, experimental in a way but looking into the future with ambition. It regards conservation and development policies, enforcement by the European Landscape Convention, and beyond, but above all in the alpine mountains and areas, improvements that coincide with the centrality of the landscape project as far as the necessity to encourage different treatment to the construction models and settlements in the Alps by which an urge towards architectural quality capable of relating coherently to the context is fundamental.
The idea of ALPS is that in Davos, Switzerland, another location pertaining to the Alps, the idea of Alps is to have a periodical meeting about the economic topics. For some years now, Trentino successfully hosts the Festival of Economics, therefore the alpine setting, most of all Trentina, turns out to be particularly suitable for the discussion of important actual and emerging issues, like the economy and landscape which are not very far apart to relate physical space and what part of it should be developed at different levels. Therefore landscape, not because it is a trend as has been stated, but because it is an economic, cultural, social and indentifying resource as well as an occasion to unite the project to different scales, from its territorial dimension to an architectural one.
To consider landscape, not as a background nor a cumbersome "monument", but as the face of a society rich in features or the image of a collectivity built in time overlaid by various layers of long

and progressive transformation which have not been excluded and not reduced in aesthetic value.
We still have the need to understand how to unite this period, individuate it from ephemeral trends and render it the result of research, but some results emerge from a series of performed experiments, that makes us hope for original and contemporary, as well as functional – as defined by Manuel Gausa - centrality of the landscape.
The urges and issues are numerous, and from the conflict with reality, reflecting on the condition which this resource has assumed in our country, from a great deal of research emerges the landscape project which a great part of the Italian culture caught off guard, extending and intenly defending – often contradictory – its heritage, above all with public safety measures.
And if in more occasions it is possible to accept progressive changes in the landscape project, it is due to the strong political urges of the EU joined by the possibility of including the value of the landscape in all the action planning, transformations, government acts and urban or territorial changes, as well as the unification among simple and correct construction processes and new directions of architectural quality and settlements. Starting from this first edition, ALPS is an initiative created in Trentino, by a university which intends to progress and perform research, around the active synergy by the innovation that it is capable of producing, as well as by administrations, autonomous province and local organizations.
A Biennial that regards an arc of facts, Italian and European, that today, throughout the Alps, that has a population of about sixteen million, with a consequent high impact by settlements, tourism and fruition of the locations which imposes the need to reflect upon the models in use and the issues to bring forth.
From this first edition and in the following ones, ALPS intends to become an open and permanent workshop; to combine with similar initiatives; to compose the center of attraction for research; to become the "common house" to internationalize advanced research of the various issues that are the base of its thematic origin.
An "incubator" of innovative and original ideas, of projects and investigations, creating atlases with a divulged permanent center with the capacity to attract people and activity. With the use of accessible instruments and speech, that communicate not just with the staff, but widely comprehensible, directed towards the construction of a new "environmental" conscience that will constitute and connect the "constraints" and "safeguards" along with "project" and "quality". It will take the place of, in the perennial conflict between nature and settlment, through the project's instruments, with new forms of equilibrium between the various parts of the different landscapes.
Trentino can be a privileged spot to relaunch, keep together and develop these significant experimentations: the "Cycle of the Months" of the Castello del Buonconsiglio, on of the effective, evocative representations of the transformation of man on the landscape, it is the key icon of this long journey. The journey begins from the presence of architects, from the expressive power like Adalberto Libera, that goes through the years of arduous and perpetual experimentation of the urban topics and regards the museum network and research centers, at a European and international level in art, sustainability, as far as the agricultural landscape among the best ones in the Alps that clearly characterize the places of Trentino.
ALPS Biennial, measured by this reality and its glance turned towards Europe, it aspires to become an extraordinary soundboard, attractor of scholars and high cultural tourism, an engine of innovation and development models.

Pino Scaglione
Faculty of Enginereeng, Trento University

The Brenner axis as opportunity of collaborative practices among territories

The realization of the Trans European Transport Network (TEN-T) will produce further territorial hierarchies within the EU space. In fact, if TEN-T is going to develop territories that will be able to take advantage of the construction of the Corridors, it will weaken, at the same way, territories that will be not in the position to interact with these major infrastructures. At the moment territories are positioning themselves in competition with neighbouring areas in order to maximize the potential advantages coming from the new infrastructures. Instead, it would be opportune for neighbouring territories, in order to calibrate their own efforts and cope with common difficulties, to practise collaboration rather than competition. Collaboration is, in fact, a much more advantageous practice if a common ground on mutual benefits is established and negotiated by the different territorial stakeholders. In the following notes, upcoming collaborative practices are envisioned among the territories sited on the Italian side of the Brenner axis - which is in its turn a segment of the European Corridor I – considering the construction of this infrastructure as an opportunity to experiment a new territorial governance. Such collaborative practices are suggested, anyway, on one hand by common characteristics of these territories and on the other by existing experiences of collaboration among them. The materials and results discussed, relate to the research work recently performed by the Italian Society of Urban Planners and the Department for territorial development, planning and coordination of the Italian Ministry of Infrastructures (Ministero delle Infrastrutture, 2007a,b).

Towns and territories along the Brenner axis

Along the Italian side of the Brenner axis, outlined by the incisions of the Isarco and Adige valleys, lines up a system of small and middle-sized towns, among which Trento and Bolzano come out. These towns constitute connective nodes of both important communication routes that depart transversally from the main valleys, and minor roads, which develop along lateral valleys to end in their tops. At the southern end of the axis, Verona plays the role of collector and separator of fluxes, not only commercial, casting itself as a sea port in the land while evoking a city image suggested by the scholar Scipione Maffei in the eighteen century. Historically, the history and the role of the above mentioned towns are profoundly intertwined with the history and the role of the Brenner corridor, that from the pre-industrial epoch has represented the principal infrastructure used by continuous fluxes of commodities, moving up and down the River Adige, coming from Germany and from various alpine valleys, which needed to be managed and organized.

In different measures to the past, today the futures of these towns appear as well linked to their territories where, in the last 30 years, took place a local development certainly differentiated but equally dynamic. In other terms, a relevant percentage of the revenue is today produced by several local contexts with which towns have established tight relationships. In Alto Adige-South Tyrol are the districts, where tourist and agricultural activities mix together, the agricultural and food chains of production, the specialized manufacturing products that constitute territorial “multinational companies”, that is territories able to face international competition on the basis of a local and integrated system of production and/or services supply. Also in the Verona province the shoes production, the marble extraction and working, the machines production, the thermo mechanical devices production, the agricultural and in particular the wine production, take place in the districts. However, the exchange activated by these productions has its engine in the commercial intermediation operated in the town and particularly in the activities that intervene in the Quadrante Europa – the “harbour” of Verona - one of the most important Italian transport infrastructures as far as intermodality and logistics integrated systems are concerned. In this framework, Trento, Bolzano and Verona represent as many strategic places for these local contexts, given that notwithstanding the achieved well being they continue to present a shortfall as far as urban characters are concerned. Hence, differently to what happened in other Northeast Italian areas, there is not in fact an urban evolution of such territories stimulated by the relevant economic growth. On the contrary we find two different dynamics: that one which affects the towns and that one which affects other centres. In other words Verona, Trento and Bolzano move at a different speed in comparison with other urban centres.

This can be recognized not only in the Verona province, where the size of the chief town overhangs all the other centres but also in Trentino, where Rovereto plays a relevant cultural function, and in Alto Adige-South Tyrol where Bolzano is actually located in an urban polycentric system in which historical and economically vibrant towns such as Brixen and Meran take part. Briefly, we can say that differently to the other urban centres, major towns are the sites where the most important initiatives take place, including the ones dealing with education, training and research. It can be explained by the fact that major towns are not only the places where public and private decisions are taken, but also the only places that offer a sufficient critical mass as to warrant the efficacy of decisions.

We can draw an example by looking at Bolzano. The Autonomous Province of Bolzano has for decades – even for reasons we could agree with - notoriously hindered the growth of the major town. It has in fact tried to develop a polycentric urban system, while placing and reserving a certain amount of resources for Meran, Brixen, Brunik, Sterzing and respectively all the other centres distributed along the valleys. However, whereas an investment made in Bolzano immediately proves to increase and reproduce urbanity, in another centre it does not: it becomes an incremental advantage, not a multiplier.

That said, Verona, Bolzano, Trento – but it is quite redundant to dwell on this aspect - compensate the deficit of urbanity of the local contexts supplying advanced services, developing innovation, managing and selecting fluxes. The tight relationships, which took place among towns and the contexts of local development, have combined to create territorial systems highly competitive by promoting both the synergy of different territorial vocations and specific roles and territorial characters. With a further advantage for the Autonomous provinces of Trento and Bolzano: that one represented by the self-government that has ensured in the course of time effective and coherent policies.

The success achieved by these territories, confirmed by both the high revenue and the quality of life of their inhabitants, is due to separate development paths, meaning that it is quite difficult to find significant synergies among them. Therefore, the choice made by the territories of Bolzano, Trento and Verona of acting on their on account, if not in competition, even facing the globalization challenge, could be considered in continuity and coherent with the past. Such choice appears, besides from the behaviours of several administrators, even from the most recent programmatic documents drawn up by the provincial institutions. They are the two strategic documents drawn up by the Autonomous Provinces of Bolzano and Trento with reference to the drawing up of the National strategic framework 2007-2013 (Provincia autonoma di Bolzano, 2005; Provincia autonoma di Trento, 2006) and the Preliminary document supporting the choices of the Territorial coordination plan drawn up by the Province of Verona (2006). Even considering the strategic plans drawn up by the towns (Città di Bolzano, 2006; Comune di Trento, 2003; Comune di Verona, 2004), do not appear significant references to fields of common initiatives among them. In the case of Bolzano synergies are envisioned with several European towns but not with Trento.

Experiences of collaboration among territories: the major infrastructures along the Brenner axis

There are certainly cultural, political and historical reasons that have contributed to prevent a long time any forms of cooperation among these territories. However, where economic opportunities have become real and crucial, collaborations between different territorial actors – both private and public - have been very successful. It is what can be seen in some valleys of the Dolomites, where tourist operators acting in agreement with administrators, have created the biggest ski carousel in the world: the Dolomite Super-ski system. Something similar has happened and is happening in the Brenner axis with regard, in particular, to the railway high capacity. It could not be otherwise considering the relevance and role of this natural passage linking the North and South of Europe in the past, present and future.

The objective of creating a fast railway link between the Inn Valley and the Adige Valley goes back to the time when the aim was to create the conditions for stabilizing and consolidating relations and exchanges along these valleys. Later, – in the 80s - exchanges between Veneto and Bayern are encouraged in order to reduce distance between territories. In the mid 90s, the railway line, which avails itself of the Brenner tunnel, became an European project that started being formally realized. It was in 1996, that studies and plans for the basic gallery of Brenner were sponsored with the creation of the Brenner Basis Tunnel, an European company where the Italian Railway Network, the Austrian Republic and the Tyrol Land work together. The idea of the gallery and subsequent hypotheses, were thought through locally and have for some time involved different administrations and stakeholders operating together. A clear example of collaboration we can refer to is the Brenner Railway Community Action, an organism developed in 1991 characterized by the presence of the Provinces and the Lands of the territories crossed by the Brenner axis, the Chambers of Commerce of Verona, Trento, Bolzano, Tyrol and Bayern. The aim of such collaboration is twofold: partners have the opportunity to make joint decisions in relation to the development of the existing railway line and the construction of the new Brenner line and they share the responsibility to inform the population living along the railway of the project development. In the Action Community multiple interests had been compared and had subsequently converged. The territories located before the Alps and on the other side of the Alps do gather together the origin and destination of fluxes and are interested in keeping this role. Diversely, the territories that are crossed by the railway and invested with commodity fluxes – which are mainly facilitated by heavy goods vehicles - are interested in deviating at least part of this transport on the railway. However, without referring to the most involved territories that have specific roles and functions in actually developing the railway, territorial leadership of the Alpine territories transcends the management of emergency. As a matter of fact, the railway in Trentino and Alto Adige-South Tyrol crosses both provinces, representing on the one hand a penalizing factor and on the other an economic opportunity which goes beyond the coming and going of tourists. Furthermore, without going too deeply into the past, the realization of the Brenner motorway has favoured the relocation and growth of local transport enterprises, which have quickly gained a leading position in the market.
It is at the level of process management and big transport infrastructures that territorial leadership reveals itself more strikingly. In order to clarify this idea, let us consider that the Autonomous Region of Trentino Alto Adige-South Tyrol, the two Autonomous Provinces of Trento and Bolzano, and the Councils of Trento and Bolzano control the Brenner Motorway Spa over 50%. Now besides having the benefit of the A22 motorway this partnership includes substantial financial shares of other transport companies including the railway. Moreover, it is involved in the implementation of both the Mantova South-Cremona motorway and, as a future prospective, the Chioggia- Mantova North motorway.
In other terms, with regard to great fluxes of traffic, which cross the alpine territories, these latter ones respond through not only using traditional instruments of territorial government but also investing capitals in those companies that can support effectively territorial management. So that we find the influence of the Autonomous Provinces of Trento and Bolzano in the capital of strategic companies starting from the Brenner Basis Tunnel to the Valerio Catullo Airport Spa, the company that controls the airport of Verona-Villafranca and then the traffic flows of a basin constituted by Verona, Brescia, Mantova, Vicenza, Rovigo, Trento and Bolzano and also the airport Gabriele d'Annunzio of Brescia-Montichiari. We also have to bare in mind the multiple initiatives of the local construction enterprises, which aim through consortia to get into the big business through the realization of works both in the basic tunnel and other features of the new railway line. Going back to the corridor, territorial leadership also manifests itself in reference to propose solutions regarding the crux of the high railway capacity drawing up. The two Autonomous Provinces tend to prefer a solution, which encloses new railway tracks underground, which rectifies that one proposed by the Italian Railway Network. The aim being to avoid that the principal purpose of the new infrastructure, which is for both the Provinces to transfer further heavy road traffic to the railway in order to improve the quality of life of the territories involved in the project, be eluded exacerbating the problems caused by the existing situation, Moreover, the three territories, strong in their experience in fluxes management, do intend that the entire mobility of the corridor could be reorganized by a specific authority in order to create synergies between the various road, railway, energy and communication networks from the perspective of sustainability and economy of transport.

Scenarios of collaboration: landscape and environment

Environmental protection and landscape conservation, in territories where both environment and

landscape are crucial factors of development, can represent as many fields of collaborative practices. Leaving aside the Stelvio National Park, were experiences of common administration have well established roots, by way of example can be indicated on one hand the Baldo Mountain and on the other the Garda Lake, which both extend across the Trento and Verona provinces.
The Baldo Mountain chain lengthens by the eastern side of the Garda Lake, between the hollow of Loppio and the plane of Caprino Veronese, being delimited on the east by the Lagarina Valley, where the River Adige runs. It is a recreational area, with winter sports infrastructures, but mostly a protected area with a Special Protection Area of 6500 hectares on the Verona province side, called Baldo Mountain West and two Sites of Community Importance on the Trento province side, which together cover a surface of 2600 hectares, called Baldo Mountain-Valdritta Peak and Baldo Mountain of Brentonico. If the western side, which faces the Garda Lake, presents steep slopes and thick vegetation, the eastern one slopes down slightly to the valley revealing from time to time a remarkable landscape that expresses a perfect balance between natural features and traditional agricultural practices. Moreover, there are an extraordinary presence of endemic species and precious sites of reproduction of migratory birds.
From time some subjects, among which environmental associations, are intentioned to transform the Baldo Mountain in a large protected area as well to guarantee the continuity of both the landscape and the natural conditions. But discussions between these subjects and the institutions is occurring in fact separately, given the difficulty in having the provincial administrations sat down at the same table. On the contrary, a joined initiative of the Autonomous Province of Trento and the Province of Verona would produce positive effects not only on protecting environment and landscape but also on the attractiveness of their territories. The Garda Lake, which is part of the territories of three provinces and three regions, is notoriously the widest lake of Italy. As far as water resources and hydraulic dynamics management is concerned, the lake is under the jurisdiction of the River Po Basin Authority that performs this task in concert with the Autonomous Province of Trento, which Public waters utilization plan is equivalent to a basin authority of national level plan. Moreover, to coordinate interventions concerning the lake and its hinterland, with reference in particular to the environment and land use change, water quality, safety, tourism flow and cultural activities, was created the Community of Garda that collects 70 municipalities located in the provinces of Trento, Verona, Brescia and Mantova. The relevance of the problems, above all the environmental ones, raised by this wide lake demands however a further engagement, that one of the major institutions that have in great measure the responsibility of both the territorial transformations and their impacts on the water resources. They are problems punctually indicated by the River Po Basin Authority following a research carried out on the alpine lakes. First of all the inadequacy of the management of water resources with reference to their manifold uses, which is reflected by conflicts among users, above all tourism operators and farmers. Moreover, the growing difficulty in conciliating the need of water regulation – but also of water consumption – with the preservation of water natural ecosystems. Finally, the preservation of water quality considering the high human pressure.
Today there is more awareness, in comparison to the past, of the fact that a solution to these problems can only arise from the collaboration between the institutions and the different subjects, both public and private, concerned. Especially in a context where does not emerge a decision maker endowed with a particular authority over the others and even an authoritative subject, as proved by the experience of the River Po Basin Authority, is in need of consensus to operate.

Corrado Diamantini
Faculty of Engineering, University of Trento

References
Città di Bolzano (2006), Idee 2015. Pensare la Città, Bolzano.
Comune di Trento (2003), Piano strategico della città di Trento, Trento.
Comune di Verona (2004), Idee al centro della città: il Piano Strategico della città di Verona, Verona.
Ministero delle Infrastrutture - Dipartimento per la Programmazione ed il Coordinamento dello Sviluppo del Territorio (2007a), Il territorio come infrastruttura di contesto. Contributi alla programmazione 2007-2013, Roma
Ministero delle Infrastrutture - Dipartimento per la Programmazione ed il Coordinamento dello Sviluppo del Territorio (2007b), Reti e Territori al futuro. Materiali per una visione, Roma.
Provincia autonoma di Trento (2006), Documento strategico provinciale preliminare, Trento.
Provincia autonoma di Bolzano (2005), Studio per la predisposizione del Documento Strategico Regionale Preliminare per la politica di coesione 2007-2013, Bolzano.

Alpine landscapes in the north-west

Transformations

Only by following the infrastructural corridors of the valley bottom, climbing the recently urbanised slopes and penetrating in the rural hamlets, abandoned or reclaimed by the new tourist projects that it is possible to observe the full impact of the transformations in contemporary settlements in the Alps. It is here, where the three-dimensional is not only represented by the architectural 'cultivation' of the land, but also in the substrata itself, that the processes of construction and rewriting of the territory become fully evident.

From this point of view the Alps appear once again as they did during twentieth-century Modernity, almost a strategic laboratory, in which to measure – in the intersection of nature and man-made structures, between the historical palimpsest and contemporaneity – modern needs and in particular to experiment with and clarify new figures and projectual practices.

Here in the Department research unit, we have worked intensely in recent years on the settlement, infrastructure and landscape changes in the western Alps. In the studies published in Approfondimento Valle di Susa del Piano Territorial della Regione Piemonte (study of the Piemonte regional authorities' territorial plans for the Susa Valley) the entire axis of the transalpine corridor became the location in which to understand the logic of contemporary settlement practices, in the meeting and conflict between local and super-local contentions. The recognition and the tracing of the settlement patterns thus became the basis for projectual prefiguration on the scale of the valley.

Similarly, the research carried out during the doctorate on the lower Aosta valley made it possible, through the historical reconstruction of recent processes of transformation of the territory, to understand the logic that lies behind – in the interweaving of planning and individual action – each distinctive modificatory action, but also the specificity of the Valle d'Aosta model with respect to that of the valleys of western Piemonte.

Additionally, the recent research under the new Piano Paesistico (building restrictions plan) of the Piemonte regional authorities into the settlement patterns, has made it possible to reconstruct on a vast scale the continuity and differences in the configuration of the Alpine landscapes of the north-west, also highlighting the relationship that binds the transformations of the internal mountain areas with the dynamics of the piedmont territories.

Man-made landscapes

We must add to this work on the territorial settlement patterns the specific study on a small-medium scale of the man-made landscapes. For some time, through research conventions, we have supported local communities in the western alpine valleys. In Ostana - Oustano in Occitan – in the upper Po valley we are, for example, planning with the residents the new entrance to the principal village, with the inclusion of new constructions, the planning of open spaces and the organisation of an open-air rock gym.

Just a few hundred metres away, we are building a sports and wellness centre, which will support the policies for the valorisation of the area, in a perspective of compatible tourism: a building with zero energetic impact, thanks to the combined use of solar, photovoltaic and geothermal technologies. Even the stone walls of the building are paradoxically innovative, since experiments on the layering of walls has recovered – in spite of the difficulties created by the fact that the area is seismic – the bearing function of the material, nowadays used merely for cladding and facing.

Further up the valley, in the centre of the hamlet of Miribrart, we are organising a project for a cultural centre, which will become a place for meeting and research, and for studies on linguistic minorities. In this work, side by side with local administrators and residents, the threads of centuries of history – frayed by the great transformations of recent decades – are being woven into contemporaneity, in a performance that sees everyone as players and actors.

Research

Then there are the research projects on rural and modern architecture in the mountains, on the alpine landscape. A 'deposit' that derives from the congress on alpine architecture promoted by the

Politecnico di Torino in the fifties, and which exists locally in a 'seam' of research that has never since been interrupted. So there exists, to speak of recent works, the Atlante dell'edilizia montana nelle alte valli del Cuneese (atlas of mountain constructions in the upper Cuneo valleys), of which various volumes have been published, edited by Lorenzo Mamino and Paolo Mellano. Other recent publications are Architettura alpina moderna in Piemonte e Valle d'Aosta (modern alpine architecture in Piemonte and Valle d'Aosta) by Antonio De Rossi [Allemandi, 2005], and the collective volume Paessaggi in verticale (vertical landscapes) [Marsilio, 2006]. Or other books, such as Abitare le Alpi and Terre Alte (living in the Alps and Highlands), which gather studies carried out by lecturers and researchers in the Department in recent years.

Architecture

While these are the paths followed within the university structure, there are also individual journeys. In the Occitan valleys a group formed by Massimo Crotti, Antonio De Rossi and Marie-Pierre Forsans is creating for a private operator, in a wood on a south-facing slope, a volume with pure forms destined to become a wellness and meditation centre. On a parallelepiped that juts from the slope, with bearing structure, internal and external claddings in wood, it sits on another volume completely in glass, recalling the alpine-expressionist Glasarchitectur of the early twentieth century.
From inside it gives the impression of floating in space amongst the trees, looking out onto the magnificent Monviso, which dominates all the valleys of the Cottian Alps.

Antonio De Rossi
Department of Architectural Planning and Industrial Design of the Polytechnic University of Turin

Landscape design
IUAV research program

Based on the notions and objectives proposed by the European Landscape Convention, the Venice IUAV University is committed to promoting research and education in the field of landscape (seen as "an area, as perceived by people, whose character is the result of the action and interaction of natural and/or human factors" (Art.1), and therefore "an essential component of people's surroundings, an expression of the diversity of their shared cultural and natural heritage, and a foundation of their identity" (Art.5).
More specifically, IUAV is committed to working in the field of education and research in the area of landscape design, that is management and implementation techniques for conservation and transformation processes of the landscape.
This activity of research coordination has started with the setting up of a specific Research Area within the University just a few months ago, and of a number of Research Units responsible for current and forthcoming projects.
For IUAV, which, with its three Schools, is specifically focussed on design (architecture, urban areas, and spaces) based on art, architecture, urban and spatial planning, putting landscape design at the core of its interests means to start multidisciplinary research projects, aimed to know, interpret, design and build "landscapes", with a view to virtuously transforming them ("actions, from a perspective of sustainable development, to ensure the regular upkeep of a landscape, so as to guide and harmonize changes which are brought about by social, economic and environmental processes" (Art.1).
This multidisciplinary approach to research includes aesthetic, cultural, environmental, social and economic aspects of landscapes, seen as a "complex project".
"The viewpoint of landscape design has the special ability to identify or establish relations between elements of different nature, both material and immaterial, rather than between objects which are defined per se" (Zagari).
The "relational" aspect of landscape design, together with the central issue of time, make this research area very specific and unique, highlighting on the one hand context-related values, both in geographic and historical and cultural terms (relations with places and local identities), and time-related elements (seasonal changes, relations with climate conditions), and on the other, highlighting interdisciplinary connections with a view to a closer cooperation between professionals of different scientific backgrounds (geography, earth sciences, ecology and environmental sciences, architecture, landscape art and architecture, urban and spatial planning, history and representation sciences).
The relational character and the core elements of time and movement in landscape design (rooted in the history of garden art, in the design of public spaces and landscaping, starting from the experiences of classical Greek and Roman tradition and oriental tradition, until the eighteen-century "Pittoresque" trend) connect artistic and architectural research in this area with the scientific and aesthetic-philosophical thought found in Heidegger's reflections on space and inhabiting, with the phenomenology of perception, of topology and fractal geometry, with artistic experiences linked to space, senses, vision, hapticity, etc., and with related research works on representation techniques.
This research area is in line with major contemporary art and architecture trends and experiences, that could produce fruitful exchanges with the international scientific community. This explains the significant contribution provided by areas such as aesthetics, history and landscape representation.
Landscape design is currently becoming more and more important due to the ecological-environmental problems and man-caused transformations affecting the planet.
Landscape design therefore incorporates traditional architectural-urban themes, that can fall within the framework of "urban design" and its research techniques ("urban morphology"), but at the same time also extends to geographic-territorial areas, well beyond the transformations caused by human settlements, and which can be defined as "the built environment".
Following on the pioneer intuition of its "founder", Giuseppe Samonà, and based on the theoretical and methodological production of major representatives of Italian architecture in the past fifty years, such as Giancarlo De Carlo, Carlo Aymonino, Aldo Rossi, Gianugo Polesello, Vittorio Gregotti, the Venice School has

always insisted on extending its interests and design techniques to the city, the region, the territory. This approach has helped produce high-profile theoretical and applied research, thus able to meet the need for innovative instruments and new techniques in the field of landscape design and management.
This explains the particular contribution to research provided by disciplines like urban and architectural design – together with geographical and environmental sciences - and the fundamental contribution by the more specific area of landscape architecture and landscape urbanism, that rely on the involvement of authoritative national and international contract professors that IUAV has recently recruited and who can certainly give an innovative thrust to this study area.
Research based on the topic of landscape and applied to highly complex and stratified contexts subjected to major processes of transformation (as, for example, the ecosystems of the Venice Laguna or the Po Delta, industrial and residential developments in Mestre, the Veneto "diffused city", mass tourism in the Veneto-Friuli sea resorts or alpine areas, historical contexts like the Veneto Villas or small cities on the mainland around Venice, and the network of rivers) will open the way to extremely important socio-political applications, that are fundamental in the cooperation with administrative authorities (regional, provincial and municipal bodies), with environmental and other agencies (water conservation authorities, mountain communities, etc.) and closely connected with policies for the protection and improvement of the environment and the landscape.
At the same time, this type of research can be the basis for methodological studies and innovative experiments on the application and implementation of instruments of governance, planning and policy-making in the area of urban planning. These innovative instruments will be closely connected with policies for landscape and environmental protection, improvement and planning and with new approaches to environmental-oriented urban planning, which were once of minor importance with respect to housing policies. This will open the way to a large area of research works and investigations into planning policies and instruments for the governance of spatial transformations (with particular reference to protected or fragile territories because of their hydro-geological, natural or historical-archaeological characteristics, and also with reference to territories marked by major development and transformation processes, due to huge housing developments, tourism, industrial and infrastructure growth, the mine industry, etc.).
Moreover, a specific research area will be devoted to the introduction of "Landscape Observatories" in Italy, as proposed after the recent review of the Urbani Law by Minister Rutelli.
For all these reasons, the research contribution provided by the sectors of landscape and territorial planning is particularly important, specifically for their close connection with geographical and environmental subjects.Therefore, the innovative contribution of research lies in the combination of the more traditional analytical and design skills of architecture and urban planning (see the studies of urban morphology, urban-scale design experiments and the studies on housing phenomena) with the inputs derived from landscape architecture (recently strengthened by close relations with important international experts), together with a more marked integration with geography and technical-environmental subjects, a revival of historical studies on landscape, and a greater focus on aesthetics and art, as related to landscape, and studies on landscape representation.
This wide-ranging approach will involve experts from all three IUAV Schools and will open up new and fruitful relations with nearby Universities (Ca' Foscari, Padova, Trento etc.) and with Italian and European Universities that already participate in the research work and conferences recently organized by IUAV (see the series of international meetings Dessiner sur l'herbe, the recent foundation of the European Network Uniscape and other similar initiatives).
This coordinated research work, here briefly summarized, comes alongside with, and derives inspiration from, the reorganization of the whole teaching system implemented over the past four years, with the start of a two-year graduate course on "landscape architecture", and the implementation of some parallel cultural initiatives (above all the already mentioned Dessiner sur l'herbe conferences).
The best and most innovative results achieved in this field come from the so-called integrated workshops,

where – working on common fields of application – it has been possible to successfully carry out a common multidisciplinary work between architects, designers, urban designers, landscape architects and other professionals, with a continuous exchange and true and proper "integration" of know-how, methods and instruments.
Project design – its definition – can come above all from this exchange and close collaboration. A fundamental contribution has been provided by IUAV over the past four years, with the involvement of major European landscape experts, who have been offered teaching contracts: Paolo Burgi, Joao Nunes, Imma Jansana, Manuel Ruisanchez and other international experts, thereby promoting an important process of internationalization specifically focussed on landscape.

Renato Bocchi
Director of DPA Department, IUAV-Venice

Ticino is an alpine town

The house at Maroggia of 1957 is for me one of the most successful buildings. In a certain way it is an abstract architecture, a constructive geometry. In front of a falling rock there is the opposite of a pure geometry. Here you will not find the so called integration. This house is detached object so as to become an object which is in itself absolutely rigorous. (1)

The words of Rino Tami, acknowledged father of the modern architecture in Ticino, express in a very clear way the behaviour of the architect facing its own context. When you build in the Canton Ticino you have to establish a particular relationship with the landscape. This was true in the past and it is so today. And it is true whether you oppose pure geometries or you look for an integration with the place. The pure geometric form which is able to include in an harmonic relation all the elements suggested by the architectonic theme is for Tami the real value of the new architecture.

At Maroggia again, in a geographic context where the architect has to deal with a rocky and steep land facing a lake, Rino Tami completes the context relations theme with other two projects: the adjusting to the natural shape of the land by a gradual section with three holiday houses built in 1954 and the holiday house of 1963, which is a building measuring the land slope and becoming a direct link between earth and water and where a boat finds place in the cellar and a car on the roof. We have therefore three behaviours: opposition, integration and mediation or measuring, three ways of reading and dealing with the context; behaviours that with these houses become real and visible.

To work in this particular context implies a relation with a complex and specific land where natural and artificial landscape cohabit, where valleys tend to fill up and buildings tend to climb beyond mountains foot. A place which is becoming more and more a natural space as a result of the disappearing of those activities that in the past made mountains a built landscape. Architects are always asked to have a constructive relation with the territory, nobody can avoid to try and translate the natural context.

Ticino territory is in major part made of mountains. It has few agricultural planes, many scattered villages usually placed upon the top of ancient river debris deposits or on the terraced slopes, and it is inhabited up to a limited altitude. In the valleys today we find the agricultural activities and the main urban expansion. These valleys in the past, before reclaimed land operations, were unhealthy places covered by rivers and cane damps.Here nature and artefact are strictly connected in the shaping of the territory.

A relationship that will be always taken into consideration by modern and contemporary architects, to such an extent that the projects will become also a tool to investigate the reality in order to build a new environmental balance. In this sense the project is to be considered a sort of investigating practice able to identify the territory transformation mechanism, to find the critical conditions and anticipate the evolutions.The purpose of the research lead for about five years by the Project Atelier of Mario Botta at the Architecture Academy of Mendrisio in Switzerland, during lessons managed by Gabriele Cappellato, Domenico Lungo and Mauro Cereghetti, was to elaborate a method to analyse and investigate the territory that takes into consideration both the natural and artificial elements of its morphologic character.

It is a question of pointing out construction objectives and peculiarities of the intervention areas, and in general the relation between urban and natural landscape, in order to elaborate an architectural project which find a precise and stable territorial placement.

Thematic charts are created through a selective observation and subsequent translation of the territory main elements. These charts are drown in different scales so as to better see the peculiarities and identities of the context.Observation and translation – this last one made through representation tools like drawings, photos, descriptive notes, altitude models – are useful to find out laws and transformation mechanism of the territory and the specific language of the context.

As mentioned, these charts are the result of a selective observation of urban landscape, a selection that is already an intention of transformation.

This method should lead to a project of the ground, where ground is meant as urban fact able to host an architectural object that express unity between the building and its physical support and an interconnection with the context.

Domenico Lungo
Architect, teacher at the Academy of Architecture of Mendrisio

Notes

*Ticino is an Alpine town, a new type of open and spread town that covers valleys from Piazza del Duomo in Milan to the foot of Gottardo mountains. Aurelio Galfetti Progetto e territorio. Il progetto Alptransit Ticino, in Aurelio Galfetti e Letizia Tedeschi (a cura di). Progetto e territorio, Mendrisio 2001, Accademia di Architettura Università della Svizzera italiana, p. 84.

(1) Rino Tami in AAVV, Rino Tami. Segmenti di una biografia architettonica, Zurigo 1992, ETH, p. 50.

(2) Rino Tami, De l'antigéometrie. Lettre tessinoise, in Werk n. 9, 1946, pp. 314-316.

(3) You must be able to build a new landscape rather than fit into the existing one. But to do this it is necessary to have a precise knowledge of the history, geography, architectural and socio-economic elements in order to give back its identity to the place where you intervene. This can be achieved by a research engagement in various disciplines like anthropology, geography, history, the study of settlements, their typology and morphology, and in the end with the study of the architectural project, which before being a tool of reality modification is a fundamental instrument of knowledge. Luigi Snozzi, Il sito – La natura e le opera dell'uomo, Abitare n. 206, 1986, p.103.

(4) All human interventions in the nature modifying its original shape are, in general terms, architectural operations as they deliberately produce new structures, new relations between form and space, which in their turn, determine either an aesthetic enrichment or deterioration of the landscape. Rino Tami, L'autostrada come opera d'arte, in Tita Carloni (a cura di). Rino Tami, 50 anni di architettura, Bellinzona 1984, Edizioni Casagrande, pp. 122-123-125.

Analytic Project for an Alpine Valley

The Palamela building at Non Valley

The place appears as a mountain landscape designed by typical topographic elements of a low mountain valley: the different inclinations and conformations of natural slopes allow farming in the low valley and in the first declivities: the artificiality geometric of apple trees rows highlights, with linear parallel paths, it reveals the shapes, as if they were a great Land Art intervention, planned with aesthetic intentions.

The outline of "Palamela" building arises from morphology suggestion of that territory, marked by rows of apple trees where the espalier cultivation accentuates the outline of land ownership following precise guidelines, dictated by a combination of orographic criteria and a favourable sun exposure.

The image you perceive is like an industrious and rational patchwork which is the landscape the architectural project compares with: a whole of geomorphologic figures - shaped lands in centuries of farming - and parallel lines which engraved them.

Another system of signs try to fill together new buildings for the various activities of Palamela, to the agricultural land on which it will be built and it overlaps, without erasing this stratification of man-made tracks constructed with natural elements - earth and trees, both forced to an artificial landscape project.

The contact line of every single building inside the "Palamela", to the smooth slope of soil becomes a part of the plan, like geometric drawings of a carpet. The square general form of the weft doesn't interfere directly with the floor but connect single building to the external landscape.

Eleven parallel body beams, 136 meters long and 5 high, are lifted an average of three meters height from the mild slopes of ground; this structure of perfectly horizontal beams, spaced of eight meters, takes the step of each plot of land within is inserted which corresponds to the distance between each row of trees. At some points the soil comes to lap its undulations to the low page of the beams that seem to fly without gravity: quite all pillar disappear hidden within the undulations of the ground or inside the walls of internal buildings. These ones - exhibition spaces, classrooms, conference hall, shops, offices and refreshment rooms - are designed as independent and free pavilions within the mesh of beams that hold the semitransparent covering of connective spaces.

At first level the space between beams is often the connecting way to offices, included by the eight meters step of structure, as they were the moulded tubular elements hanging to different pairs of beams. It forms thus a mezzanines and balconies system, which allow you to explore Palamela spaces in different angles and heights.

In reading and interpretation of the agricultural land shapes governed by human actions, such as crops with their irrigation systems, the nature of the mountain area appears and insinuates into artificial signs and overlaps the paths of agricultural colonization and the local infrastructure; a landscape architecture project must be able to consider the changeable role of single parts and attribute values in composition to both new or already present elements in the place.

Altitude resort at Mount Bondone

Looking to an appropriate style and usage of a vernacular, often superficial, represent two widespread attitudes, in designing tourist equipments for alpine environment, inside the ideal conflict between conservation and reproduction of a priority value of territory. Landscape maintenance in mountain natural context is a necessary, but contrasting factor for tourist soil use: settlements development will be grow through the consumption of natural context.

Production and conscious implementation of new landscapes is the aim of this landscape architectural design research, not only in terms of preservation and conservation. In fact, natural and human landscape characterizes cultural identity in alpine regions, but also from his aesthetic perception becomes significant economic resources trough tourism.

In this project for an altitude settlement, architectural design and landscape architecture are applied to the study case of Monte Bondone, an alpine environment, 1,600 m., in Trentino region.

The project is such a kind of split architecture, adapting buildings to the natural morphology to compose a new landscape and to ensure best sightseeing to all rooms. From the access way the resort is facing

similar to an urban square front. From this point of view It shows up the main public facilities, open even to non-hotel guest: the auditorium, the first shape we meet, seems suspended almost to float above the pool -looking similar to a small mountain lake basin- derived in a hollow of the slope. The structures of this main building consist on laminated wood beams, and the coating surface is in natural wood. The second element facing, which completes the building front, is the restaurant, facing south to the square with large windows acting as solar collector. The roof of the restaurant is a large sheltered solarium that extends to the steep surface rising for free climbing. This ascent closes the front to the west side and is to function as a solar chimney to capture the thermal radiation, as well as visual appeal. Between the two volumes of the square is wedged the access porch to internal areas of the hotel, which leads guests to the reception and rooms.
These are standardized in two repeated variants, with different combinations in distribution: tower blocks and two-storey block. The first is composed of four columns distributed by a system of central routes at ramp; they are oriented according to cardinal points and facing, with large wooden balconies, to the best views of the landscape, mountain sloop and Adige valley; the south walls, more to be seen from the square than to offer visual from the rooms, are covered with solar thermal panels that create a chromatic contrast with the natural wood brise soleil.
Four single cottage houses complete the resort's landscape composition, at the lower side of the site, in ideal continuity to the broken lines of two storey terraced rooms departing from the rooms tower.

Claudio Lamanna
Faculty of Enginereeng, Trento University

The Palamela Conferences and Exhibitions Centre for the Valle di Non, Trento, is a plan developed in April 2006 with Andrea Lazzaroni. Collaborators: Silvia Filz, Fabio Pasini, and Nicola Realis.
Project for a mountain resort for mount Bondone, Trento, 2007-2008; design: C. Lamanna; collaborators: A. Lazzaroni and D. Cappelletti; digital modeling and render: P. Tamin

The cultural landscape of the Right Bank of the Adige in Vallagarina
An outline of an enhancement project

«The history of a place ought to be its "self-realization". That which was present at the outset as possibility, is uncovered through human action, illuminated and "kept" in works of architecture which are simultaneously "old and new" [and] which transform nature into the "cultural landscape"». So wrote Norberg-Schulz regarding the relationship between physical space and human activity, recognising in the balance between these components, the creation of a "cultural landscape" and therefore the development of places for living. His words express the reality of the Right Bank of the Adige in Vallagarina particularly well: "an anthropological place" in the full sense, to use the definition given by Marc Augé, in other words, a concrete and symbolic construction of the space which proffers itself as a keystone of sense to its inhabitants and as a keystone of intelligibility to its observers.

The territory of the Vallagarina opposite Rovereto is a large, natural, south-facing amphitheatre which has created itself over time, grafting a beautiful mosaic of forms and colours produced by settlements and agriculture onto the orographic and hydrographic characteristics of the land. Urban centres and rural hamlets, carriage tracks and paths, cultivations and terraced vineyards, woods and pastures create a sense of continuity from the valley floor, to the hills and mountains encircled by the channel of the Adige river to the east, the ridge of Bondone Stivo to the west, the col of Covelo to the north and the plains of Mori to the south.

Over the centuries, these physical characteristics have favoured authentic socio-economic integration which is reflected in the history of the "Comun Comunale": the ancient medieval mountain-agricultural communes (vicinia) which survived until the formation of the town councils at the beginning of the '800s. Despite the definition of these administrative boundaries, the strong supra-council character of the territory has never been lost, and in the spirit of this uninterrupted tradition, in 2007, the five present-day councils of Isera, Nogaredo, Villa Lagarina, Pomarolo and Nomi set up an Inter-Council Commission for the Development of the Adige Right Bank. One of the first tangible moves of the commission was to establish a collaborative relationship with the University of Trento, and with the Province, to share an ambitious aim: the launch of a joint project to establish an "Adige Right Bank agrotourism area" for the enhancement of the economic system, local industry, the territory and the environment, as well as the promotion and coordinated management of cultural and tourism activities.

As part of the enhancement project agriculture will play a strategic role in protecting the rural landscape, in strengthening the local wine-producing industry, in incentivising enogastronomic and craft activities rooted in the territory, and in initiating development policies which are both sustainable and respectful of the environment. It is only from a starting point such as this that it will be possible to create a series of organic steps of care and maintenance, aimed at transforming the whole area into a "cultivated garden" which will one day become the central attraction of the new "communal landscape area".

The aim of the programme, which is shared by the Inter-Council Commission and by the University research group, is to turn the idea of a landscape as a "total environmental body" into reality, whose rational form is produced and shaped by agricultural activity. This form will not focus «on conserving or reconstructing separate natural values, [but] on recognising the material nature of the whole anthropogeographic environment as usable and continually meaningful». To quote Vittorio Gregotti further, «this does not mean imagining the construction of a physical environment from which to influence or direct human behaviour, we wish simply to render the physical environment more accessible» preserving its total usability as an essential value, presenting once more «the living body of nature of which we are part as communication and knowledge of new possibilities».

The initial phase of describing the urban centres and the surrounding area has already been undertaken as part of the practical workshops of the courses of 'Computer-Aided Design' and "Urban and Environmental Surveying and Topography" in the fourth and fifth years respectively of the degree course in Architectural Engineering at the Faculty of Engineering of the University of Trento.

Simultaneously, consideration has begun of the possible structure which an "extended" project could take, which will mature in the light of a collective strategy of redevelopment of the whole of Right Bank of the Adige in Vallagarina, and which it is hoped, will ignite a "self-feeding" and "self-maintaining" process within the territory based on chain reactions. For example, favouring attractions aimed at sustainable and niche tourism such as short visits to discover the local identity which could become the main source of internal income for the territory itself: a public initiative such as this could have an immediate impact on private individuals thus soliciting independent entrepreneurial activity.
The starting point for the project could be the reconstruction of a network of cycle tracks and pathways through areas of particular historical relevance and natural beauty. Such a network is already partially in existence in the historic pathways connecting the five municipalities horizontally and vertically. The reconstruction of ancient paths through woods, panoramic areas and biotopes, vineyards and agricultural buildings, churches and castles, villas and historic homes could, in a relatively short time, create a rich system of relationships between the natural context and the various "artefacts" within it. In this way, the image of the path would be the symbolic form and aesthetic instrument on which to base successive phases of the project. Walking has always led to the creation of settlements and new types of sociality; by walking humans discover and construct the landscapes which surrounds them.

Giovanna A. Massari
Faculty of Enginereeng, Trento University

Zero energy house

Summary

The Gruppo Polo – Le Ville Plus building firm from Cassacco (Udine-Italy) and the University of Trento (Italy) are developing a prototype of a smart green building where a family of four people will live and that will be monitored for one year to check the correspondence to the project purposes. The total cost of the research project, included the construction, has been financed by the Friuli Venezia Giulia Region and by the Gruppo Polo – Le Ville Plus. The building is called "casa energy zero" referring to the fact that it does not use energy coming from conventional nets or from nonrenewable sources mainly of fossil origin. In addition the building is classifiable as autonomus house because the consumed energy is produced in situ by alternative and clean sources.

The main features of this smart green building are:

- carbon neutral;
- built with renewable materials and innovative building elements producing clean energy (sunspace, LVP intelligent window® , etc.);
- low energy consumption and with bioclimatic characteristic;
- integration between energy systems using alternative and clean sources;
- use of intelligent systems to manage clean energy sources in order to guarantee both inner environmental comfort and energy saving.

In order to test and validate the research expected results, the theoretic behavior of the prototype hypothesized during the design phase will be compared with the continuous on site monitoring of the functioning and performance of the active and passive systems, paying attention to the energy saving and the users' comfort conditions. The building is now under construction. It will be completed in Autumn 2008 when the monitoring and evaluation phase will start.

Introduction

This paper deals with a research activity carried out at the Laboratory of Building Design of the University of Trento (Italy) aimed at the development of an integrated design process of a prototype building, whose performance will be monitored and evaluated on a real scale model. The main features of the design process are:

a. use of natural materials both for the bearing elements, made of wood, and for the finishing realized with dry systems;

b. attention to the energy performance of the envelope both in winter and in summer period, working especially on their structure and composition as well as on the inner joints (between the base-elements) and the outer ones (between the sub-elements);

c. integration with energy systems using alternative and clean sources: passive solar systems (sun space, Trombe wall, natural ventilation), thermal and photovoltaic solar systems, biomass and geothermal systems;

d. installation of an intelligent system for the managing of both the active and passive solar devices in order to minimize the total energy consumption but assuring in the meantime the best inner users' comfort conditions, even through self learning procedures;

e. development of innovative building elements as the so called "LVP intelligent window®" that will generate low speed air draught in order to contribute to the cooling and warning of the rooms together with an intelligent system for the draught modulation and optimization.

The prototype will be monitored to check the correspondence to the project purposes. Comparative analysis with simulation model will be performed.

In the following chapters, the most relevant aspects of the project mentioned above will be deeply analyzed and explained.

The Bioclimatic Concept

For what concerns the bioclimatic strategies, the building (design by arch. Arnaldo Savorelli – Solarch Studio in Bussolengo – Italy) presents both passive elements for winter heating and for summer ventilation and cooling. First of all, it must be noticed the particular position of the construction inside the building site, situated at the northern side in order to let the widest part of the garden and the livable spaces directed to the South. The whole shape is interesting and studied in accordance with the local climate. The main body of the house, in fact, has a compact rectangular plant with an unique roof pitch facing the North with a double result: to protect the house from the northern cold winter winds and, in the meantime, to expose the widest part of the southern façade to the warm sun radiation during the cold season. Moreover, there is a little difference in altitude from the main roof and the secondary one on a lower level: it allows the presence of several little windows at the top of the building that, being inaccessible from the outside, can be left completely opened even during the night in order to guarantee a proper ventilation of the inner spaces during the warm season. The southern façade, facing the garden and the pool, is a wide glass surface that takes advantage of the sun irradiation and let it enter the house till the back of the space during winter, while in summertime it is shaded by overhangs and provided with brise-soleil in order to avoid over irradiation and glare phenomena. In addition, a sun space and a Trombe wall are present. The northern façade, on the contrary, has little windows most of which are used just for summer night ventilation and to allow a proper views to the north side of the landscape. The façades facing ast and West have themselves bioclimatic features, presenting low windows but large enough to let the user be delighted of the outer space without causing discomfort coming from the apparent daily sun path. Moreover, adequate shadows are provided.

The Building Technique

The prototype is a timber framed building with external and internal timber walls. The building is built with natural and renewable materials excepted the hardware of the carpentry that is in steel. For this reason the building is classifiable also as natural building. Actually in Italy there are few timber buildings, but their construction is increasing for the raising consciousness of users in relation with environmental issues and green buildings. In Italy, the majority of timber buildings are built with panel systems borrowed from the close Austria. Only few systems are planed and made in Italy, most of all with handmade systems. For this research we chose to experiment a framed system that could be produced with industrialized techniques and that is completely designed in Italy by the Gruppo Polo – Le Ville Plus with the support of the University of Trento. The choice of this building system instead of a panel one is due to the greater building tradition in framed construction, also if limited to the Italian Alpine Region. In addition, it allows an higher constructive flexibility and it is easier to adapt to different configurations, even if the various building components are made with industrialized processes. The expected time for the construction of the prototype was 10 months, but the real time for the end of the works will be presumably 14 months. The delay is due to the experimental feature of the building site and to the necessity to modify some building details during the construction phases in order to improve their performance. The pillars have a square cross-section 16x16 cm, they are connected to the basement by steel structure and steel plug. A knee wall connects together all the posts and it closes the frame. The main beams and the secondary beams (used sometimes as wall plates) are in glue-lam with a square cross-section 16x16/24 cm. The intermediate floor and the roof are built with glue-lam beams with a square cross-section 8x24 cm and a step of 50-80 cm. In both cases, the floor is built with board and insulation materials. In particular, the roof floor has a U value (thermal transmittance) of 0,197 W/m2K. The external walls are made up by thermally insulated elements and by timber panels. With this kind of wall it is possible to reach a value of thermal transmittance of U=0,192 W/m2K (Figure 3 and 4). The basement is a crawl space finished on the extrados by a reinforced-concrete slab. In this way concrete volume, which has a great heat capacity, can accumulate energy to help the heating system in the winter season.

The inner walls have a timber framework and plasterboard cladding. Wood fiber, a natural insulation material, is positioned in the free space between the frame grid. Nowadays, in Italy the most diffused type of inner wall is built by steel section and plasterboard cladding. This solution is in contrast with the natural house concept because the steel section set can determinate a Faraday cage that can reduce the inner environmental quality for the presence of electric charges that can not be disperse. In the prototype, a new type of inner wall will be tested that has not this problem because the frame is in timber and the elements are made by industrialized processes. The horizontal elements are lists 40x60 mm, the posts are two coupled lists 30x 50 mm. The system planned in this research is patented by the Gruppo Polo – Le Ville Plus and the University of Trento .

Another innovative element planned in this research, is the LVP intelligent window®. It is built by

two glazed panels with an interspace of 30-45 cm (depending on different solutions). Each panel has two openings with a flap putted on the top and on the bottom. In order to improve the air circulation in the interspace, a small fan is positioned in the lower part. The fan is operated by a small electric motor powered by a small photovoltaic system. The opening and the closing of the flaps manages the circulation of the air inside the interspace. In this way it is possible to run warm air into the house during winter, taking advantage of the greenhouse effect. In the same way, opening the opposite flaps it is possible to extract warm air from the inner space incrementing natural ventilation. The flaps are managed by the intelligent supervision system of the house and the opening/ closing is totally automatic depending on inner and outer environmental conditions (especially temperature values).
The building is now under construction. It will be completed in Autumn 2008 when the monitoring and evaluation phase will start.

The Intelligent System

The smart solutions implemented in the prototype building focus on the followings main goals:
- to test and verify the utility and the effective use of scenarios for the flexible utilization of automated passive solar systems;
- to quantify the contribution of automated control for the lighting, shading and conditioning systems;
- to experiment the possibility to guarantee both safety and security to the house users.

The devices and the correspondent functionalities of the smart system have been specifically established, in order to manage the interactions of all the technological system components in compliance with the peculiar issues of the prototype. In particular the following input devices have been included in the smart system design: temperature and humidity sensors, magnetic contacts to check the opening or closing state of the windows, occupancy and movement detectors, illuminance sensors (IEA, 2000).
Each device will be connected with a weather station in order to monitor the outside climate conditions (temperature, illuminance level, wind speed, rain) and with supervision touch screens in order to visualized and control the parameters available on the bus.
The design of the automation system has been developed in collaboration with the bpt group, in order to define both technical characteristics and programming possibilities of each device. Moreover in this phase the wiring structure, the topology of the bus system and the position of the smart elements have been identified.
The sunspace of the building is completely automated. It is a passive solar system, used mainly to heat the indoor spaces in the winter season. The automation system gives a specific signal about the proper functionality mode based on the outside weather conditions specifically connected with the proper use of the sunspace in winter season and with its complete opening in summer time.
The implementation of its functionality program has been previewed in two specific temporal modalities: seasonally and daily running function.
The functionalities of the smart system for the sunspace are:
- automated control of the opening/closing system of the windows, in order to optimize the convective fluxes of the air and the temperature level not only inside the sunspace but also in the adjacent rooms (automated control and priority of the manual operation);
- local and remote visualization of the windows opening/closing state and of the sunspace shading system according with the best position dynamically calculated;
- detection of the temperature values in the sun space.

The cooling system of the building is based on natural ventilation strategies. The functionality of the automation system for the natural ventilation improvement in the inner space is focused on the activation and the trigger action of the windows automated opening system. The main input parameter of this regulation function is the local detection of the inside temperature in order to support the air fluxes. The opening modalities of the opening systems are the same described above for the sunspace.
The building is equipped with shading systems. Their automated control is applied in different complexity levels: from the simple motorized action of the shading system to the complex control of smart shading systems, able to change properly the brise-soleil position according to indoor and outdoor environmental conditions (temperature and illuminance level). In this way, by means of the automation control system, it is possible to adjust both the slope level (angle of descent) of the brise-

soleil elements and their movement speed (step by step or up and down).
The heating system of the building is controlled by the automation system. It is previewed, indeed, the integrated control of the heating system by means of the simultaneous use of radiant heating, solar panels and pellets boiler with height efficiency (the so called "integrated fireplace"). The whole system is regulated using a supervision system with seasonal mode. It is based on the subdivision in thermal zones of the radiant heating system.
The smart functionalities of the control system for this specific application involves the integration of the radiant heating with the solar panel, the proportional opening in continuous of the thermal valves of each single zone, the separate and differentiated activation of each defined thermal zone and, at least, in addition, the possibility to get, a remote control of the whole heating system.
The photovoltaic panels are connected to the automation system only for what concerns the data related to the hourly production of photovoltaic energy. It is indeed useful a comparison of these data in relation with the weather parameters values recorded by the outdoor weather station, correlated with the sun position and the sky conditions.
The smart system has been included as tool to guarantee the users' safety in the experimental house, because it is able to monitor the domestic environment for what concerns faults and malfunctions of the systems or fire dangers. Moreover the automation system could help the normal manage of the domestic environment, for example by the automated opening of heavy shading systems.
With smart systems it is possible to have, as well by remote position, a constant security control of the building, through outside and boundary alarm and detection systems. At the same time it is possible to visualize the visitors' identity using the connection with video-phone or mobile-phone. For this issue, the same magnetic contacts on the windows and occupancy detectors installed for the energy saving management could be used.
Significant data about the daily use of the building elements are controlled and monitored by the bus net of the devices installed. The supervision system allows indeed not only the recording of environments parameters but also the users' behavior analysis. With these data it will be possible to improve the theoretic model of the building analyzed in relation with both weather conditions/building constructions characteristics and the user' action in real use situation (Reinhart, 2004).

The on Site Monitoring

Even in Italy, summer average temperature are slowly increasing causing brief but very intensive muggy periods. The design and the construction of a light envelope building in a temperate Mediterranean climate is therefore a challenge directed towards the investigation of two main aspects: the possibility to guarantee adequate summer comfort conditions in bioclimatic free-running buildings, that is design with great attention to the local climate (most of all with reference to the sun position and prevailing winds direction); the necessity to provide building elements with an high thermal capacity in order to diminish temperature rises. This second aspect has been recently faced by the Italian regulation (Legislative Decree 311/06) providing a minimum mass value of the elements of the envelope of 230 kg/m2 if the average daily solar global irradiation of the site in July is over 290 W/m2. The mass, however, is not the only parameter to be taken into consideration speaking of thermal inertia and, most of all, it is also important where massive elements are positioned, even considering the building inner spaces.
In order to prove and to verify that this approach guarantees an high quality result, better users comfort conditions (following the recent adaptive comfort theory - Nicol and Humphrey 2002), an higher energy saving and the possibility to built using wood even in temperate climates, the research approach is based on to main activities:

1. the continuous thermal survey of the building;
2. an energy simulation in dynamic state conditions.

Continuous Thermal Survey

It will be carried on by recording data of the temporal courses of some specific environmental parameters (air temperature, relative humidity, air velocity, globe temperature, walls surface temperature) related to the most used thermal comfort indices (PMV and PPD – Fanger 1970) and to the adaptive comfort theory. Probes will be positioned in a certain number of rooms chosen for their exposure, their level and their different use. In addition surface temperature probes will be position both inside and outside the outer wall of the building together with fluxmeters, in order to reconstruct, during real life conditions,

the thermal profile of the walls and their thermal behaviour in terms of thermal inertia (phase shift and temperature decrease). In a second time, a new approach (already experimented by the authors) concerning the measurement on site of the thermal transmittance of the opaque elements of the envelope will be deepened by means of thermal fluxmeters and thermovision technique, both in a quasi steady state condition (winner period) and in thermal transitory one (spring and autumn).
The results of the research will increase a data bank concerning several thermal survey campaigns of real buildings that have been carried on by the Building Design Laboratory since 2002. In this particular experience, the surplus value (besides the possibility to monitor a building with mixed-mode systems, both passive and active, put all together one near the other in the same climatic context, with the same boundary conditions and so contemporarily assessable) is that, as far as the research goes on, some parts of the building can be modified in order to improve the thermal performance and the comfort conditions according to the output of the research itself.

Energy Simulation in Dynamic State Conditions

Once the building has been monitored, a virtual model of will be realized using specific software (EnergyPlus and its pre-processor DesignBuilder for the thermal simulation, Flovent for the fluid dynamic one) in order to determine the virtual temporal courses of indoor temperature and of the heat transfer through the building envelope as well as the circulation of the air flow in the indoor spaces and its capability to cool down the space and the structure. In a second time, a critical calibration of the model will be made in order to take into account the real behaviour of the inhabitants and their use of the building components (by means of specific questionnaires as well as a careful analysis of the recorded data), with particular reference to the bioclimatic strategies (shading elements, natural ventilation, sunspace, Trombe wall). When the annual recorded temperature trend is comparable to the virtual one (concerning both the temporal courses and the absolute values), the model can be assumed to be the "perfect virtual copy" of the building during the real life conditions for the duration of the study. Finally, it is possible to modify some building elements characteristics on the virtual model, in particular the mass value of the structure materials (but being careful to leave unchanged their thermal transmittance in order to verify only the influence of one parameter -in this case mass- on the building thermal performance), the shape and positions of the windows used for the ventilation, the disposition of the inner spaces and so on.
Following this methodology, it is possible:
- to compare the inner temperature trend in the base situation, that is the real one, and in the different versions analysed in order to evaluate the maximum, minimum and mean differences during the day when the mass of the building envelope is changed;
- to analyse the influence of an heavy envelope on indoor comfort conditions;
- to evaluate the influence of the building shape on a proper passive ventilation and cooling strategy.
The final goal is to propose guidelines useful in order to design proper bioclimatic and light weight buildings even in a Mediterranean temperate climate.

Antonio Frattari
DICA Department, Faculty of Engineering, University of Trento

References

Fanger, O. 1970, Thermal comfort, analysis and application in environment engineering, Danish Technical Press.
IEA, 2000, Daylight in Building –Solar Heating and Cooling Programme Task 21, section 6 Design Tools
Nicol, J.F. and Humphrey, M.A. 2002, Adaptive thermal comfort and sustainable thermal standards for buildings. Energy and Buildings, 34, pp. 563-572.
Reinhart, C.F. 2004. Solar Energy, 77 (1), Lightswitch 2002: a model for manual control of electric lighting and blinds, pp.15-28

Acknowledgments

The design of the automation system has been developed in collaboration with the bpt group (Villotta - PN)
The research project has been possible due to the incessant activity of Loris Clocchiatti, president of Gruppo Polo – Le Ville Plus, that has hardly longed for the experimentation briefly described in this paper in order to improve the quality of the final product of his firm towards a better and new way of living. The on site construction of the buildings has been followed by arch. Carlo Rugo and geom. Denis Giammarini. The design of the electric and heating systems has been made by p.ind. Luigi Battista.

Workgroup

Antonio Frattari (capogruppo), Rossano Albatici, Fabio Bernardi, Paolo Bottura, Michela Chiogna, Arnaldo Savorelli

Bioclimatic Architecture and Alpine Landscape

Bioclimatic buildings and new shapes in the Alpine landscape

The new emerging topics concerning the use of energy coming from fossil fuels and non renewable materials and the emission of green gases in the atmosphere, force a rethinking of the building design procedures. Considering data from the European Union offices, in fact, the 43.1% of the total energy consumption in the member States is due to the building sector, so being the first responsible of the CO_2 emissions in the atmosphere.

In this context, sustainability in the building sector has been achieved developing four main intervention strategies for what concerns both existing buildings and new constructions:

1. the use of natural materials, especially those typical of the local building tradition, both for the whole building system as well as the single building element;
2. energy efficiency, with particular reference to the passive building standard;
3. energy saving, by means of active solar systems minimizing the use of non renewable energy sources for the production oh heat and electricity;
4. bioclimatic design, that is definition of criteria (distributive and formal) that allows the exploitation of local climatic sources by means of passive devices for the inner microclimate control.

A research carried out at the University of Trento has deepened the methodology proposed in the Alpine architecture in order to achieve energy efficiency and to improve at the same time comfort in inner spaces, with particular attention to the relationship between building shape and local climate. It has been stressed the introduction of new architectonic shapes in the landscape leaning towards a new self-referential building typology, surely well recognizable and identifiable in the urban context because of its originality but often in a conflicting relationship with the surroundings, not always considering the so called "environmental characters of architecture". Briefly, four main recurring features have been identified characterizing the new sustainable architecture: unit shape, in order to guarantee high energy efficiency levels, decreasing heat bridges and the ratio surface/volume; adequate windows and shading devices arrangement; the presence of passive solar devices as the sun space; the roofing shape, generally plane or curved, slightly raised from the building and with great overhangs. The following pictures are meaningful of the relationship often conflicting between traditional architecture and sustainable one as it has been interpreted and proposed.

Rossano Albatici
Faculty of Engineering, University of Trento

National research project carried on by the University of Trento, coordinator dr. eng. R. Albatici, called "Analysis of the solar passive systems efficiency for wooden buildings in the alpine region and design guidelines" and funded by the Italian Ministry of Instruction University and Research for the years 2005-2007.

The 4th tourism

The 4th tourism, war fronts, places of memory.
The war archeology recovery as the sustainable way of a new possible tourism.

The object of the research is the war archeology of the Great War in Trentino. The study has followed from a multidiscipline trend and has been done investigating the architectural as environmental, social and economic aspects driven by the military events happened in the territory.

The research, started as doctoral thesis, is based on the study of the tourism phenomenon in the alpine area, where there has been a process of commercialisation of both the natural environment that has created an image that does not coincide with the native soul identity. Appointed the heterogeneity of the alpine region has been investigated what are the other possible tourisms and how it is necessary to adapt the offering to an ever more varied question based on a differentiation and integration of local systems using uniquely attractive features and ideas of mountains.

Catalyst of interest are the many logistical structures and infrastructure of this region which is made up in the main by a chain of mountains that has been affected by war events involving the First World War. This territory consists of a huge quantity of tracks on there, from a large number of barracks, trenches, military roads, boundary-stones and tunnels up to Italian forts and to 114 fortifications of the Austro-Hungarian line.

The study has emphasized that all these artefacts can't be considered separately but as a whole fortified system. A system is the source of their existence, not as isolated episodes but buildings linked by ballistic relations, offensive and defensive first of all. Element behind each building planning has been the camouflage and defence itself of the enemy views; every natural obstacle is used out of bounds to adapt and be confused with landscape. Every fort shape is different, it changes continuously to fit natural contours; architectural typology varies over time with the evolution of materials that is directly linked to armaments evolution.

Recovery and valorization of these several neglected buildings, doesn't require any new theft of land and it demonstrates a valid theme to depart from an offer focused largely on the only winter theme. Applying actions even minimally to make what would otherwise not even exist and to insert portions of land inside the touristic circuits.

The aim is to protect the area directing the job of holiday to new places connected with alpine tourism and bringing back those dismissed areas to find in today's use a renewed identity.

PhD Giovanna Salgarello
Didactic Assistant, University of Trento

The 4th tourism; war fronts, places of memory
The war archeology recovery as the sustainable way of a new possible tourism.
International Doctorate in Architecture Villard d'Honnecourt – 1st cycle
IUAV University Venice
Title: The 4th tourism; war fronts, places of memory
Tutor: prof. Alberto Ferlenga,: 24 july 2007

Identity landscape

There is a close, excessive connection between us and what surrounds us. A relation that encloses our capability to relate to nature, to mold, and to be transformed and changed by it. A relation that currently risks being definitely compromised.
It is action that generates landscape. Or rather that is the fruit of labor tens of thousands of generations of men in one same territory. At the same time it is the surroundings that originate the spirit of local societies which within that setting they identify themselves. There is not but one more beautiful than the other. If ever, there exists a landscape more authentic than the other, one more condensed than the other. An authentic landscape is a space which still lives from a collective and conscious contribution of planning and transformation by the community that dwells in it. Compromise is that which is invaded by detached elements of tradition and in which it is impossible to recognize one's self. To understand landscape, the «alpine» landscape, it is necessary to start from that unutterable sensation that characterizes the relationship between inhabitant (or visitor) of the mountains and the mountain itself. Or rather the sense of dismay and confusion that seizes us whenever our glance lingers on the shape, gorges, edges and colors of the mountain.
That penetrating sensation that characterizes – to say it like Merleau Ponty – " that unspoken contact with things, when they have not yet been said" or as Paul Guichonnet affirms "those ghost without organic relation with the surrounding environment". Writers, philosophers, observers have tried to describe and talk about it, creating real and true beauty of the Alps which, still today, represent the a frontier on the speculation of the landscape.
And at the same time, the suggestion of a new (but ancient) relational dimension man-nature. Until the Renaissance, if we exclude of Homer who had defined the mountains as "the monstrous burdens of the earth", and Petrarca who talks extensively about them in his famous description in a trip on Monte Ventoso, the topic of the mountain had been that of unknown 'elevated places'. Places that men had to avoid. Maybe the home of the gods, or the witches and devil's, but anyhow and area in which men could not be but faraway, both physically and mentally.
Leonardo da Vinci, in the dawn of the Renaissance, demonstrates marked theoretic interest for the mountains: he explores them, making himself in a certain way into an alpinist and then reconstructing with his drawings the contemplative dimension in the horizons of many artworks. He wrote in a passage of 'Literary Pieces': "I say, the blue in which the air shows, is not its true color, but caused by the warm humidity, vaporized into tiny and senseless atoms, which catches after itself the percussion of the sunbeams and light phase under the darkness of the immense dimness of the region of fire, that from above serves as a cover. And this will see as I see myself, who goes above Momboso, oxbow of the Alps that divides France and Italy, which mountain has its base that gives birth to four rivers, that rule due to four contrary aspects all of Europe: and no other mountain at its base has similar height."
But it was Josua Simler, that in 1576, with his splendid alpine descriptions that provided new light for the vision of the giants of the earth. He was attracted by "that immense mass, pushed so high, there it has lied for centuries without surrendering and vanishing" and consequently "who does not asks themselves in amazement on which foundation could there lean such similar weight?". Simler wrote that "the sublimity of the mountains deserves our most devoted contemplation", since in them, if observed in the particulars, "the glance penetrates you with amazement and you will find a great number of sublime and unusual things." Konrad Gesner, a few decades before, in 1541, had stated "I declare nature's enemy he who does not consider the tall mountains worthy of long contemplation. The highest parts certainly seem to be beyond the ordinary conditions and escape our tempests, as if they where part of another world."
The Enlightenment attempted to destroy the mythical and spectral spell that shrouded the mountain, unveiling it for what it was and what it: "a layer of rocks" – as said by Luis Trenken – from the most dissimilar origins, forced to erect by the thrust of the mighty power under the Earth." And in this unveiled mountain, with the help of exact sciences, every remaining mystery could be observed, explored, studied and climbed.
Even during and after the century of candlelight, there where those who resisted with a aesthetic-contemplative behavior, like George Simmel, an those who formerly related the mountain to the state of men who lived in it, like Georg F.W. Hegel, in 1817: "I doubt that even the most credulous theologians could observe here on these mountains would dare to attribute Nature itself the purpose of benefit for men, that instead must steal that

small and miserly amount that it can use, who may never be safe from being crushed by rocks or avalanches during its miserly theft while it removes a handful of herbs or not to destroy in one night the arduous work of their hands, its hut and cowshed." But yet: "Neither the eye, nor the imagination of these shapeless rocks can find a point in which what can stop for pleasure or find an occupation (...). The reason in the thought of the life of these mountains or the type of sublimity that ascribes to them, does not find anything that will impose and snatch its amazement. The view of these eternally dead rocks has not offered anything but the monotonous representation, in the long run: it is like this".

George Simmel, in an essay dedicated to the "Alps", in 1892, was on of the first to give the mountains a lyrical voice, giving thickness and breath to those emotions that for millenniums had remained shut in the hard heart of the inhabitants from the valleys below. He wrote: "the impression that the mountain gives us is a symbol and presentiment of the fact that life redeems itself, potentiating itself to the maximum in what can no longer enter its form and rather dominates its and stands in front." And still: "When, like in the Alps, the forms are brought together casually, whithout existence of a uniting global line, not even a single one would find its place in the whole and therefore remain isolated, if the mass of the matter were imperceptible, uniform within its peaks transforming their isolation into a unifying body."

The identity of the mountainous territories is indissolubly linked to its landsape. Both in individual and collective terms. There is a logical chain, ephemeral but essential, that links the individual landscape and local society who has built it. A chain composed of "language" and "form" of the open space. This relation, intact until the twentieth century, suddenly torn by modernism, where generational construction of landscape has been substituted by the technological conquest of the mountains: with skiing establishments, uncontrolled urbanization and out of scale human industrial pressure.

The mountainous landscape, in order to survive modernism's nightmare which is unseperatively linked to the economic-touristic dimension, prisoner of a exploitive-destructive relation and relegated to sport activities, will have to recover its relation of theory and practice with emotion, flowing into the constructive-contemplative necessity of the landscape. It is exactly the emotion of contemplation; the emotion of the project and the masterly achievement; the mountain as the evaluation of our ego and as a constructive context of the community; the mountainous horizon, not as place of abominal actions, but as a mirror that reflects our identity.

Alessandro Franceschini,
Faculty of Enginereeng, University of trento

Perceiving landscape

The social perception of the landscape is an highly topical research theme. It's shared by all of the subjects which – from sociology, to geography, to town planning and architecture - are interested in studying, describing and projecting the territorial transformations.

Recently, in particular from the promulgation of the European Landscape Convention (2001), it has acquired a new centrality. The Convention, in fact, defining that the landscape "means an area, as perceived by people, whose character is the result of the action and interaction of natural and/or human factors" proposes a new approach to the theme.

More specifically, the social perception emerges as a central question, where it also assumes a constituent role for the landscape that, just as perceived, can manifest those characteristics on which founding the transformative interventions is possible.

However, in practice, already from some time, the investigation of the landscape social perception has been revealed an essential element to define shared scenarios for the territorial planning and to assure their actual effectiveness and sustainability.

A such awareness has been derived from that studies which – as long as the Sixties – mostly by some geographers, has interpreted the landscape as a manifestation of the local societies, in terms in which it represents " the uses of its territory by a community" (Turri, 1974) and expresses peculiarity and sense of belonging. This view of the landscape as the outcome of human activities (Cosgrove, 1984; Debar¬bieux, 2007) proves to be still today an interpretation very effective to understand the relations between the nature and the society, from the perspective of asserting the central role of that subjects and that forces that live and rule the territories. So, the reflection about the social perception of the landscape can take a double relevance. On the one hand, it is possible to reach a definition of the landscape itself, through the grasp of the perceptive mechanisms which, moving from individual acts to shape collective representations, contribute to make explicit the idea of the landscape. On the other hand, this reflection allows to understand a more far-ranging and complex sense of the landscape (Castelnovi, 2002) as a system of awarded meanings, that are the needs, expectations and motivations to the landscape subtended. Starting from these considerations, a space for a research emerges in terms of a research which, moving from understanding the social perception of the landscape and thought the construction of shared representations, proposes itself in a planning perspective to find in this kind of representations the significant elements to ground effective landscape politics and to build the consensus for the real actions of development and preservation.

To pits itself against such kind of objectives, the research has to face a multiplicity of themes. If, from one side, these themes express the complexity in several levels, very hard to synthesize, from the other side they become the not-renounced contents to not lose the various "pieces" of the perceived landscape, in the gap between the perception of the real and the return of its perception.

In this sense, building a multidisciplinary approach is essential, because it has succeed in understanding the multiple dimensions contained in the vision of the place, both as the same watching acts and as expression of sense, culture and expectations as regards that place. However, understanding such a vision is unescapable if a research about the perception of the landscape is carrying out within the disciplinary tradition of planning and architecture, endemically moved from a planning tension.

To develop an appropriate methodology, it is necessary at first understanding the elements contributing to the perception which, even if an individual act, is affected by a set of collective experiences.

In fact, the landscape has to be considered as a complex system in its multi-dimensions, made of physical/natural, symbolic/cultural, physiological/personal and intersubjective/collective elements (Backhaus e Strem¬low, 2007), integrated and interrelated and deeply connected to an interior dimension (inscape) referred to the personal and collective imaginary of everyone.

Studying such a landscape, as the synthesis of the various dimensions expressed in perceptive act, is composed of a process which from the visual act lets to understand its images to find the vision.

Watching, image and vision are in a sense the key actions to explore to understand the perceived landscape. In their progress they represent one of the central question of the whole research, though: the passage from the more individual dimension of the perception to the collective one.

The visual act, in terms of watching, makes reference to the experience of individual observation of the places, own of every subjects. The image is considered as the expression of the individual elaboration of the views. With reference to these images is then possible to interpret the vision, as the collective image which contains values and disvalues and the projection of desires that houses into the landscape "what we want to be" as community in a territory, by the way in which the landscape is perceived and told.
The synergies deriving from a such structured study are the results of the development of a procedure able to work on the evolution of the identification processes and to set the diversities, to determine shared landscape images, expressing a global sense (Dematteis, 1999) also intended as a project of horizontal communication between society, culture and territory.
With reference to the continuous process of the actions and meaning attributions, the landscape is characterizing as a palimpsest of a society in evolution. Assuming such a process way also in the mechanisms of understanding the landscape, we propose a sort of semiotic analysis (Castelnovi, 2002) to conduct with an almost archaeological attitude which, through reading the more recent signs (relational and relative values, demonstrations of belongings and differences), let us draw the sense of the identity of the society itself.
Moreover, conceiving the planning perspective also in a political sense, we wish that – in parallel with the transformations of their territories whose the landscape is a central element – the contemporary societies, made of a complex of cultural and ethical references, can find in the landscape perception a way to interpret constructively their identity (Remotti, 2007). In fact, it can represent the meeting of values and meanings attributed by the inhabitants – the old and the new ones, the insiders, the outsiders (Cosgrove, 1984) – moving form the common experience of the same landscape, hic et nunc, in the perspective of different cultures. In this sense, the contemporary alpine context offers itself as a very interesting workshop. The alpine landscape shows some characteristics contributing to define a mental geography (Dematteis, 1999) getting from a contradictory and multiplicity imaginary, partly animated by contemporary experiences, needs and phenomena, partly founded on the defence of some stereotypes the same inhabitants couldn't renounce, such the one of the "invention of the Alps" built to stimulate the 19th-century tourist route. Who lives today the mountain looks to his/her landscape thought its territorial contradictions which express the eternal challenge to find a balance between the economical and infrastructural development and the desire to preserve a rustic and traditional modus, always renovated to propose itself as the expression, not only visual, of the contemporary of the Alps (De Rossi, 1999).
However, the same ways of thinking and living the alpine landscape are going to deeper diversifying, depending on being in the condition of the tourist who live it in the quick holiday space, playing to identify with the local life style, or being in the position of the alpine populations reclaiming urban life style and at the same time the preservation of their landscape heritage.
So, the Alps has revealed a space of continuous reflection, where is possible to start stimulating experimentations to understand its social perception.

Cristina Mattiucci
PhD Faculty of Engineering, University of Trento

Bibliography

Backhaus N. Stremlow M. (2007) *Alpine views: from imagination to action in Proceedings of the ForumAlpinum 2007.*

Castelnovi P. (2002) *Società locali e senso del paesaggio in A. Clementi (a cura di) Interpretazioni di paesaggio Meltemi, Roma.*

Cosgrove D. (1984) *Social Formation and Symbolic Landscape, Croom Helm, London.*

Debarbieux B. (2007) *Social demand for landscapes in Proceedings of the ForumAlpinum 2007.*

Dematteis G. (1999) *Una geografia mentale, come il paesaggio in De Rossi A. et al. Linee nel paesaggio, Utet, Torino.*

De Rossi A. (1999) *Trasformazioni fisiche e costruzione dell'immaginario nelle Alpi Occidentali in Diamantini C. e Zanon B. (a cura di) "Le Alpi. Immagini e percorsi di un territorio in trasformazione" Temi Editrice, Trento.*

Remotti F. (2007), *Contro l'identità, Editori Laterza, Bari.*

Turri E. (1974) *Semiologia del paesaggio italiano, Longanesi, Milano.*

The infrastructure as a landscape "occasion"

The word landscape has been interpreted over time in different ways: often assuming an almost mythical identification, decontextualized from a reality altered by men, but more frequently it has been read as a group of signs left on the territory from the different communities that used it as a survival means. Today, it can be considered as a "complex system of relations", that can be understood trough the same signs, that correspond to the individual beings and to the social community that draw them.
In the modern world, a globalized world, where the mobility and the communication can be perceived at every level, where everything appeared to be continuously changing, the concept of landscape seems even more connected with these changes, highlighting its dynamic dimension that follows the needs and the requests for a solution to the problems of the social contexts it emerges from.
And if the landscape is the manifestation of these needs and requests, the roads, the highways, the electric systems, the railways, the dams, the ports, finally the infrastructures, should be considered landscape in every respect, because they belongs to the will and to the transformation ability of the human communities.
From this point of view, infrastructures couldn't and shouldn't be considered as an element that cuts the landscape, that is not connected or is even clashing with it, as a sign that is conceptually different from it and is generating separation and rupture: infrastructure, as João Nunes wrote, " sows the growth and development opportunities of an urbanity stain gathered in one point where people meet, and start to live." (1)
It becomes a central element of landscape construction, stimulating growth and development, or simply change and transformation. Already in 1930, as Serena Maffioletti wrote, Le Corbusier guessed the designing opportunities offered by infrastructures in the landscape, writing in Sur le 4 routes: " A road is not a kilometrical entity: it's a plastic event inside nature. Exciting things have been often backed by geometry and nature. [...] The road can be enriched and cuddled by good projects: it's route, the settlement of it's borders, claim for consideration and love as every spirit work." (2)
Usually, communication networks (road and railways) has simply hold the functions of transit and transport, trying to the facilitate the connection between the starting and the arrival point of a route, exemplified by the road signs on the highway, almost trying to stress that the start and the end of the route are more important of the space between them. Exactly on this space, that is commonly considered a non luogo we should focus our attention, trying to change the perceptive indifference of those who are driving by into curiosity, and furthermore to transform this same space into a design opportunity.
As Paolo Bürgi wrote," Interstices become gardens, green areas glimpsed while running turn into parks; We discover that highways have focal points, but also borders, embankments, strips, empty spaces. Even the areas below the highway viaducts, can develop into modern designed spaces." (3)
Only in this way, the infrastructural non luogo can change into a space that is natural and designed at the same time, expression of balance between men and nature, a milestone for local identity.
From this standpoint, landscape and infrastructure cannot be seen as opposed entities, but as parts of a single process producing a sense of balance between those who want progress at any cost, and those who reject any kind of change.
It seems important to understand and value the identity of places. Still remaining aware that identity is an ongoing process, continuously transforming and reinventing itself, occasionally showing new features previously hidden or unspoken, giving new connotation to traces that have lost their original meanings. Following the same approach with the alpine landscape, the dialogical relation between place and infrastructure disclose it's value. In this case is necessary, on one side to safeguard the ecosystem through projects that compensate the problems created by the infrastructure; on the other side, taking into consideration the expressive needs of the places often related to tourism, to design reconciling functional and aesthetical objectives. Swiss tradition has been always steered in this direction, working out interesting design projects focusing mainly on the highway's problem. It is worth reminding the works of Rino Tami, who innovated integrating in the alpine landscape both the highway structural elements

(tunnels, bridges, viaducts) and the non-structural ones (petrol station, halting places).
Another significant project in Switzerland is the new Gottardo railway connecting Zurich and Lugano ("Alptransit San Gottardo" 1993-2014) designed among others by Flora Ruchat-Roncati. Several kind of solution have been used along the route, a tunnel for 2/3, to solve the different functional and topographic needs of the places. The various solutions turn out to be a single figurative structure remarking the surrounding landscape. The project become a tool with a double function: it facilitates the perception of the landscape and creates the opportunity for orientation, fruition and identity for the local population. Similar is the case of the Transjurane A16 highway (1989-1998) by Flora Ruchat-Roncati and Renato Salvi. The section between Porrentruy and Delemont interacts with the landscape by the means of tunnel portals that become transition points between the inside and the outside, keeping the rhythm of the route and being easily identified by the drivers. But the most peculiar elements of the project are the ventilation chimneys, that talk with the landscape becoming a balcony, and the sound barriers that turn into closed trenches. The vast landscape is not anymore a simple ground for the highway, but a real artistic part of the project. Very interesting is also the Espace Géronde by Paolo Bürgi to be found at Sierre (Sous-Géronde) on A9 highway. The project is here considered a way to convert an uncharacterized place into a new public space in the middle of agricultural fields and vineyards. The infrastructure is the occasion for creating the landscape. The highway lanes are underground square tunnels that emerge by the lowered ground only for the ceilings that draw the overhanging amphitheatre. People can use the amphitheatre for sunbaths, swimming or shows, without imaging or feeling that below the ground are road coming from France and Italy.
It is clear that in this case we can not simply talk about a proper environmental introduction of the infrastructure in the landscape, but more accurately of how to manage the infrastructure to ensure that it can become, as Paolo Bürgi wrote, "an occasion for a dialogue with the territory". (4)

Chiara Azzali
PHD Student, Dica Department, University of Trento

Notes

(1) J.F. Nunes, in www.proap.pt

(2) Serena Maffiletti, "La strada ci usa", in S.Maffioletti, S.Rocchetto (a cura di), Infrastrutture e paesaggi contemporanei , Il Poligrafo 2002.

(3) Paolo Bürgi, "A due velocità", in R.A.Iarrera, Autostrade come progetto di paesaggio, Gangemi editore 2004.

(4) Paolo Bürgi, "Autostrada e Paesaggio, conversazione con Paolo Bürgi", in R.A.Iarrera, Autostrade come progetto di paesaggio, Gangemi editore 2004.

Bibliography

J.F. Nunes "Infrastruttura e paesaggio/Infrastruttura è paesaggio", in Un mediterraneo. Progetti per paesaggi critici, a cura di Daniela Colafranceschi, Alinea 2007.

R.A.Iarrera, Autostrade come progetto di paesaggio, Gangemi editore 2004.

J.F. Nunes, in www.proap.pt

S.Maffioletti, S.Rocchetto (a cura di), Infrastrutture e paesaggi contemporanei , Il Poligrafo 2002.

T.Pelzel "Infrastrutture come occasione di trasformazione di paesaggio" e "L'autostrada Transjuranne", in Casabella n°732 aprile 2005.

AA.VV. Nuove infrastrutture per nuovi paesaggi, L.Ponticelli, C.Micheletti (a cura di), Skira editore 2003.

Extraction landscapes

The abandoned extractive areas in the mountain environment: planning approaches

Collaboration, earth, landscape, human: these are the key words that underline today the necessity to research the critical balance between human settlement and landscape.
The collaboration is more pressing for the particular areas, where the production settlements, especially the extraction activities, use/consume the soil, without arranging a fair refund of the soil. The balance is more delicate in the mountain context, characterized by extraordinary landscape value, where the soil consumption and the territorial changes by human activity, are more underlined.
The natural scenery and the cultural features of the territory above are strained by the signs and over development that have unshaped the natural profile and morphology compromising the continuity and identity of the site.
"Landscape protagonists/antagonists" are the altered sites, the "exhausted soils" that Lynch describes as "rules of the big spaces consumers – the kings, the army and the extractive industries-that, without the masters, can be transformed into parks and gardens for their humble successors". (1)
The key to re-establish the balance between the landscape is to find a new significance of the degraded areas. This doesn't mean a restoration to mask the ineffaceable territory's wound with a "mimetic re-naturalisation". The goal is to consider the abandoned areas, now hidden and inaccessible for the community, such as added value, such as new occasion to plan enjoyment for the people. The history and the for-use of the site, are the basis where is possible plan new spaces, new functions.
In the opinion of Lynch for a continuous transformable landscape is important "to maintain the history witness, such as evolution reference, that continues to increase the landscape critical depth and safeguards its evolution and particularity." (2)
According to the "European Landscape Convention" the extraction landscape, has been to re-valuated in order to obtain their sustainable development based on a balanced relationship between social need, economy and environment. The goal is to find the linkage between the quarry's activities and the tourist, cultural and social future, and to transform the degraded landscape in a new occasion to create, to think new landscape in a bigger plan to:
'Landscape management' means action, from a perspective of sustainable development, to ensure the regular upkeep of a landscape, so as to guide and harmonise changes which are brought about by social, economic and environmental processes;
'Landscape planning' means strong forward-looking action to enhance, restore or create landscapes".
(European Landscape Convention, Florence, 20 October 2000)
From this viewpoint, negative topics as "refuse", "recycling", "waste", "wound" become occasion for re-think and create landscapes.
For the different sites and ways in the alpine environment of the extraction activity (flat country quarry or mountain quarry) we need to use different approaches and problem solving strategies to a redevelopment.
The project idea of giving new significance to this areas ranges from the local scale to large territory and can imply "re-naturalization" (more or less spontaneous) of the ground, or the creation of new facilities for the community. New topics come out from the study of the relations between:
-Cavities/soil's regeneration: a natural and agricultural revalorization can restore disused areas.
A possible development is the safeguard of naturalistic oasis which are the consequence of a spontaneous evolution of the sites running wild. In this case new ecosystems can originate ("The Third landscape" by G. Clement). Another possibility is the experimentation of new tilling. (3)
The restoration of Schumel Quarry, a mountain quarry in Switzerland, emphasizes the relation between excavated soil and regenerated soil. A particular microclimate (strong wind, sudden changes of temperature) have developed cavities in the soil, caused both by erosion and washing away phenomena, and generated new habitats favourable to a new spontaneous vegetal colonization.
The project (realized in 1988 by Stökli, Kienast & Koeppel) emphasizes/enhances the spontaneous natural process and safeguards the new vegetation by means of bioengineering and drainage technologies. A similar example is the restoration of Musital quarry by the same planers.

-Excavation-production reject\art: means for a revalorisation of disused or dumping areas can be searched among projects of landscape and land art. The refused sites design becomes the occasion to create sculpture in a territorial scale. In the reuse as public park of Motto Grande Quarry, Switzerland, Bürgi underlined the history of the site (in particular the public protest against the deforestation caused by the realization of the motorway) through an artificial design. The planner utilized natural elements to design a rigorous geometric lay-out. The circular space delimited by poplars recalls the natural sculpture of Roberth Smithson or Richard Long.
-Quarry\project: the reuse topic combines with environmental, social and cultural rehabilitation of the abandoned areas through the architectonical design. The fields of application spread from culture and leisure time recreation areas to new residential zone. The masterly example is the project of the Maison des Jeunes and the ground in Firminy, 50 km near Lyon designed in the sixties. The site quality –abandoned quarry with its natural and artificial presence- struck Le Corbusier. Two elements, one opposite the other, close the quarry designing two artificial fronts such as underlining the artificial and natural presence. (4). The quarry's artificiality is emphasized by the strong sign of the Maison: 110 metres linear structure. The Maison appears as a mounting in the rock and simultaneously harmonizes with the environment. Nicoleta Trasi said about this project: "the particular morphology of the territory suggests the project powers and directions." (5). Strong signs, intentionally oversized walls with pedestrian crossings and housing design the topographic project –unrealized- for the Monte Ricco quarries in the Colli Euganei (Purini, Manichini, Staderini e Thermes). In Murisengo, a flat area near Torino (30 km), the restoration of an abandoned chalk quarry emphasizes and re-produces public space (hidden and forgotten by the people since long time) establishing relations with the nearby landscape. Small signs and natural engineering materials design the public park.
"The first project actions were to re-model, re-form, to give back the light, re-create relation between the cut off places. [...] The main goal was to transform a close site into an open, identified, crossable site." (Alessandro Alì, 2007)
The multi-phases plan (that regards simultaneously the quarry activity and the reuse of disused site) is the principle adopted for the restoration project of the Northern Quarry in Paderno Dugnano (designer: Maurice Cerasi; site: Milano, 1984-2005). Two service towers, an open theatre, sport and enjoyment facilities are integrated/designed in a geometrical composition. The particularity of this project is the co-presence of active extraction machineries as integral part of the project. In this case the project restoration is a "global" and harmonious plan that incorporates all the extraction phases: from the identification of the sites of the quarries, to a definition of dumps, to a re-thinking of abandoned areas. This is a very interesting approach applied to an extraction landscape ongoing transformation.

Emanuela Schir
PHD Student, Faculty of Engineering, University of Trento

Notes

(1) K. Lynch, *What time is this Place?*, The MIT Press; New Ed edition Cambridge, 1976
(2) (5) Trasi N., *Paesaggi rifiutati paesaggi riciclati. Prospettive e approcci contemporanei.Le aree estrattive dismesse nel paesaggio: fenomenologia di un problema progettuale*, Editrice Librerie Dedalo, Bari 2004
(3) Clément G., *Manifeste du Tiers paysage*, Sujet Objet Eds, Paris 2004.
(4) *Carnets, III (1954-57)*, ed. Herscher, Paris 1982

Bibliography

Contemporary Landscape in the World, Process Architecture, Tokio 1990
Trasi N., *Paesaggi rifiutati paesaggi riciclati. Prospettive e approcci contemporanei.Le aree estrattive dismesse nel paesaggio: fenomenologia di un problema progettuale*, Editrice Librerie Dedalo, Bari 2004
Simonetta Zanon (a cura di), *Cave. Per un atlante storico geografico delle cave del Veneto, Reinvenzione e riusi*, in "progetto Interreg IIIB, area Cadses, Rekula", Fondazione Benetton Studi Ricerche, Treviso 2006

Extraction areas and alpine landscape
Designing in degraded lands

Landscape architecture needs to be defined within a theoretical and practical framework for the development of ideas and projects.
Landscape is henceforth defined as the overall environment modified by the presence or the active involvement of man within it; the latter does actually define architecture, in its anthropogeographical acception - the definition used in social and geographical disciplines. The environment structures are recognized by the authors as an integral part of the landscape because the actions of man have, more or less coherently, built it as such.
The historical construction of a landscape takes place through target-reaching or purely conservative decisions of undetermined residualities and of the creation of a "collective vision" by the media, the agencies linked with tourism and by the stereotypes of the Alpine region which are often so sedimented as they are far from the true nature of the places they supposedly refer to. A landscape isn't such without man using, observing and living it. It is a vision that also feeds on perception, that is the result of the cultural experiences of the users who are out to conquer new perspectives, observation dynamics and meaning through the artistic creation of the surrounding environs.
It is necessary to investigate landscape architecture, understood as a total project regarding the physical space lived by man on Earth and the different dimension scales, bringing the landscape up as the core material of the architectural project to use for the purpose of shaping the territory.
The PhD Civil and Environmental Engineering Working Group at the University of Trento (1) in line with the European Landscape Convention, took on the challenge of discarded landscape and identified the Cembra valley as a degraded territory where complex issues are interwoven; these are often linked to porphyry extraction and related activities in the region. The landscape identity has been modified over the years by the proliferation of extraction sites, the spreading of wastelands and the divestment of exhausted sites. This process has produced a crisis of the landscape's natural and cultural features. The morphology, identity and continuity have been twisted by the scars left from the processes of production and exploitation.
The Avisio torrent, through its incisive flow neatly separating its banks, produces two extremely heterogeneous territorial entities which base their economic activities on the optimization of environmental resources: on the one side the terraced viticulture, on the other the porphyry quarries. Agricultural exploitation has undoubtedly influenced the historical evolution of the dwellings represented by compact and distinct clusters of rural nature positioned at regular intervals halfway up and layed on natural terraces dating back to the Glacial Era and connected to each other through agricultural paths. The excellent preservation of the valley's terracing determines a well-defined and sedimented territorial structure: any "idea" on the landscape necessarily has to face this issue. Only after War World 2 has the porphyry extraction become a relevant economic activity while viticulture on the terraces possesses an intrinsically unchangeable and persistent character for the reasons stated above.
The porphyry extraction activity contrasts with the same idea of identity; it is perhaps because of this that tourism, an activity strongly connected to local identities, has never really taken off. The quarries appear like enormous, empty and "negative" spaces stolen away from the mountains and which, in reverse, could contain entire cities. The quarries correspond to a territorial, design-free patchwork that doesn't bring a precise idea of landscape with it - although the landscape itself is in a constant movement and transformation flow. If such idea existed, some methodological principles could be found on a large scale and subsequently applied to a specific site. The empty spaces generate the sense of a long wait and of the transformation of time; this is associated with a more intense perception of the physical and sensory reality: the absence of a presence or rather the presence of the absence. Architecture, by way of working on, with and through the landscape, could try and answer this absence of a presence. The project can keep together the elements of this territory: like parched concavities that are waiting for new fertilization. It is only with a project that the extraction landscape of the Cembra valley could in the end go back to being usable in its materiality, for tourism too - a sector looked at with interest by the entire valley.

The research conducted so far has evidenced the valley's unexpressed potential which could be linked to a slow and rural type of tourism connecting the viticulture heritage with the relevant historical and naturalistic sites with the porphyry quarries.
The study defines some methodological principles for the extraction landscape project: excavation/soil regeneration, excavation - discarded element/art, void/energy production, quarry/architectural project which, going over traditional environment restoration interventions (i.e. the case of the quarries where the formal construction results tend to be concealed or camouflaged for the human exploitation of the environment), set out to actually build on these formal structuring, inevitably linked to the extraction activities, for the purpose of putting the foundation of new rules and new identity-building processes for the territory.
The study of the relation between the elements making up the territory, the critical comparision with similar approaches to the same issues in analogous contexts, has allowed for a focus on the extraction areas not as "emarginated" and "discarded" but as part of a whole usable system, therefore bringing into the equation the prestigious agricultural areas, the natural parks, or indirect relations (i.e. the vision of a moving observer through distance, along transport roads, or from a static point of view, in the proximity of an extraction site for example).
The research aims at the definition of a planning process through a number of pilot projects for a homogeneous, continuing and ever evolving extraction landscape.

Claudia Battaino
Faculty of Engineering, University of Trento, research coordinator for the Cembra Valley

Notes

(1)Research Area Architecture for the city and landscape(1), C. Battaino, Cembra Project, Phd Students E. Schir, L. Zecchin

Bibliography

- *C.Battaino, Cave, castelli, cantine, in J.M.Palerm Salazar, Paysage sin-con texto, Ed. Saquiro, Tenerife 2009*
- *C.Battaino, Progettare nei paesaggi estrattivi, DICA Report di Ricerca 2007*
- *C.Battaino, G. Cacciaguerra, L. Zecchin, Islas en la isla in J. M.Palerm Salazar, Projectar el Paisaje. Territorios en transformación: Barranco de Badajoz/Güímar, 2007*
- *C.Battaino, Cave per il disegno del territorio in C. Lamanna, G. Cacciaguerra, C. Mattiucci, Infrastrutture Canarie, due progetti a Tenerife, 2006*
- *C. Battaino, Isole nell'isola, Progetto per l'area estrattiva del Barranco de Bajadoz a Guimar in C. Lamanna, G. Cacciaguerra, C. Mattiucci, cit. 2006*

Marginal landscapes
Architecture and design for alpine and mountain zones

Contemporary landscapes and territories are described by many researchers and the media as fluid spaces (Z. Bauman 2003), in which the borders are ever-increasing and the damage caused by its transformation is occurring at an ever-faster pace. A collective imagination has thus developed, linking the proliferation of new technologies and globalization with the reduced impact of the tyranny of distance.

"Marginal landscapes" is the title of the research that is developing in the Doctoral School in Environmental Engineering at the University of Trento, Architecture for the city and landscape, XXIII cycle, inside the PhD Working Group "Cembra Project" (1).

The research in the "margins" study characterizes the valleys and territories of the Alps and mountains utilising the application of the general principles introduced by the European Landscape Convention (Florence 2000) for the "management and enhancement of landscape".

One focus of the research will be the Cembra Valley in Trentino, to investigate the possibility of integrating the diversity of the landscape: the areas of porphyry mining, wine production, wine cellars and environmental concerns.

The study, to be included in the Research Program of National Interests (PRIN) of the Research Unit of Trento, "Rejected Landscapes; studies and projects about marginal architectures and areas of low and medium mountain" (2), aims to examine through the "architecture of relationship", tourism projects linked to the quality of local products and the Cembra valleys.

The object of the research and investigation from a theoretical and planning perspective, on the theme of "marginal", understood as "spaces", is to focus on the two converging aspects of space, between the physical and morphological reality, its different uses and of overlooked spaces. It covers landscapes situated on the boundaries of heavily-developed areas whereby growth tends to produce and accumulate refuse such as production packaging or sites whose function directly pollutes the environment. Also included are those sites of undiscovered potential that have until now been overlooked.

The restoration of marginal sites and their "revalorization" (development) has been referred to in a vast array of interdisciplinary literature: from the analysis of the confines between town and country with the key word being "confines" (P. Zanini 2000), to "sahel", open spaces "devoid of agriculture" on the edges of urban spaces (E. Turri 1983), to the spaces without any specific use "terrain vague" (I. De Solà Morales 1995). In the literary field, the theme of marginalization was explored as a narrative instrument (Breton 1924, Debord 1973). In art, "the entropic landscape" (R. Smithson 1967) and the "actual land" (Stalker 1995) are studies referring to the unifying traces of connection between marginal spaces and widespread development.

If the theme of marginalized landscapes had been widely studied from an urban context, the results would produce little research in reference to alpine settings or areas with the characteristics of "archipelago towns" (M. Cacciari, R. Bocchi) dominated by the architecture of empty spaces.

In mountain settings the most relevant aspects of the theme can be traced back to the existence and creation of marginalized areas that have been refused or simply not considered, areas that have become dumping grounds for industry in respect to the privileged zones within the region, to the abandonment of areas as a result of their isolation and to the eventual loss of their identity.

The theme of Trentino connected to porphyry is a real problem because the mining industry by nature alters the landscape: emerging markets, the reduction of primary resources and environmental concerns, but within an unpredictable timeframe. This is one of the major issues in this area: the necessity of proposing new visions for a changing landscape, introducing sustainable figurative options and reconfiguring the "naturality" for its future evolution" (JM Palerm Salazar).

In the Cembra Valley of Trentino, characterized by intense mining activity, and in which the degradation of the countryside is widely accepted as the result of heavy industry, the most relevant aspects of the

argument can be ascribed to the magnitude and speed of the transformation of the landscape, to the accelerated expansion and exploitation of the earth, to the propagation of dumping grounds, to the disused mining sites and concentration of new mining areas.
The deliberation on marginalized, degraded landscapes and the resulting impact on quality of life developed within Europe during these past years, has produced a wealth of ideas and projects that form the reference point of the study. One of these is the European project "Rekula" (Restructuring Cultural Landscapes Interreg IIIB 2003-2006) which refers to "cultural landscapes", or rather, landscapes that have been transformed by man with the aim of creating profitable, formal and functional spaces (3).
The necessity of observing the theme of marginal landscapes from the perspective of architectural planning and regulations evolved from the conviction that the problems of marginalization and its related issues (borders, marginalized areas or activities and their impact on living conditions),and the theme of "regeneration" of degraded sites, necessitated an integrated approach between human intervention that produces rapid changes in the environment, spatial configurations, sustainable technical solutions and relevant constructions with relationship to the identity of the territory (P. Zanini). Within the scope of the architecture, the comparison is turned towards similar experiences in alpine regions for the enhancement of the marginal valleys and the enhancement of the tourist zone.
The construction of places for alpine tourism, even in marginal areas, has always been carried out via architectural points, in valleys and also in high altitudes, projected as 'net architecture'. It deals with large hotels, nursing homes, alpine shelters, camps, territorial highlights for diverse use/ construction of the landscape.
Some of these contemporary projects are associated with the care and attention to the 'territorial elements' of the project, as with the rediscovery of working with the complex morphology of the land and the use of traditional materials. It deals with salvaging a specific architectural know-how, of its physical and formal anchorage, of its material consistency, as Adolf Loos had anticipated in 1913, it requires horizontal elements firmly anchored to the place. As is the case with the thermal baths of Vals by P. Zumthor, in the marginal valley of Grigioni, where the building is made out of materials solely from the site where it was built: mountain, stone, water. 'To build in the stone, to build with stone, to build into the mountain, to extract from the mountain, to be in the mountain'. The building seems as though it's a huge stone, bored and porous, a mono-substance monolith, firmly anchored to the green slope of the mountain that continues above the green covering. A series of natural stone layers continue, like the typical dry mountain stone walls, contemporarily determining the sections, the internal plans and prospective of the building; architecture made out of what is strictly necessary.
The 'reduction' that works on the necessary feature of alpine architecture is the operative approach, common also with other contemporary projects for tourism in marginal alpine areas. In particular, in shelters in high altitudes (Refuge Plateau de Saleinaz, De Montmollin & Widmer, Svizzera 1996, Refuge Cristallina, Baserga & Mozzetti, Svizzera 2002, Refuge Tschierva, Ruch and Spirig, Svizzera 2003), the volumetric abstraction and the reduction of materials involved create a dialectical report between minimal architecture and natural context. The defined geometric forms are in contrast with the organic landscape. Within the theme of "marginal zones', the rapport between architecture and landscape will be researched through some key-words, maintaining the functions of the planning analysis of method and content. Tenable energy is of particular importance in architectural experimentation in high mountains, where the climate and orography of the project is a mediation between the exigencies of the context and the building techniques. As with the Vigilius Mountain Resort (Matteo Thun, Alto Adige, Italia 2003) or the nursing home in Carinzia (Wissounig, Dietger, Austria 2005), realised in wooden structures with elements in prefabricated wood, assembled on site, with façades that protect from over-heating in summer and having green roofs. Horizontal construction, following the level curves

for a major integration/interaction between the building and the ground, is a continual planning, like the Wellness Hotel St. Anton (Dietrich Untertrifaller, Austria 2001) where the building blends with the slopes incorporating open spaces, active interfacing between internal and external.
Figurative and material analogy with the landscape is another key word. The ground, the weft of the walls and the existing signs, define the basis of a new transformed typography by means of the project. The morphology of the site lends itself to architectural manipulations, such as cuts, raisings, stratification of the elements of the landscape, at the end of which, it is no longer simply laying out the limits between nature and artifice, between landscape and architecture. In the Blumau thermal baths (Hundertwasser, Austria 1999) the lawns cover the sinuous curves of the ground in the form of undulated architecture. In the project of the swimming pools on Lake Caldaro (next ENTERprise, Italia 2006), the surfaces seem to ripple, setting a new underwater typography. Beyond the formal results, what is interesting is the continuous working with the 'ground line' in pursuit of camouflaging/unveiling architecture.
Valorisation projects in marginal areas through tourism, which seem to be applications as a way of understanding architecture with respect to the landscape, custodian of these values which Heidegger defined as 'permanence': recognition understood as a measure. That is, the structures become special 'gauges' and instruments of knowledge of alpine space.
The aim of the research is to delineate conditions of "regeneration" for the "marginalized landscapes" of the mountain zones that are sustainable solutions in the construction and transformation of the territory. It is necessary to invest an attitude of "system of relationships" into the landscape-architecture project: an open process, beginning from the spaces at the borders, refused or forgotten (4). In line with the inclusive notion of landscape – archaeological and rejected sites are also included within landscape –the objective is to verify the existence of a space (theoretical or operational) for the project, that offers more than design of new uses or re-usable options for the site; the aim is to highlight the diverse natural and cultural aspects of the marginalised landscapes, to make architectural innovations with the elements of connection and accessibility (touring-architecture for souvenir landscape) and to utilise recycled products to create architecture.

Luca Zecchin,
PHD Student, Faculty of Engineering, University of Trento

Notes

(1) Research Area Architecture for the city and landscape, C. Battaino, "Cembra Project", Phd Students E. Schir, L. Zecchin

(2) Associated Investigator of the Research Unit prof. C. Lamanna with prof. C. Battaino. Team: C. Azzali, G. Salgarello, E. Schir, L. Zecchin

(3) The principal thematic and methodological approaches of the research are also attributable to: Regeneration from a Natural Approach (Third Landscape, G. Clement), Planning and Redesign of the Landscape (Perice valleys in Piemonte; Quiarry of Cursi in Puglia), The Interpretation from a Land-as-Art Approach (R. Morris, R. Smithson), The Project of Regional Landscape Sculpture (S. Aronson, E. Chillida), The Creation of Energising Landscapes (E. Battle, Y. Roig, T. Galì) and Restoration in Artistic-Cultural Terms (P. Burgi).

(4) Spaces under research.

Superfluous spaces: places of an unresolved nature, marginalised by geomorphology, altitude or abandoned after being previously exploited; their origins are varied: agricultural, industrial, urban, or tourism-related etc.

Production spaces refused: quarries, electrical wires etc., usually places without architectural planning.

Refuse spaces: disposal sites of waste material or forgotten architectural sites and areas, to which renewed value can be restored (fortresses, castles, masi etc.).

Architectural terms and themes.

Marginal zones/ regeneration: the regeneration of degraded or abandoned sites, based on the environmental, cultural and economic needs of the regions;

Marginal zones/ connections: decisions as to the continuation, or not, of the land's spaces and functions, systemising its "crucial places": compositions, by way of traces and connections to a new story of complex landscape; "livable infrastructures" of relationship (S. Sassen);

Marginal zones/ planning: minimal architectural-landscape planning, being relevant in that the landscape-system is not recognisably undergoing change; earmarking projects for the fruition and perception of the territory; integrated systems with the production and tourism sectors that create an identity for the landscape.

Bibliography:

Zygmunt Bauman, Modernità liquida, [2000] tr. it., Roma-Bari 2002
Francesco Careri, Walkscapes. Camminare come pratica estetica, [2002] ed. it. Torino 2006

Guy-Ernest Debord, *La configurazione del territorio*, in *La società dello spettacolo*, [1967] tr. it. di Pasquale Stanziale, Viterbo 2002
Robert Smithson, *The collected Writings*, a cura di J. Flam, Londra 1996
Ignasi de Solà-Morales, *Urbanité interstitielle*, in *Inter Art Actuel* vol.61, Quebec 1995
Stalker, *Attraverso i territori attuali*, a cura di Jean-Michel Place, Parigi 2000
Piero Zanini, *Significati del confine. I limiti naturali, storici, mentali*, Milano 2000
Architecture Margin Landscape
Claudia Battaino, *Architettura del benessere nella Stiria meridionale*, in AR n.35, Udine 2005
Claudia Battaino, *Progetto per la penisola di Cavallino nella laguna di Venezia*, Gorizia 2004
Claudia Battaino, *Forti, architettura e progetti*, Nicolodi editore, Rovereto 2006
Adolf Loos, *Regole per chi costruisce in montagna*, in *Parole nel vuoto*, 1913
Bruno Taut, *Alpine Architekture*, 1919
Peter Zumthor, *Pensare architettura*, [1998] tr. it. di Maddalena Disch e Francesco Dal Co, Milano 2003
Peter Zumthor, *Atmosfere. Ambienti architettonici. Le cose che ci circondano*, [2006] tr. it. di Emilia Sala, Milano 2007

For the alpine architecture

The Alpine landscape and its continuous process of transformation is the centre of discussion between the relation of local architectural tradition and the new modern architectural trends. The old formal trend wants to transform the Alps into a theme park, aimed to imitate the past and its traditional icons.

The Alpine landscape, in its complexity shows deep scars due to the fast and irreversible process of transformation that, during the 20th century, brought a new form of progress. A new form of living the mountains developed with the construction of winter attractions, turistic houses and the exploitation of water resources. Is there a contemporary architecture?

Today, we can speak of architecture that wants to test the traditional places and improve a new interpretation. Light, materials, landscape, natural contest are all important themes but at same time it's important to think the role of contruction as proof of all the artistic and social forms typical of the Alpine contest but with the urban culture influece.

There are a lot of architects who created new typologies of colletive buildings but Gellner and Loos are the most important ones for the new conception of living in alpine landscape.

Greta Brugnoli
Architect, Didactic Assistant, IUAV- Venice

Alps, landscape, ski-tourism

The ski landscape, mountains and tourism

The Dolomite area mounted on the provinces of Bolzano, Trento and Belluno represents an important paradigm of territorial system development of the mountain prominent for its touristic vocation. The mountainous landscape is of multiple form and not a sequence of various locations that follow one another around the massive Sella, each one marked by a rocky background different from one another but rather by the seasonal variations. The featuring objects of the landscape, rocks, woods, meadows, remain more or less unchanged except by the presence of snow. It is the presence of a ski system strongly structured to determine the scale of the territorial affairs. The mountain territory is in its function, deformed between winter and the rest of the year. I think that the definition of landscape that from the relative European convention which result of the relation between the population and their territory can contribute to distinguish and attempt to recognize the ways in which the peculiarity of this specific lanscape can vary; as well as to distinguish the established ties with the local population's landscape and the touristic population. First of all, the relation is of symbolic affection since the landscape represents a sort of map of experiences and facts that make up the population's personal history. The physical places are also the places of personal memories, from childhood to adulthood, and they mark a diachronic and textual course of their own existence. Obviously cultural elements are embeded in personal aspects as well as shared valued beyond a local scale between the remnants of a romanticist vision of the mountain, even by the shift from the symbolic dimension to an iconic structure composed by simulacrums. It is testified by the construction produced in the last few years in the Dolomite area that has demostrated a drammatic drift towards a Tyrolean style based on the acritical association of the elements of language derived from the material architecture. Chalets and cottages are furnished with embroided cloths with bay windows, turrets and battlements in the belief that they represent the highest form of traditional architecutre to increase touristic activity. The neo-tyrolean style has been diffused pervasively along the network of the ski system as well as appearing in the Veneto territory where the appearance and characteristics were more autonomous a few years ago.

Instead, tourist are accustomed to aknowledge the ski slopes and lifts as ordinary objects of the experience during their winter vacations. The cabins, lifts and skiers are the protagonist of an persistent and intense vitality that manifests itself through the colored spots on the white and versatile background constantly changing from the earth and sky's perspective. Endless flows of tourist populate the ski circuits like Sella Ronda, following signs and arrows, constantly overflowing the various panoramas. The ski system is similar to blood circulation, where the red blood cells flow endlessly without really aknowledging the places where they flow through. The skiers slide down the slopes and go back up the mountain, captivated by the fascination of going back down rather than by the view. Landscape is unperceived and transfigurated as a simple icon. The attributed affection occurs on the base of an induced projection, ultimately a synthesis of affection. Away from winter, the ski establishments show evident signs: pylons and cablecars, forest corridors, snowmaking machines. These are signs that show the unfunctional networks of the territory, awaiting the next winter, a sort of "summer hibernation" but in the mean time totemizes the territory. The contellation of facilities that unfold along the meadows, pastures, woods, radically changes the nature of the mountain locations. It drives them towards a network no longer uncontaminated. The landscape of this mountain is the last result of a multiple industrial process: the production of the infrastructure and the establishments in this setting and like such industrialized ones but at the same time is an active component of a finalized process of the production of services that have been developed by the population that inhabit it.

Thomas Demetz
Architect, PHD Student, Faculty of Architecture of Genoa

Energy Sustainability and Landscape Sensitive Design

The bilateral Japan-Italy workshop entitled "Designing New Landscapes", held at the school of architecture in Pescara with students from the 4th and 5th year Urban Planning and Design programme and Doctorate Students in Urban Planning and Architecture, was aimed at developing a new philosophy of "Landscape Sensitive Design". The main points of this approach include a focus on context, the consideration of time, the co-evolution of the artificial and natural world and the fertile contamination between paradigms of urban and landscape planning. The workshop was based on the following question: if we assume the values of the landscape and the idea of energy self-sufficiency as determinant for any project, is it possible to harmoniously insert new forms within the landscape, creating works of architecture and infrastructure that are respectful of historically inherited values and, at the same, capable of configuring a contemporary landscape that is rich in both quality and identity? The work group (coordinated by Massimo Angrilli) together with the tutors Aldo Casciana and Filippo Priori, developed the project with the support of a board of consultants representing various professions. The consultants were asked to assist with the construction of the programme-project based on their own specific points of view, coupled with an openness to reciprocal contaminations: urban planning; landscape ecology; energy engineering; history and restoration and, finally, architectural design. This board of consultants was assisted by a group of professors invited to act as guest critics . The critics were asked to comment on the intermediate development of the projects, offering observations and critical input focused on improving their content and quality.

The Functional Programme

The project area is located in the so-called Palentini Planes, in the Municipality of Scurcola Marsicana, a small town at the edge of the Apennine Mountains. More precisely, it is a level area measuring approximately 20 hectares situated in proximity to the "Magliano dei Marsi" interchange along the Rome-Pescara highway. This interior area of the Abruzzo Apennines currently demonstrates a great deal of interest, spearheaded by a group of local businessmen, in the development of a research centre for renewable energies, with annexed facilities for energy production using photovoltaic and wind powered systems. One particular reason for this interest is related to the demand for renewable energies that make use of the by-products of silicon produced by an important electronics company located nearby. This interest in renewable energies is accompanied by local real estate development that includes the construction of a residential complex for tourism composed of villas, destined primarily for out-of-region buyers in virtue of the area's proximity to the aforementioned highway interchange. In light of these objectives, the first questions that we began to ask were related to their compatibility with the characteristics of the local landscape and context and, in particular, with the existing urban systems in the area. The first choice, already fully related to a landscape sensitive approach, led to the elimination of the real estate development that, what is more, was in clear contrast with the local landscape planning instruments and plans for the development of the area. The work developed during the workshop thus began by facing up to the difficult topic of the production of energy that, as is well known, in Italy constitutes a difficult issue given the need to respect a consolidated environmental and landscape culture. The numerous conflicts related to the development of green energy systems (wind power, hydro-electrics, solar and photovoltaic) highlight a paradox of environmental culture. It cannot be taken for granted that the production of green energy guarantees the sustainability of a landscape or the public acceptance of an intervention. A design approach is thus required, on a case-by-case basis, to resolve these conflicts, evaluating the admissibility of various interventions and identifying the most appropriate solutions to various issues at stake.

Design and Context

In a context with such an elevated landscape value, whose "figure of meaning" is defined, above all, by its geomorphologic characteristics - a 'bowl' between mountain slopes - the site is also distinguished by a weak urban structure that allows for a reading of its agro-environmental matrix, remnants of historical-cultural traces and the forms impressed by historically consolidated uses of the territory (transhumance, agriculture).

Framed between the peaks of the Apennine mountains, the site can be described as a "closed room", where the horizontal conditions of this reclaimed plane are exalted by the verticality of the mountain slopes. This contrast, almost cinematographic, is rendered even more dramatic by the historical settlements that occupy the slopes, overlooking the plane below, the only evidence that the area was once a lake. Flanked by the infrastructure of the highway, the eastern edge of the site assumes a dynamic character, while its centre is crossed by the Roman constructed Tiburtina Valeria. The specific area interested by the project is now used for agricultural practices and apparently devoid of any specific qualities.
However, the reality of the site is much more complex: the richness of this context is to be found in the stratification of "memories" and the multiple meanings (landscape meanings) that they give to the area. The primary meanings are related to the memory of the ancient Fucino Lake, originally drained by the Romans, and the historic battle between Charles of Anjou and Conradin Duke of Swabia , an event that conditioned the evolution of European history, evidence of which can be found in the ruins of the Abbey of S. Maria della Vittoria, constructed by Charles I to commemorate his victory.
Further meanings are derived from the vast operations of agricultural reform, successive to the definitive reclamation of the Fucino, which subdivided the vast plane into cultivable lots and attributed property rights to local farmers from the various towns overlooking the now dry lakebed. The most ancient period of the site's history is to be found in the important archaeological excavations in Alba Fucens, an area of national interest, and in the traces left by the Romans, in particular the Via Tiburtina. This historical situation is accompanied by the importance of the modern Telespazio technological facilities located in the Fucino basin. The project proposed for Scurcola denounces, first and foremost, the need to contextualise the new facilities within the landscape of reference, assuming its geographic, morphological, historical, ecological and settlement-related characteristics as part of an integrated and trans-scalar vision. In coherence with the principles of the European Landscape Convention, the local landscape was considered not as a static reference to be conserved with restrictions, but as a living reality in continuous evolution, whose values can be continuously reinterpreted, together with the historical and archaeological significance of the site, all of which must be projected into the future. In this way the contemporary functions of research and the production of renewable energies are integrated with the past, tempering the mono-functional qualities typical of energy producing facilities and designing new approaches to the sustainability of local development. The identity of the site is emancipated from its inherited traditions and nurtured by strong references to historical materials and symbols, interwoven with the modern quality of advanced technologies, inspired by the avant-garde Fucino Space Centre (Telespazio).
What emerges is a multiplicity of interventions, at various scales, that confront the large scale of this "landscape room" of the Fucino basin and, at the same time, the proximity of the inhabited centre of Scurcola, redefined by a new network of relations that expands into the landscape. Fields of energy production, the historical centre, the archaeological excavations in Alba Fucens, the remnants of the Roman period and the Tiburtina Valeria, together with rural spaces that are converted into opportunities for experimenting with the sustainability of the landscape and its transformations, as part of the search for a new meaning that is coherent with its history and its future potential.
At the urban scale the project pursues three different strategies: the first is focused on the historic centre of Scurcola and the development of residential spaces for tourism and a diffuse hotel. This strategy is aimed at satisfying the need for residential spaces for tourism in the most sustainable manner possible, achieved by investigating the inherent potential of the existing abandoned structures in the historical centre, rather than developing new areas and consuming more land for the construction of new homes.
The second strategy involves the central theme of the workshop: the Energy Park, to be developed as part of an overall design strategy. The third strategy involves the archaeological excavations in Alba Fucens, of value to the entire nation. Here the Master Plan calls for a number of actions, including the creation of a new National Museum for the display of the more important relics found on site and the construction of a new roof structure to protect the excavations. The latter can will be covered with photovoltaic panels to

produce the energy consumed by the new museum.
The Energy Park, defined as part of the second strategy, proposes the definition of a multi-functional programme that unites the production of energy using photovoltaic panels with activities of research and experimentation and cultural and recreational programmes – qualifying the area as a park – and, finally, its pre-existing vocation as a space of cultivation and pasturing. The principles that support the production facilities are only partially a result of the rational qualities of this sector (spacing between panels and orientation); the form of the solar fields is, in fact, based on the implicit geometries of the local context, primarily defined by the Roman road and the grid of drainage canals. The only exception is to be found in the end area of the solar field, whose design reflects the irregular forms of the fields. The design is intentionally accentuated and modelled to obtain a succession of small, inclined surfaces (30 degrees) to be used for the fixed solar panels, creating a 'corrugation' of the ground plane. Inside the solar fields we find an elliptical area that is used to host events and installations that recall the famous Battle of Tagliacozzo. The ground plane has been lowered to the level at the time of the battle, established by studying the remains of the Abbey of S. Maria della Vittoria, erected the following year.
The park is reached from the Via Tiburtina, which is to be requalified as an itinerary for the discovery of the local territory. The new plan features connections with the Alba Fucens excavations to the east and with the medieval centre of Scurcola to the west.

A Manifesto for Landscape Sensitive Design

The workshop concluded with the definition of a number of "manifesto principles" for an approach to "Landscape Sensitive Design" (LSD), confirming that this process develops its configuration based on a sensible reaction to the landscape in which it is located, seen not as a backdrop for architectural objects, but rather a "liquid space" into which to immerge new forms that, in turn, become inseparable parts of the same landscape, intentionally and intelligently modifying it. This configuration is to be understood not as definitive, but rather as only one of the possible configurations assumed by a site as a result of the transformations that take place during its temporal evolution.
This attitude of landscape sensitive design thus allows for the insertion of the landscape within design choices, intentionally modifying the context based on an approach that refuses the idea of mimesis or the opposing concept of self-referentiality. Landscape sensitive designs express their position through a confrontation with context, with the objective of entering into "resonance" with it and overcoming the common and widely practiced attitude whereby architecture, when it confronts the landscape, assumes forms that are extraneous to its disciplinary language and attempts, often in highly improbable ways, to become a surrogate of the landscape (the tree-house; the rock-house; the topography-house). The approach to the architectural design of Landscape Sensitive projects can be reassumed in the ability to consider the landscape as a "contextual totality with a specific individuality" (Clementi, 2002), that we must make an effort to understand, in intellectual and emotional terms, "listening" in a non-evaluative manner and entering into empathy with context.
At the conclusion of the workshop, the group formulated a number of principles, considered like an open list, for the development of a Manifesto of Landscape Sensitive Design.
1_Multidisciplinary Approach / Privileging a multi-disciplinary approach to design.
2_Transcalar Approach / Assuming the trans-scalar condition of the landscape as a key to interpretations and strategies of intervention.
3_The landscape is a living body that evolves over time / A consideration of landscapes as dynamic realties in constant evolution, subject to changes imposed by time and life cycles.
4_The relationship with historic and contemporary landscape meanings / Establishing relations of meaning with the historical and contemporary signs expressed by the landscape.
5_Guiding sustainable change (Energy-Ecology-Social) / Assuming energy, ecology and social sustainability, as guiding criteria for design transformations.
6_Natural and historical networks / Interpreting historical and natural networks as design matrixes.
7_Multifunctional programs / Structuring programmes that favour variety and multi-functionality in the use of the ground plane.

Massimo Angrilli
Architect, Professor at the University of Pescara

Alpine geography
Landscape
Networks
Cities

Alpine geography

The Alps (Alpes in French, Alpen in German, Alpe in Slovenian) are the most important mountain range of Europe. By agreement, the Alps start west of the Colle di Cadibona and end in the west of the city of Vienna, covering a distance of about 1.200 Km in an arc shape between northern Italy, southeast France, Switzerland, Liechtenstein, Austria, the south of Germany and Slovenia.
They reach their maximum width between Verona and Munich. The highest peak is Mont Blanc that with its 4810,90 m it is considered Europe's rooftop; followed by Monte Rosa (4634 m), Dom (4545 m), Weisshorn (4505 m) and Cervino (4476 m). Other important peaks are Gran Paradiso (4061 m), Bernina (4049 m) and Monviso (3841 m).
The Alps are inhabited by about 16 million people. In occasion of the IX Italian Geographic Congress in 1926, subdivision of the alpine system were established on the basis of the "Names and limits of the large parts of the Alpine System".
The pinciple division individuates three great parts: Western Alps, Centeral Alps and the Easter Alps, subdivided into 26 sections e 112 groups. The Western Alps stretches from Colle di Cadibona to Col Ferret; the Central Alps from Col Ferret to Brenner Pass; the Eastern Alps from Brenner Pass to Fiume.
These three large parts are subdivided further into:
Western Alps: Maritime Alpps, Cottian Alps, Graian Alps, Provenza Alps, Dauphiné Alps, Provenza Prealps, Dauphiné Prealps, Savoia Prealps.
Central Alps: Pennine Alps, Lepontine Alps, Rhaetian Alps, Bernese Alps, Glarus Alps, Swiss Prealps, Lombardy Prealps, Bavaresi Prealps.
Eastern Alps: Noric Alps, Dolomites, Carnic Alps, Julian Alps, Karawanken, Salzburg Alps, Austrian Alps, Stiria Prealps, VenetianPrealps, Kras.
The SOIUSA (Suddivisione Orografica Internazionale Unificata del Sistema Alpino)classification has been officially presented with the objective of standardizing the denomination used by in the states of the alpine area. This classification. This classification constitutes 2 large parts (Western Alps and Eastern Alps) rather than the three traditional italian one, in accordance with the classification of the beyond the Alps, and further subdivision in 5 sectors, 36 sections and 132 subsections.

Trentino Dolomites, by Alessandro Franceschini

The Western Alps are subdivided in:
Southwestern Alps: Ligurian Alps; Maritime Alps and Nice Prealps; Alps and Prealps of Provenza; Cottian Alps; Dauphiné Alps.
Northwestern Alps: Graian Alps; Savoi Prealps; Pennine Alps; Lepontine Alps, Luganesi Prealps; Bernese Alps; Glarus Alps; Swiss Prealps.
The Eastern Alps are subdivided in:
Central Eastern Alps: Western Rhaetian Alps; Eastern Rhaetian Alps; Western Tauri Alps; Eastern Tauri Alps; Noric Alps; Stiria Prealps.
Northeastern Alps: Northern Limestone Alps; Bavaresi Alps; Alpi scistose tirolesi; Northern Salzburg Alps; Salzkammergut and Alta Austria Alps; Northern Stiria Alps; Bassa Austria Alps.
Southeastern Alps: Southern Rhaetian Alps; Bergamasche Prealps; Bresciane and Gardesane Prealps; Dolomites; Venetian Prealps; Carnic and Slovenian Alps; Slovenian Prealps.
National traditional classification also exists, which considers only the rich part of the alpine system on national territory:
The Italian Alps, classifyied by the Italian Alpine Club and the Italian Touring Club
The French Alps, classifyied by the French Alpine Club
The Swiss Alps, classifyied by the Swiss Alpine Club
The Austrian and German Alps, by the Geographische Raumgliederug Österreich
The Slovenian Alps, classifyied by Naravnogeografska regionalizacija Slovenije
And finally there is also a classification of the Eastern Alps according to Deutscher und Österreichischer Alpenverein and the Austrian-German Alpine Clubs.

(the map of the following pages have been elaborated by TALL/Trentino Advanced Landscape Lab, by P.Scaglione)

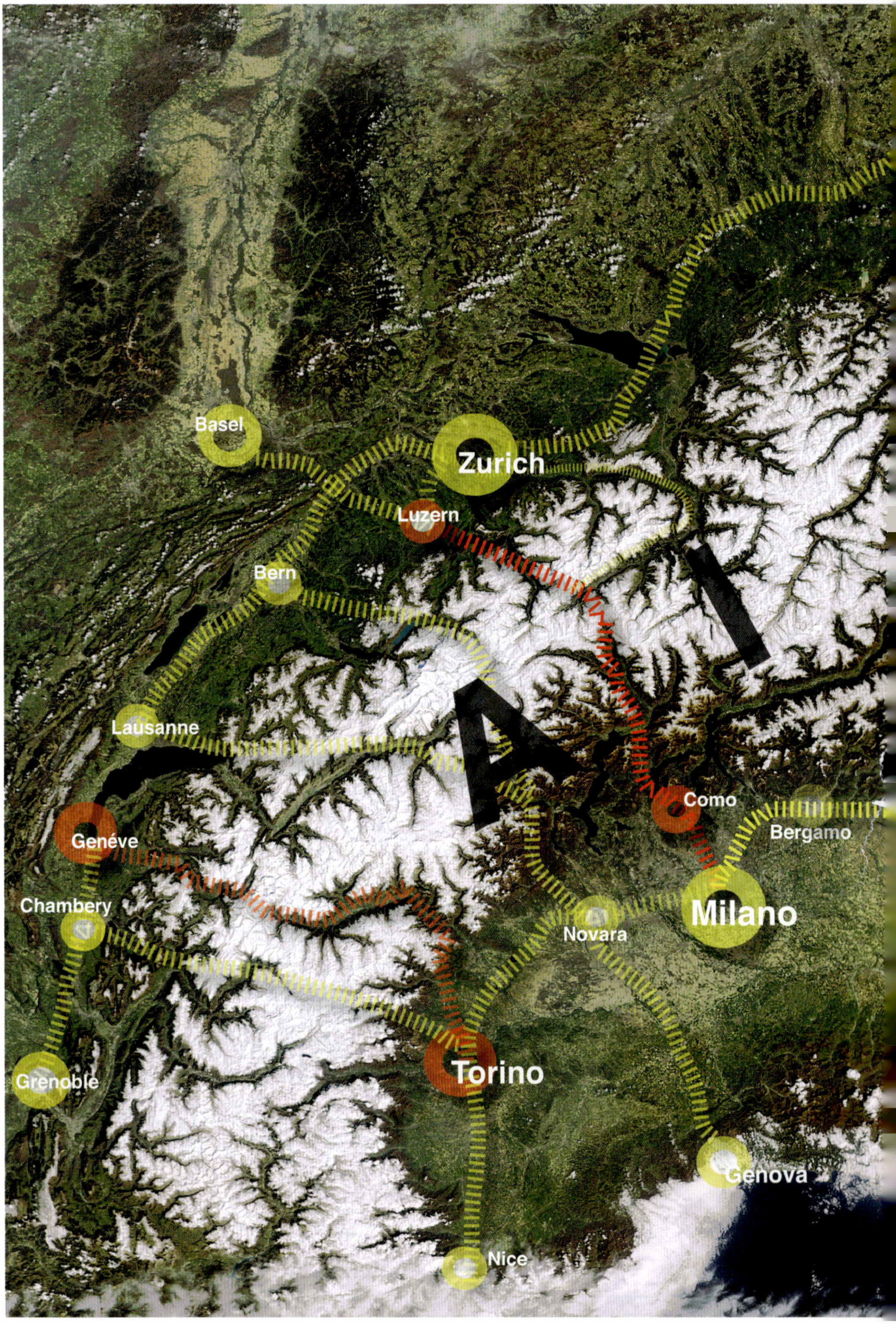
Basel
Zurich
Luzern
Bern
Lausanne
Genéve
Chambery
Grenoble
Torino
Nice
Genova
Novara
Milano
Como
Bergamo
A
I

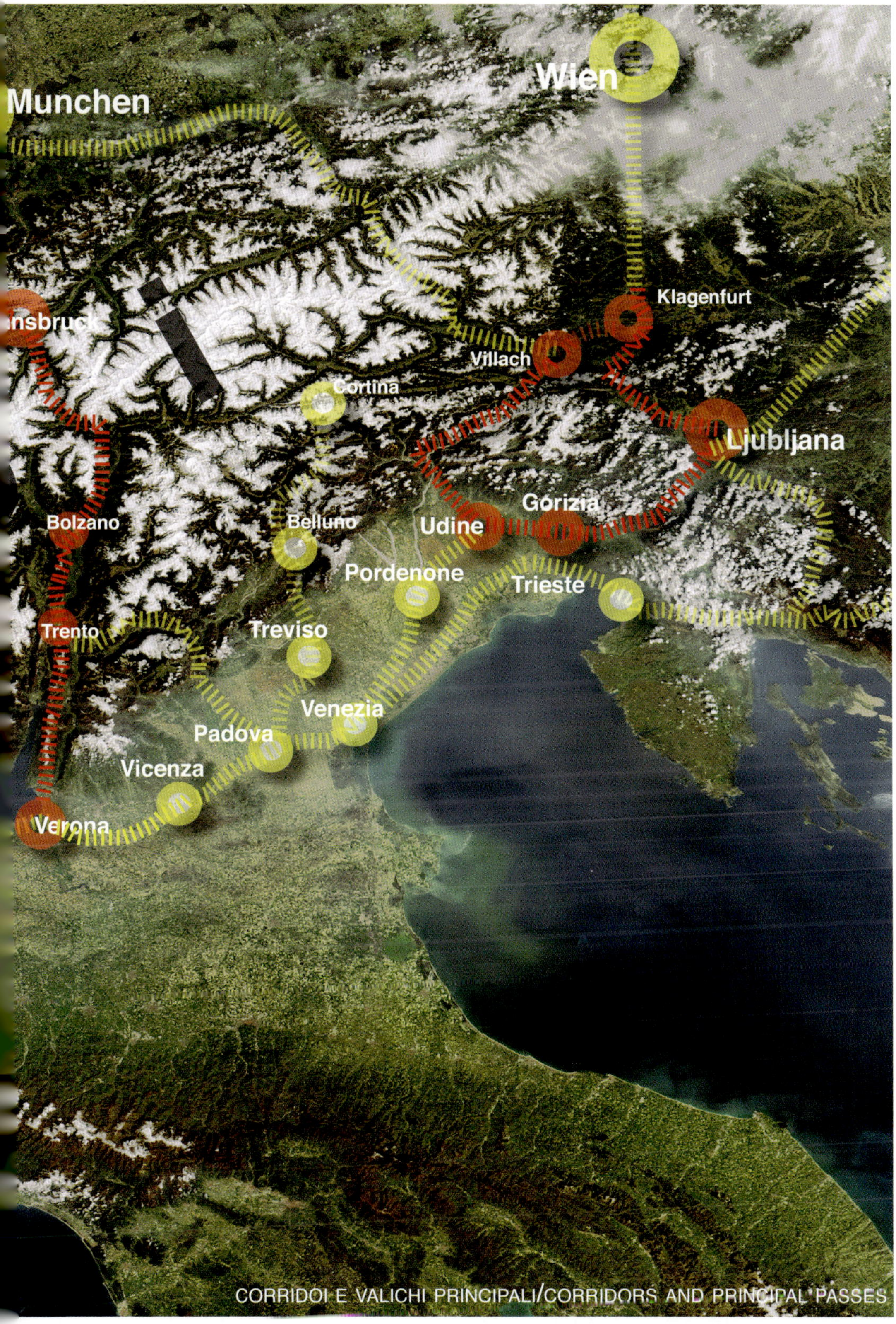

CORRIDOI E VALICHI PRINCIPALI/CORRIDORS AND PRINCIPAL PASSES

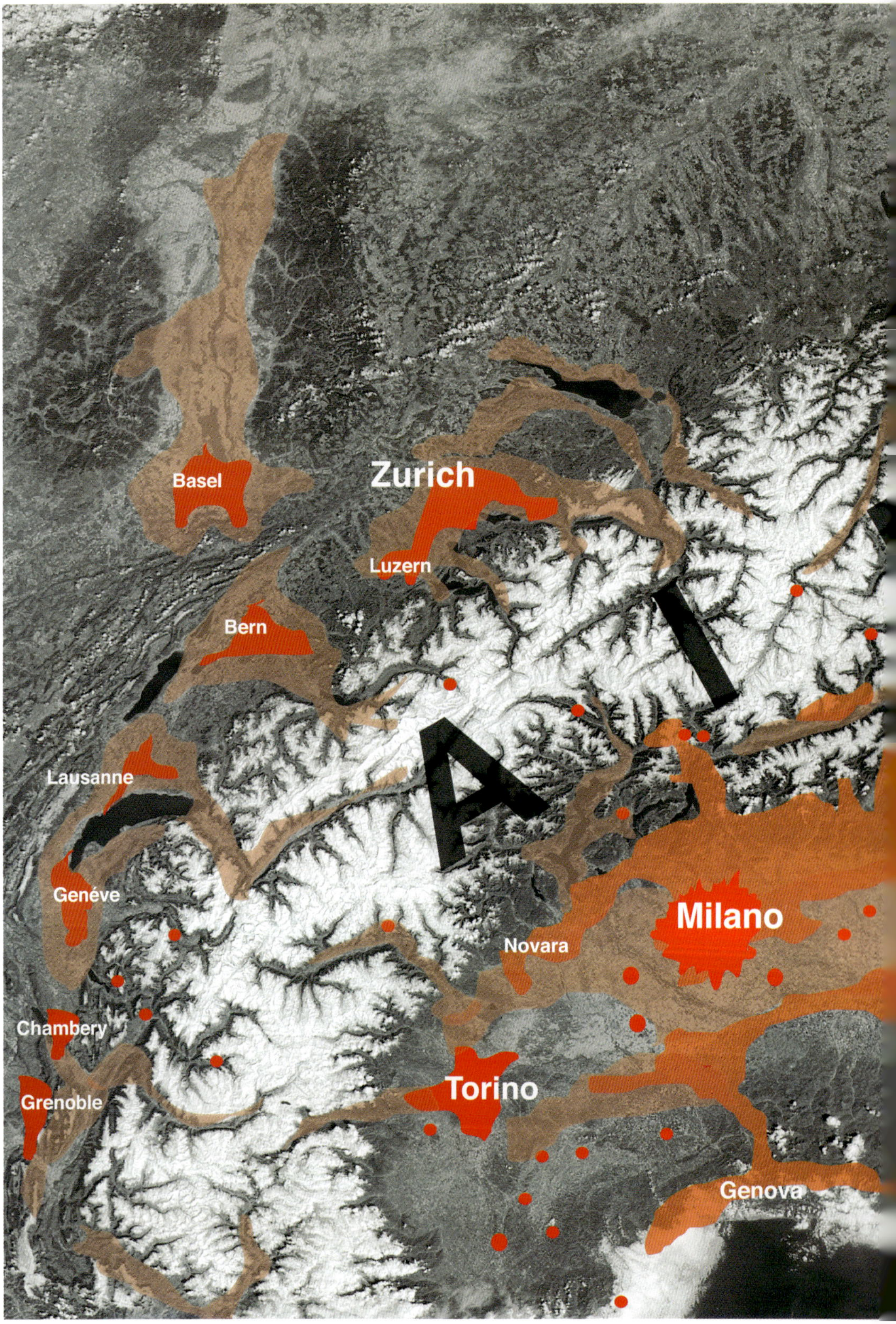

Basel
Zurich
Luzern
Bern
Lausanne
Genéve
Chambery
Grenoble
Novara
Milano
Torino
Genova
A
L

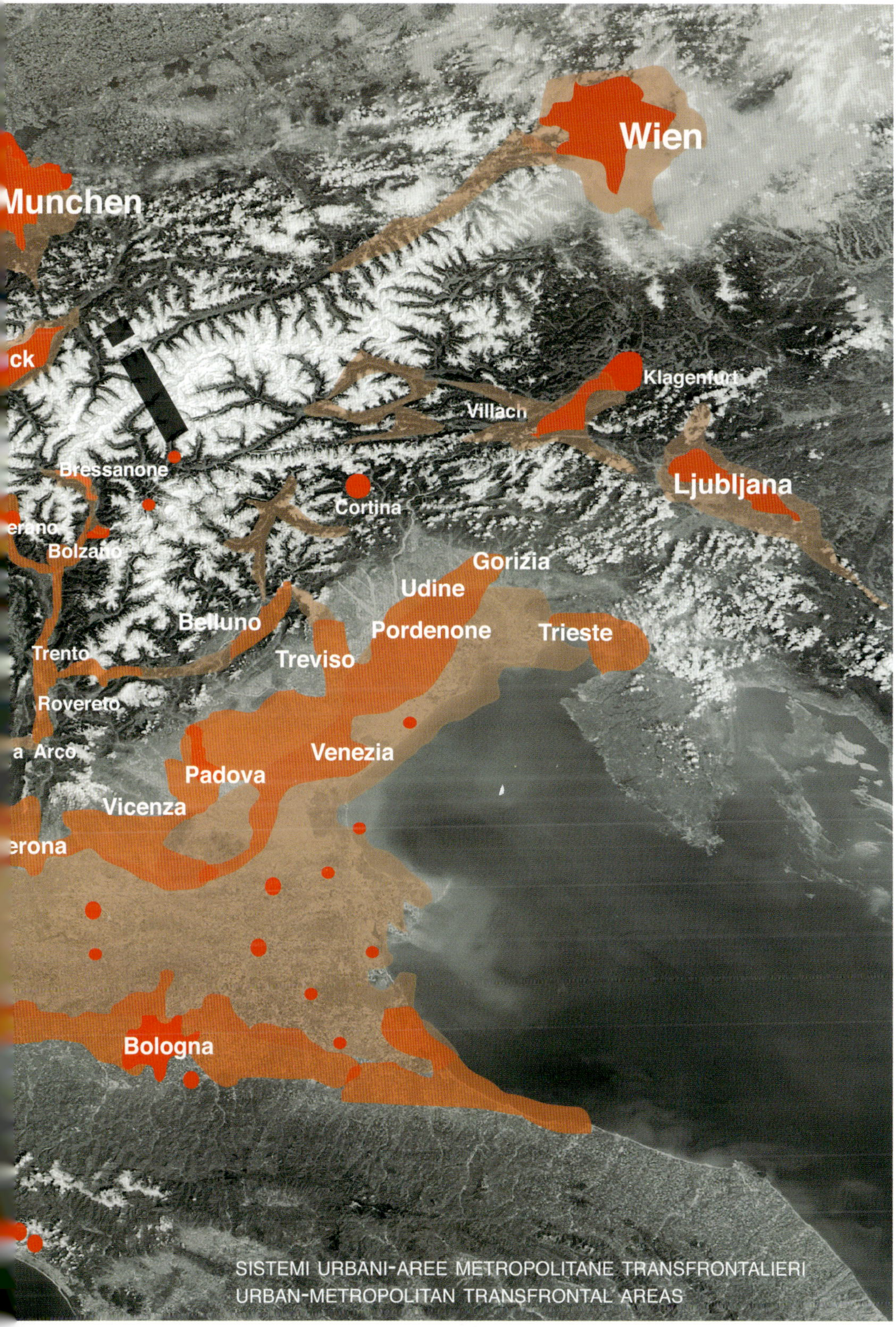

SISTEMI URBANI-AREE METROPOLITANE TRANSFRONTALIERI
URBAN-METROPOLITAN TRANSFRONTAL AREAS

Trentino Dolomites, Alessandro Franceschini

Austrian Alps, Alexander Pfanzelt

Top view of the French-Italian Alps, Dino Olivieri

Photographic alpine itinerary

Urbanization diffused
in a Valley of Val D'Aosta

Widespread urbanization
in a valley of Austria

Widespread urbanization
in a valley of Switzerland,
in an impressive night
view

The valley of the Adige in its distension in proximity to Mezzocorona (Trentino)

Widespread urbanization and infrastructure in San Michele all'Adige (Trentino)

Widespread urbanization and infrastructure in the bend of the Adige in proximity to Trento (Trentino)

Photographic alpine itinerary

Widespread urbanization of Bolzano in the natural context

Vineyards in Bolzano

Widespread urbanization and alpine landscape along the shores of Lake San Valentino alla Muta (Bz) in Alto Adige

Underground cellar in Alto Adige
architect W. Angonese

Widespread urbanization and infrastructure cultivated country (Alto Adige)

Masi, farm house, agrarian landscape in Alto Adige

Tradition and trivialization

traditional sentry boxes in multipurpose wood

Alpine house, second touristic residence

Alpine house

Traditional wooden apartment houses in the French Alps

Levicoland", or rather the Far West in the Trentine Dolomites

Agricultural deposit and traditional farmyards in Lajon (Alto Adige)

Alps and mass tourism

Autogrill on Monte Cervino

Building models of the winter tourism (Alpi Carniche)

In the snow as in the city (Alpi Carniche)

In queue for skiing,
in front of the
establishments

Park games in the
snow

Alpine apartment houses,
second touristic residence
(Dolomiti carniche)

Alpine Profile

Planning projects for the mountain and alpine landscapes

Piemonte - Landscape regional planning

PAESAGGI AGRARI E FORESTALI DELLA REGIONE PIEMONTE

TAVOLA 2.1.1
APPROCCIO FISICO-NATURALISTICO-ECOLOGICO

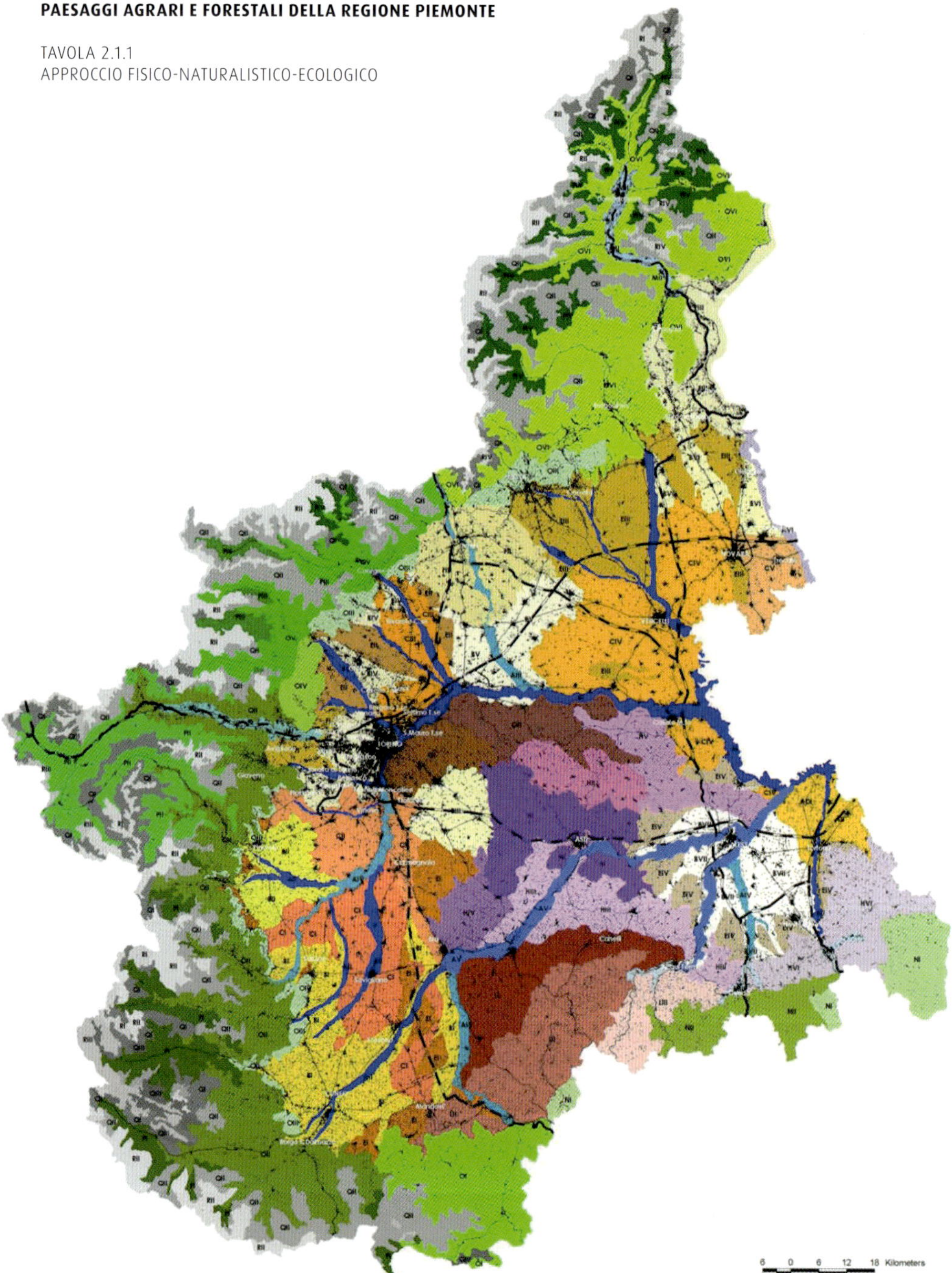

REGIONE LOMBARDIA

RegioneLombardia

Area Sud Milano

Area: 114,2 km²
Area urbanizzata: 27,5 km²
Popolazione residente: 105.000 abitanti (escluso Milano)

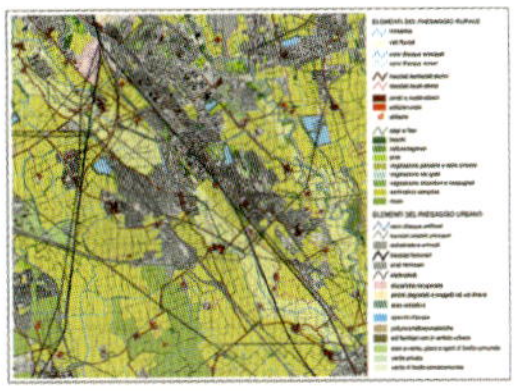

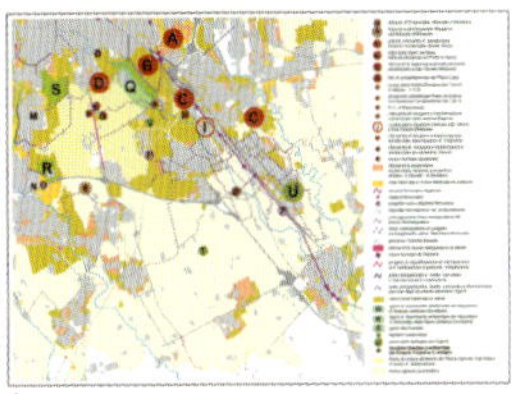

Fig. 1 - Gli elementi costitutivi del paesaggio: ambito della Valle della Vettabbia. La carta è costruita utilizzando i tematismi del Sistema Informativo Territoriale regionale, integrati e verificati dal gruppo di lavoro.
The landscape basic elements: the Vettabbia Valley. The map has been drawn using the issues provided by the regional Computerized Territorial System, duly integrated and tested by the work team.

Fig. 2 - Il quadro dei piani e dei progetti di trasformazione e innovazione territoriale in corso di definizione nell'ambito di area vasta.
The picture of the territorial transformation and innovation projects and plans to be defined at a large scale.

Fig. 3 - Stato del paesaggio nell'ambito Valle della Vettabbia: sensibilità, criticità, opportunità
Condition of landscape within the Vettabbia Valley: sensitive areas, threatened areas, enhancement opportunities.

Fig. 4 - Ipotesi di scenario strategico per la riqualificazione della Valle della Vettabbia.
Hypothesis of a stategic scenario for the rehabilitation of the Vettabbia Valley.

Definizione azione pilota

Gestione paesisticamente attenta delle trasformazioni territoriali in aree di frangia - Problematiche inerenti i rapporti tra struttura urbana e territorio agricolo.

Finalità azione pilota

Formulazione di indirizzi paesistici e di "scenari strategici" per la progettazione e gestione degli interventi in un'area periurbana a forte dinamica di sviluppo.

Enti territoriali e istituzioni locali competenti

Regione Lombardia, Provincia di Milano, Parco Agricolo Sud Milano, Amministrazioni comunali (Milano, San Donato Milanese, San Giuliano Milanese), Commissario per la realizzazione degli impianti di depurazione di Milano.

Risultati della sperimentazione:

La proposta per uno "scenario strategico di riqualificazione paesistica della Valle della Vettabbia", ambito con un elevato grado di sensibilità e per il quale urge definire incisive politiche locali di paesaggio, riconosce e riconfigura la valle fluviale; riesprime la centralità delle abbazie e dei borghi; recupera le acque per uso irriguo, produttivo e paesistico; riorganizza l'attività agricola con valenza ambientale; favorisce il riassetto ecosistemico; struttura il sistema fruitivo; recupera l'edilizia rurale con funzioni diversificate; avvia mitiga le reti infrastrutturali. I soggetti istituzionali direttamente coinvolti hanno già espresso l'intenzione di assumere l'ipotesi di scenario come base per orientare la pianificazione di dettaglio e i progetti locali in corso di definizione.

Definition of the pilot action

Careful landscape management of the territorial transformations in urban fringes - Problems concerning the relationship between urban structure and rural territory.

Objectives of the pilot action

Creation of guidelines for setting up "agreed strategic scenarios" and for "landscape planning" in a fast-growing suburban (peri-urban) area.

Competent territorial agencies and local institutions

Regione Lombardia, Provincia di Milano, Parco Agricolo Sud Milano, Amministrazioni comunali (Milano, San Donato Milanese, San Giuliano Milanese), Commissario per la realizzazione degli impianti di depurazione di Milano.

The outcomes of previous experiences:

The proposal for a "strategic scenario of landscape rehabilitation in the Vettabbia Valley", a highly sensitive area requiring immediate serious local landscape policies: recognize and restructure the valley; enhance the importance of the abbeys and villages; retrieve waters for irrigation, production and landscape use; re-arrange agricultural activities making them envornmentally friendly; encourage multifunctional eco-system reorganization; set up the recreational system; restore rural buildings for varied functions; upgrade infrastructures (in particular, powerlines). The governmental bodies directly involved have already stated they intend to base specific planning as well as local projects under discussion to be carried out in the territory considered, on the hypothesis of scenario.

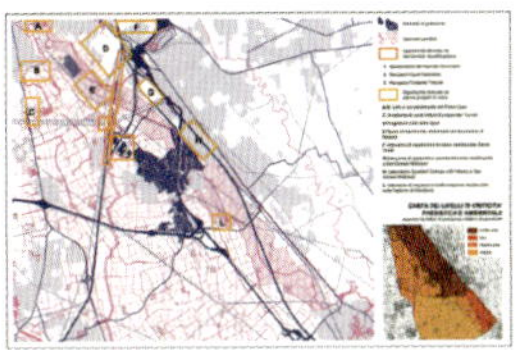

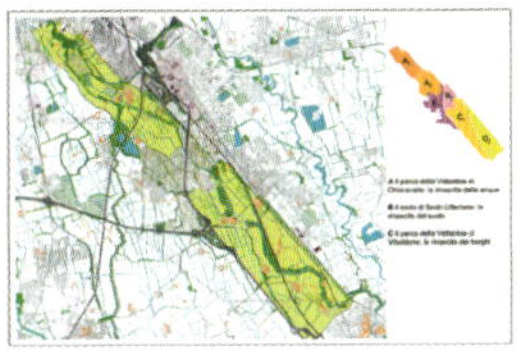

Coordinamento istituzionale
Riccardo Ramozzi
Anna Rossi

Responsabile
Marco Prusicki - *IReR*

Gruppo di lavoro
Luca Bisogni
Valentina Dotti
Francesca Simonetti

Area Montichiari

Area: 200 km²

Popolazione residente: 85.000 abitanti (escluso Brescia)

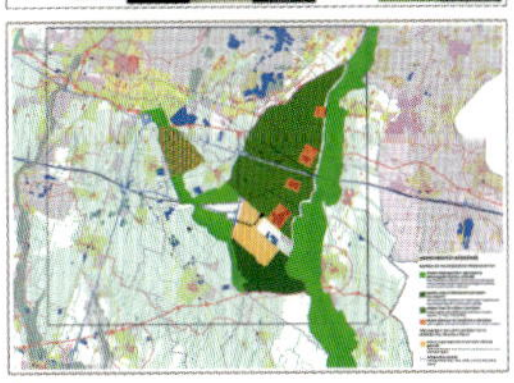

Fig. 1 - Il paesaggio bresciano: una mostra itinerante ne traccia il profilo mettendone in evidenza gli aspetti strutturali e i valori di cultura materiale e simbolica.
Landscape of Brescia area: a wandering show (or exibition) marks out its outline, pointing out the structural angles and the material and simbolical values

Fig. 2 - Le potenzialità paesaggistiche per il sud bresciano: possibili orientamenti di intervento alla grande scala
The landscape powericapacity for the south of Brescia area: possible trend (or guide-line) for attendance on large scale.

Fig. 3 - Le potenzialità paesaggistiche per l'area di Montichiari: uno scenario di intervento per il paesaggio ravvicinato.
The landscape powericapacity for Montechiari area: a perspective of attendance for closer landscape.

Fig. 4 - La Lombardia nel 1807, nel Piano Paesistico regionale e nell'organizzazione territoriale al 2004.
Lombardy in 1807, regional landscape plan and territorial organitation in 2004.

Definizione azione pilota

Gestione paesisticamente attenta delle trasformazioni territoriali indotte dagli interventi di carattere infrastrutturale in ambiti agricoli e in aree di frangia urbana.

Finalità azione pilota

Formulazione di indirizzi paesistici per la pianificazione locale e la progettazione infrastrutturale.

Enti territoriali e istituzioni locali competenti

Regione Lombardia. Provincia di Brescia. Comuni di Castenedolo, Ghedi Montichiari, Montirone, interessati direttamente da grandi progetti infrastrutturali.

Risultati della sperimentazione:

Analisi e riscontri condotte con le istituzioni evidenziano la possibilità di correlare parte delle trasformazioni inerenti il paesaggio (previste nei piani provinciali e comunali) con i grandi progetti infrastrutturali. Alta Capacità ferroviaria, viabilità sovracomunale e potenziamento dell'aeroporto di Montichiari possono giocare un ruolo decisivo per il riorientamento di alcune scelte pianificatorie, e concorrere ad invertire le dinamiche di degrado del paesaggio e dell'ambiente. I risultati evidenziano le seguenti potenzialità: un corridoio paesaggistico lungo il fiume Chiese già interessato da previsioni di piano indirizzate alla tutela. Un collegamento tra le aree estrattive a sud di Brescia con quelle di Ghedi (un corridoio esteso interessato da indicazioni di tutela da perfezionare). La possibilità di rafforzare ambiti di valore paesaggistico in parallelo alla viabilità provinciale che intersecano ambiti di pregio agricolo.

Definition of the pilot action

Management of landscape transformation due to/caused to infrastructure projects.

Objectives of the pilot action

Formulation for landscape projection.

Competent territorial agencies and local institutions

Regione Lombardia. Provinces Brescia. Municipalities: Castenedolo, Ghedi Montichiari, Montirone (that were directly concerned with the building of infrastructures on their territory).

The outcomes of previous experiences:

The analysis of the data provided by local institutions highlighted the possibility to link part of the scheduled transformations with the big infrastructure projects, high speed railway, upgrading the overmunicipal road system and expansion of Montichiari airport may play a major role in redirecting some of the planning choices and at the same time they may contribute to reverse the landscape and environment degradation process.
The results show a picture of opportunities that may be summarized in a list of general aims for desirable interventions: build a landscape and environmental corridor along the River Chiore, which is already protected by specific charters and statutory protection and preservation plans. Connect the mining areas south of Brescia with those near Ghedi. Reinforce the linear systems along the new provincial road network passing through high value agricultural areas.

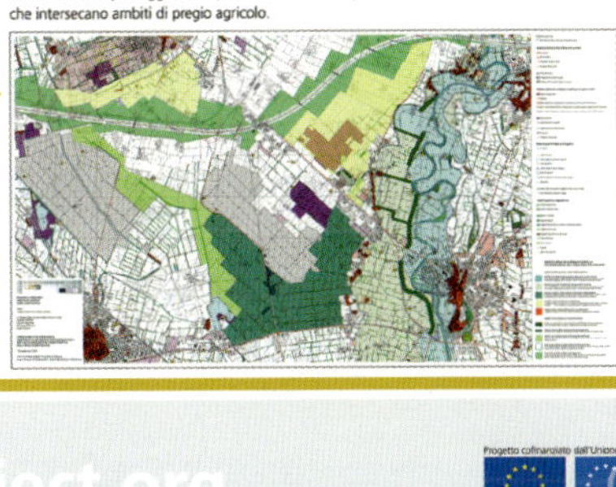

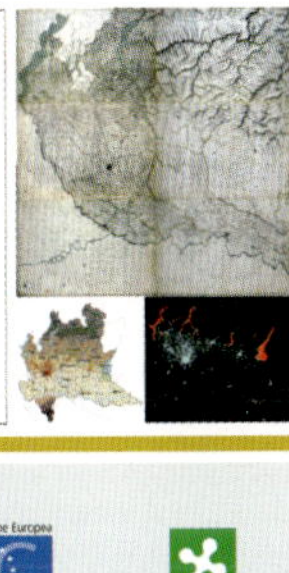

Coordinamento istituzionale
Riccardo Ramozzi
Anna Rossi

Responsabile
G. Matteo Mai - *IReR*

Gruppo di lavoro
A. Maffioli
S. Zorzolo
D. Miglietta

www.loto-project.org

Progetto cofinanziato dall'Unione Europea

INTERREG IIIB CADSES

RegioneLombardia

Landscape Opportunities for Territorial Organization

LOTO

Lombardia - Piedmontan project

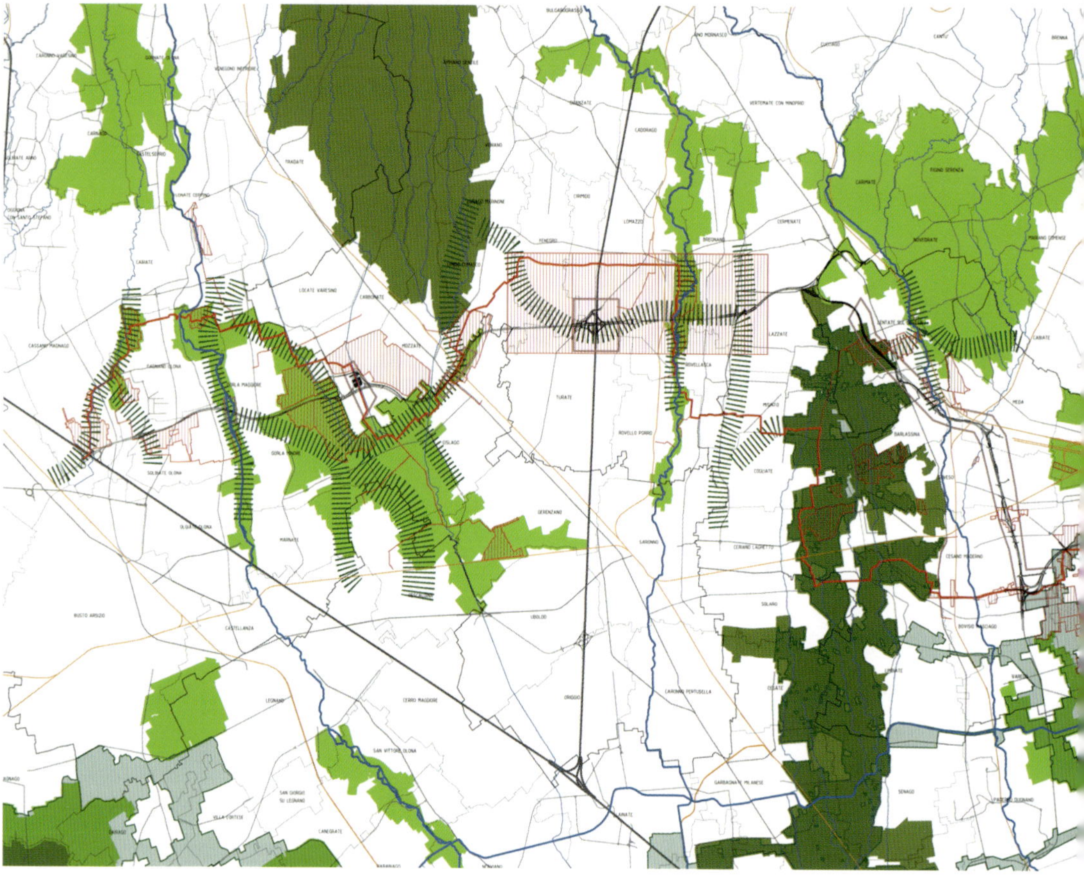

1. Planimetric map of the operations in the ecological parks and corridor settings

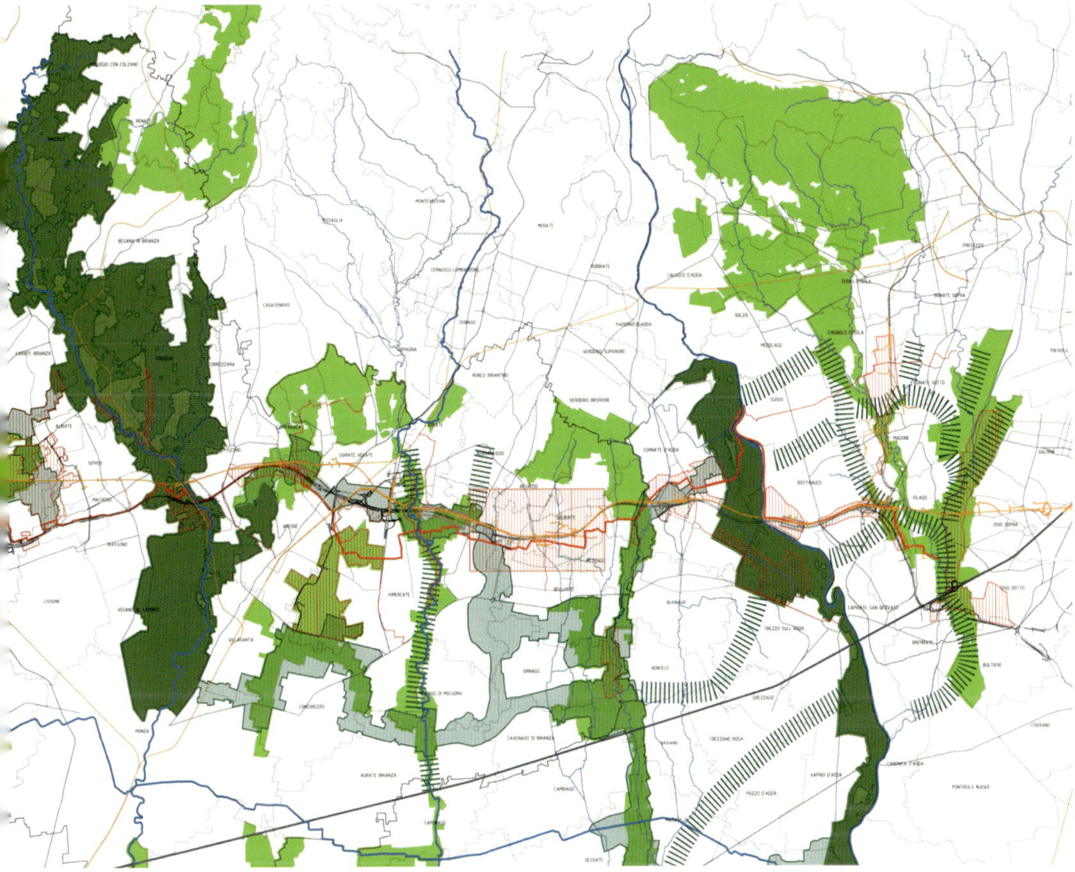

UN PARCO PER LA CITTA' INFINITA
masterplan delle compensazioni ambientali di Autostrada Pedemontana Lombarda

DiAP - Politecnico di Milano, Marzo 2008

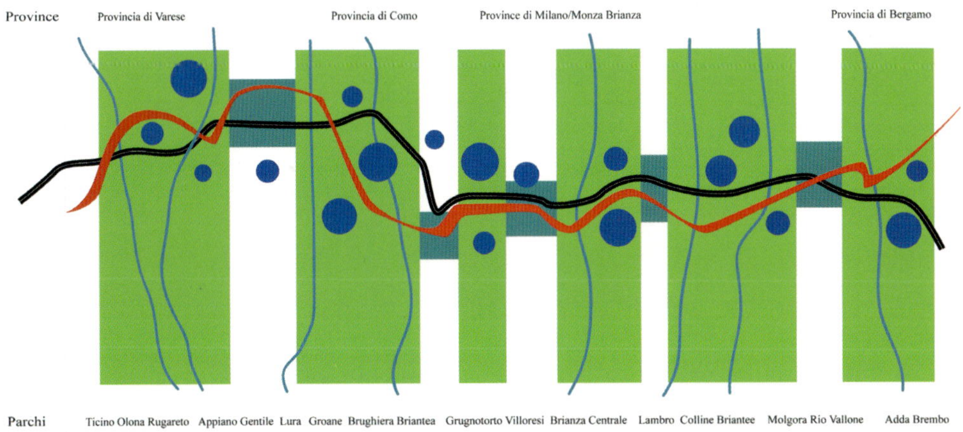

Linee blu: fiumi   Linea nera: autostrada   Linea rossa: greenway, nuovo percorso ciclopedonale attraverso i parchi   Punti: progetti dei comuni e dei parchi

Trentino - Interpreting landscape

On this page and the previous pages are some of the elaborations relative to the landscape and cities of the PUP – Provincial Urban Plan of Trentino, approved in 2008

Towards the plan for Ticino

1

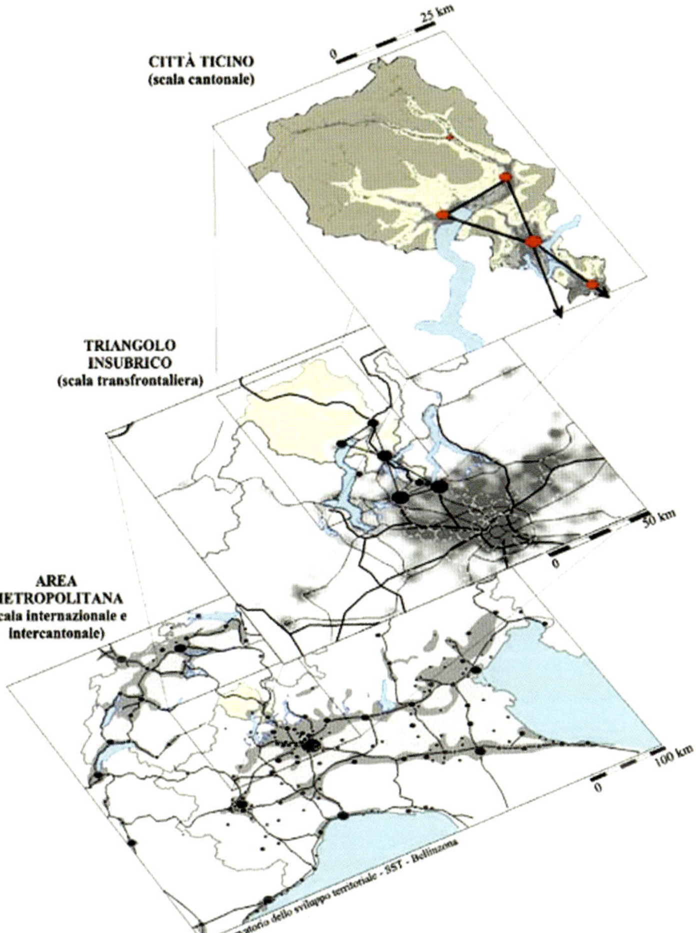

2

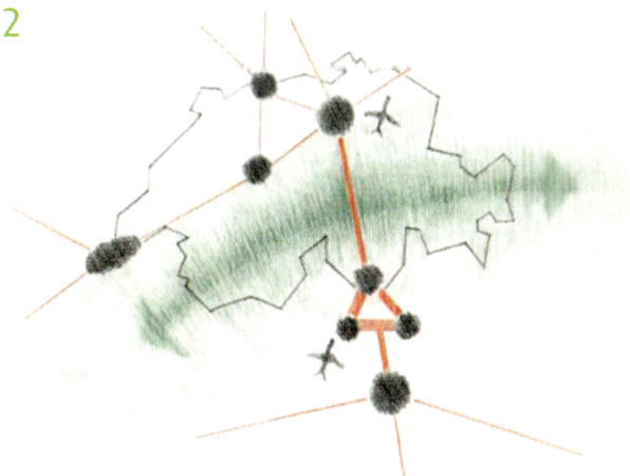

3

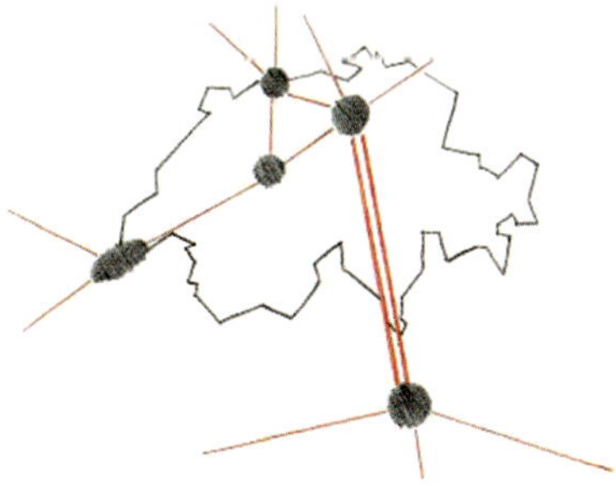

1. Master plan for Ticino: scales of the territorial model
2. Master plan for Ticino: scenario between Alps and plains
3. Master plan for Ticino: corridor scenario or double periphery

Alto Adige - reading the landscape

- Frutticultura
- Viticultura
- Prati da sfalcio
- Faggete
- Peccete
- Boschi ricchi di abete rosso e bianco
- Boschi ripariali
- Boscaglie termofile
- Boschi di pino silvestre
- Lariceti e boschi di pino cembro
- Arbusti nani
- Pascoli alpini
- Praterie alpine
- Fascia nivale

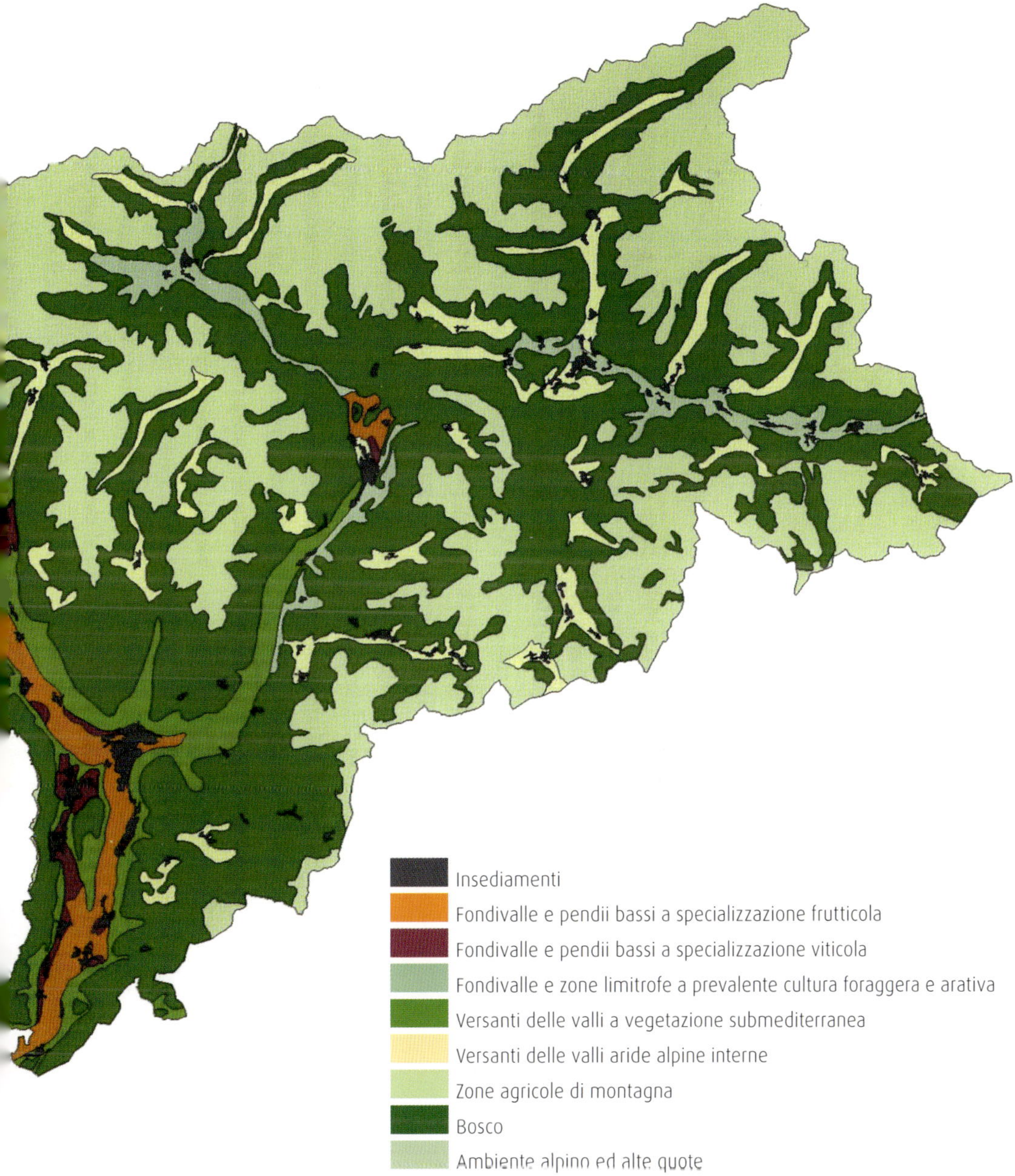
Insediamenti
Fondivalle e pendii bassi a specializzazione frutticola
Fondivalle e pendii bassi a specializzazione viticola
Fondivalle e zone limitrofe a prevalente cultura foraggera e arativa
Versanti delle valli a vegetazione submediterranea
Versanti delle valli aride alpine interne
Zone agricole di montagna
Bosco
Ambiente alpino ed alte quote

Veneto, Liguria, Valle d'Aosta
ALPTER-Terraced alpine landscapes

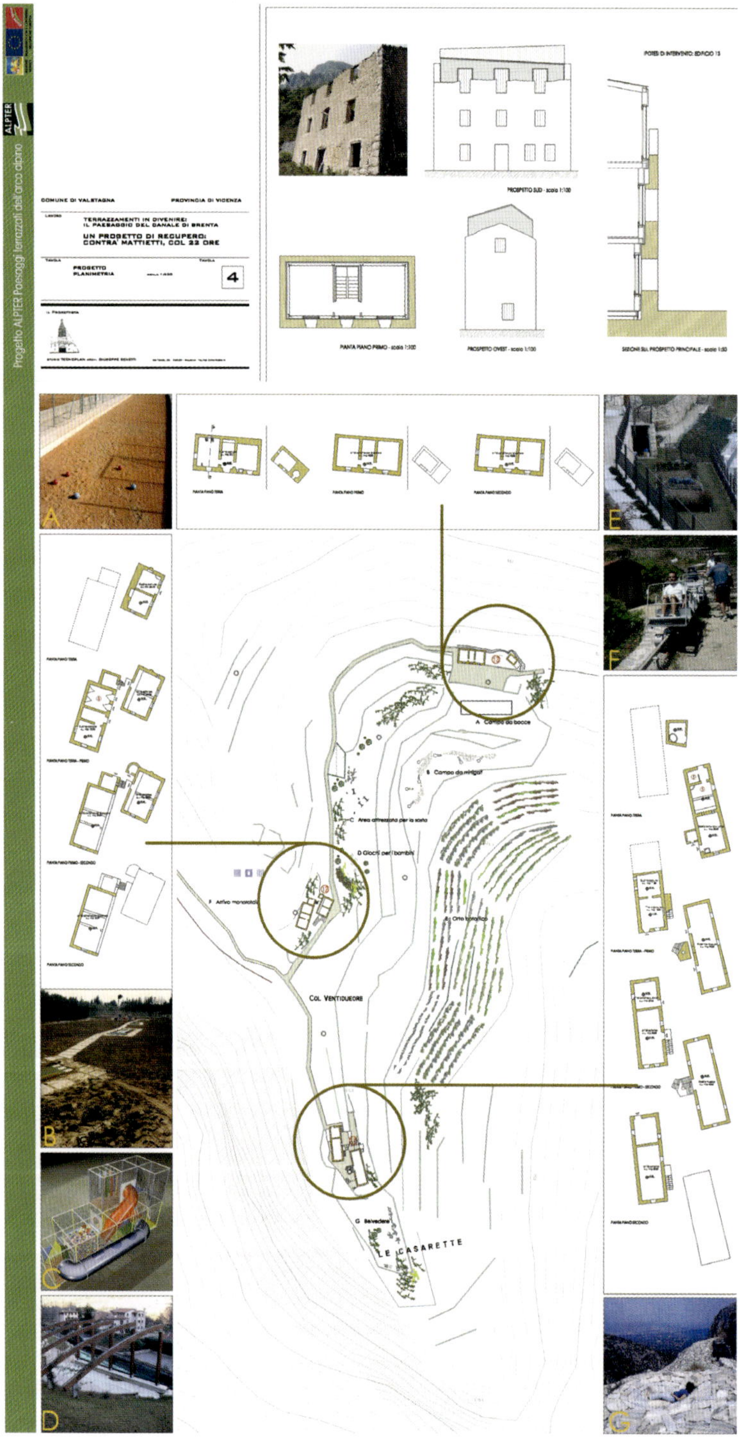

Il Progetto ALPTER

Il gruppo di lavoro del progetto ALPTER si è formato fra il 2003 e il 2004, sulla base dello stimolo che le amministrazioni regionali di Veneto, Liguria e Lombardia hanno ricevuto dai rispettivi atenei. Lo spunto veniva da una rinnovata attenzione per il paesaggio, considerato come risultato del lavoro dell'uomo e risorsa territoriale meritevole di cura ed attenzione continua, quale lo descrive la Convenzione Europea del Paesaggio. Obiettivo del progetto è la definizione di una metodologia condivisa per il rilievo dei terrazzamenti, lo studio di tecnologie e di modelli gestionali specifici per queste aree e la realizzazione di alcuni esempi concreti di recupero produttivo.

Gruppo di lavoro e Partner del progetto
Italia: Regione Veneto - Direzione Urbanistica
Regione Liguria - Dipartimento Pianificazione Territoriale, Paesaggistica e Ambientale
Regione Valle D'aosta - Dipartimento Agricoltura, Risorse Naturali e Protezione del Suolo
IREALP - Istituto per la Ricerca Economica ed Ecologica nell'area Alpina
Slovenia: Universita' di Lubiana - Facoltà di Architettura
Austria: Universita' BOKU di Vienna - Istituto di Progettazione e Conservazione del Paesaggio
Francia: A.D.I. - Associazione per lo Sviluppo Infografico
Svizzera: Regione Bregaglia
Partner osservatori: UNESCO Ufficio per la Ricerca Scientifica in Europa

Atenei coinvolti nel progetto:
Università IUAV di Venezia - Dipartimenti di Urbanistica e di Pianificazione del territorio
Università degli Studi di Padova - Dipartimento di Geografia
Università degli Studi di Genova - Dipartimento POLIS
Università degli Studi di Milano -Istituto di Geografia Umana e Dipartimento di Scienze della Terra

ALPTER Project, from the top, before and after terracing
On the sides, the project of the arrangement of terraced houses in Valstagna

A glance at the Appenino:
Umbria's Landscape Plan

1

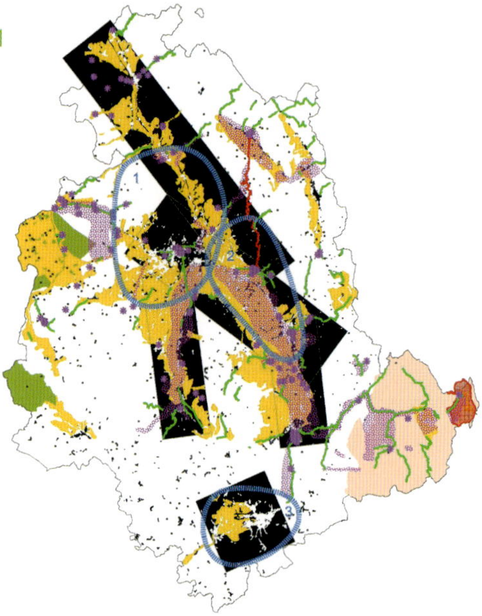

2

3

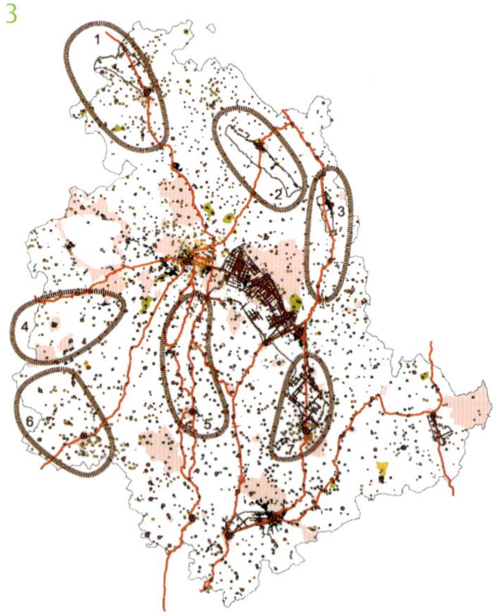

1. Umbria's Landscape Plan: charter of historical-cultural values
2. Umbria's Landscape Plan: charter of nature
3. Umbria's Landscape Plan: charter of social and symbolic values
4. Opposite page: Umbria's Landscape Plan: Urban landscapes

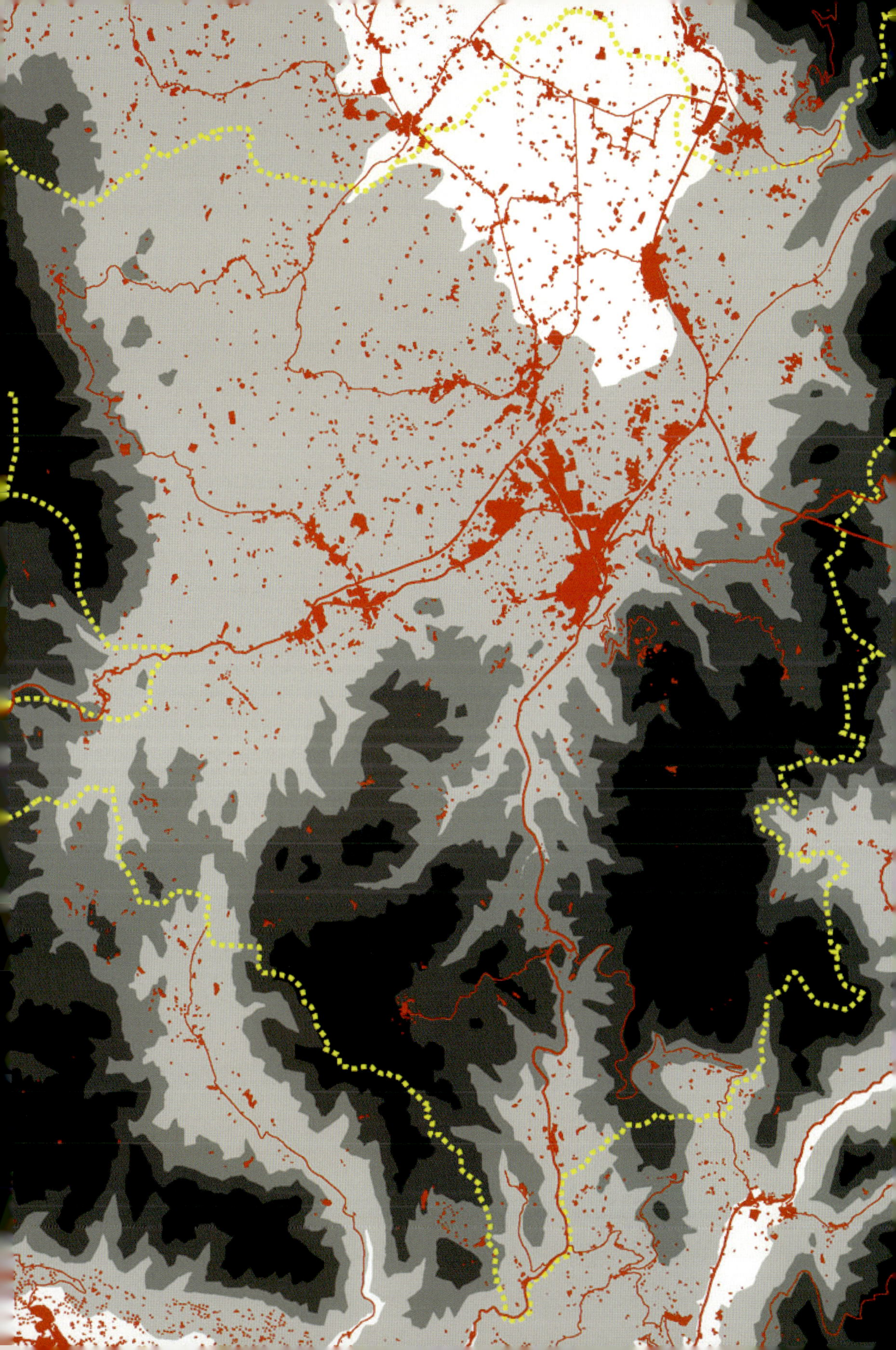

Trentino - Alpine topographies

Top view of trentino landscapes
(Laboratory of Topography, DICA, Faculty of Engineering, University of Trento)

Landscape projects between research and experimentation

Design Schools of:
Trento/Turin/Venice/Mendrisio/
Bolzano/Innsbruck/Pescara

CORRIDOIO DEL BRENNERO

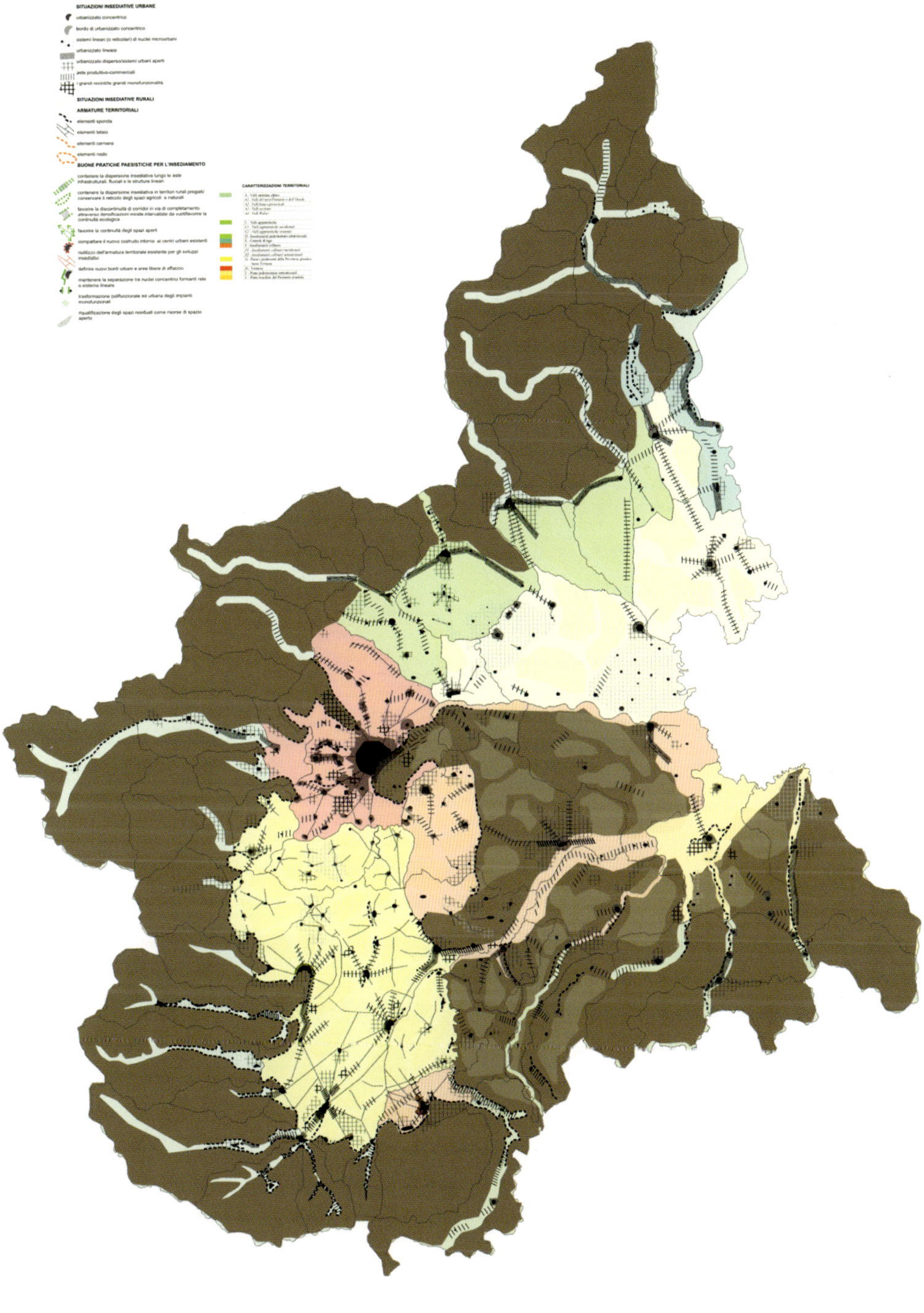

Studies for the Landscape Plan of Piemonte, group work: Polytechnic of Turin - DIPRADI
Opposite page: ITATER research, Trentino, edited by Corrado Diamantini,
graphic processing by A. Franceschini

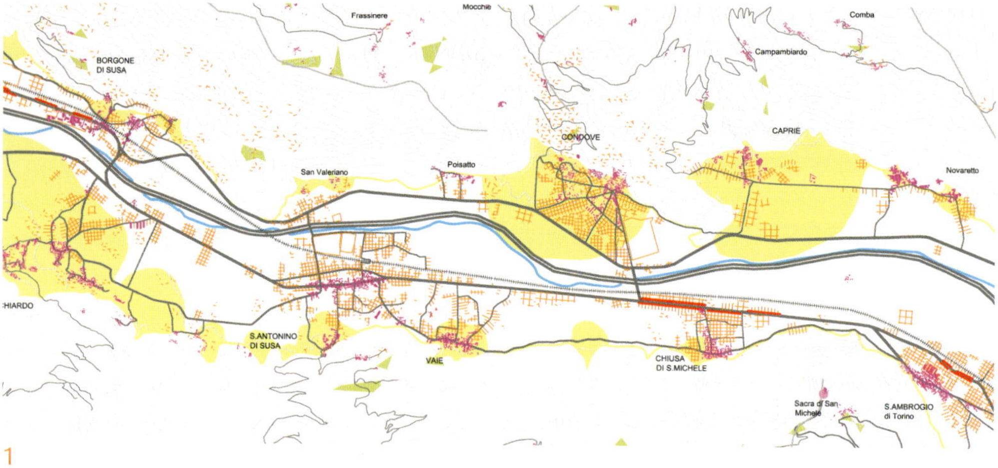

1

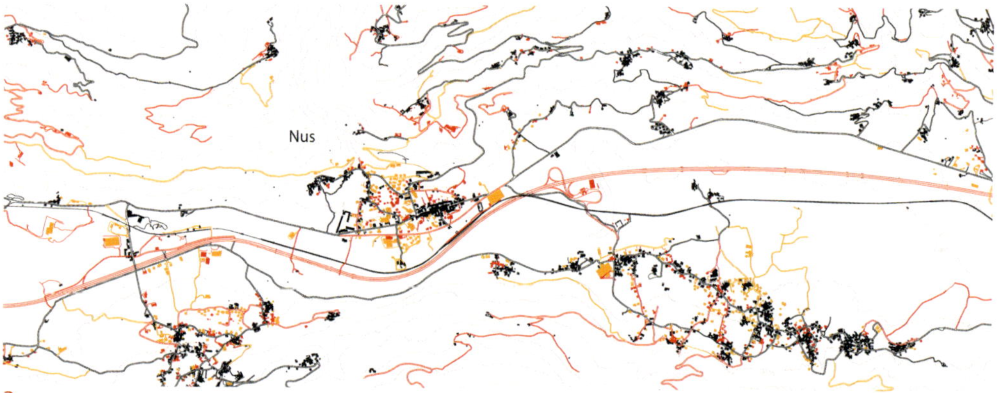

2

3

Polytechnic University of Turin - DIPRADI
1. Studies on the settlement matrices of Valle di Susa for the elaboration of the Territorial Regional Plan
2. Current modifications of the valdostano settlment landscape
3. Simulation for the new entrance of Ostana in the Po valley

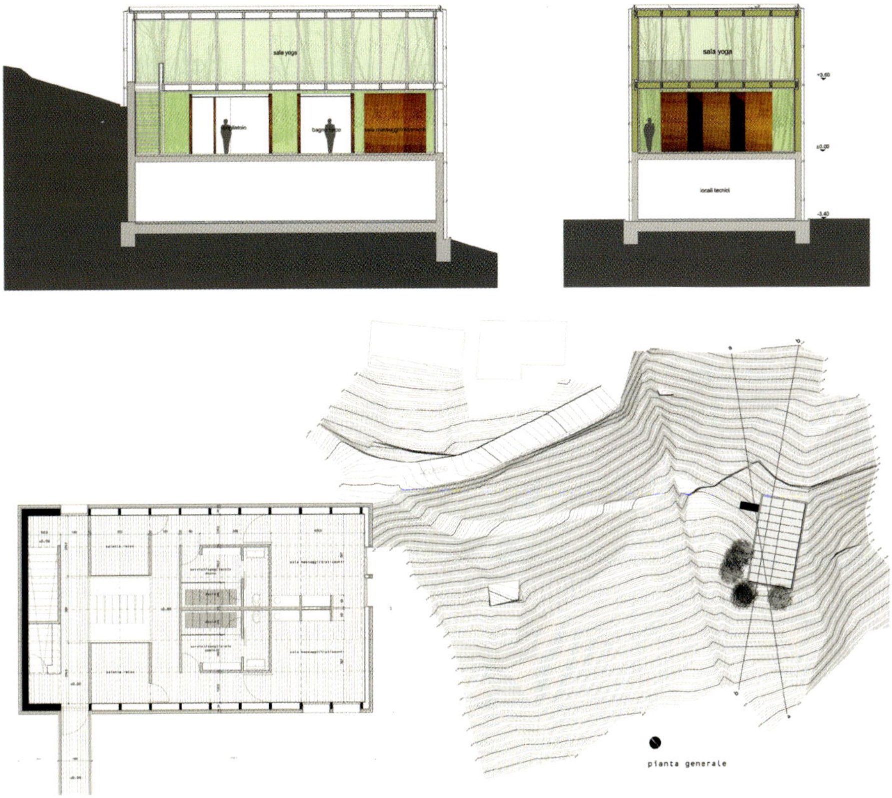

1

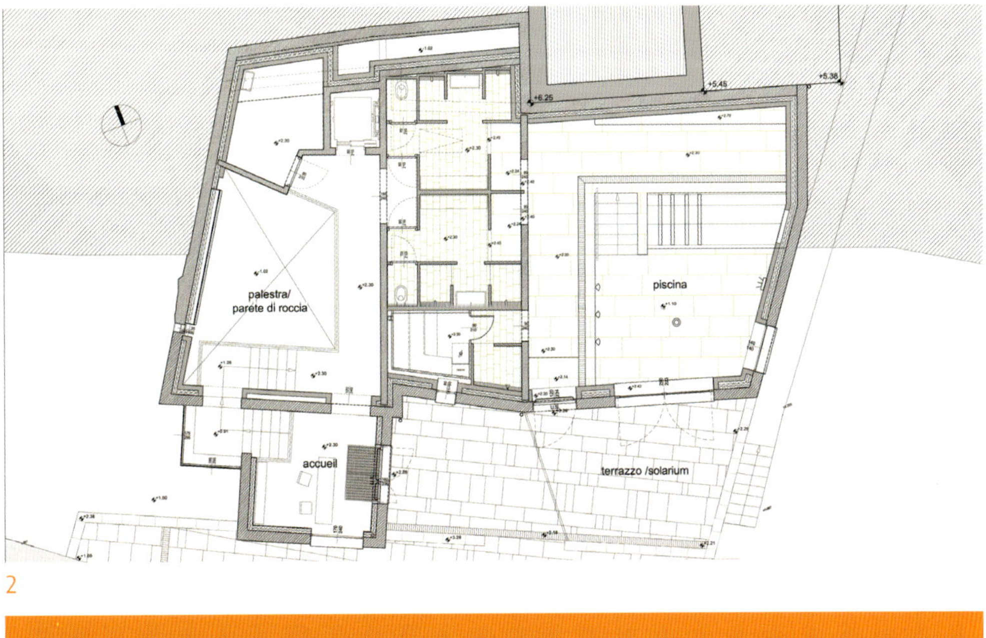

2

1. ARCHITECTURE Project for the Spa in the Alte Valli Occitane
(M. Crotti, A. De Rossi, M. -P. Forsans)
2. CONSTRUCTED LANDSCAPES Planimetry of the sports center and spa in Ostana in the Po Valley

1

2

3

4

1. Recovery of a gypsum quarry in Murisengo (Turin), A. Alì, 2007.
2. Schümel Quarry, Holderbank (Switzerland), Stöckli, Kienast & Koeppel, 1988.
3. The pond with hydroliphic vegetation
4. The pond and circular area designed by the poplar and cypress.
(Images by Pino Brioschi e Paolo L. Bürgi). Edited by Emanuela Schir

1

2

3

Claudio Lamanna, Univeristy of Trento
1. Tourist complex in the mountains within the "Patto Territoriale del Monte Bondone", 2007-2008.
2.-3. Palamela Congress and Exhibition Center for the Valle di Non, Trento, 2006.

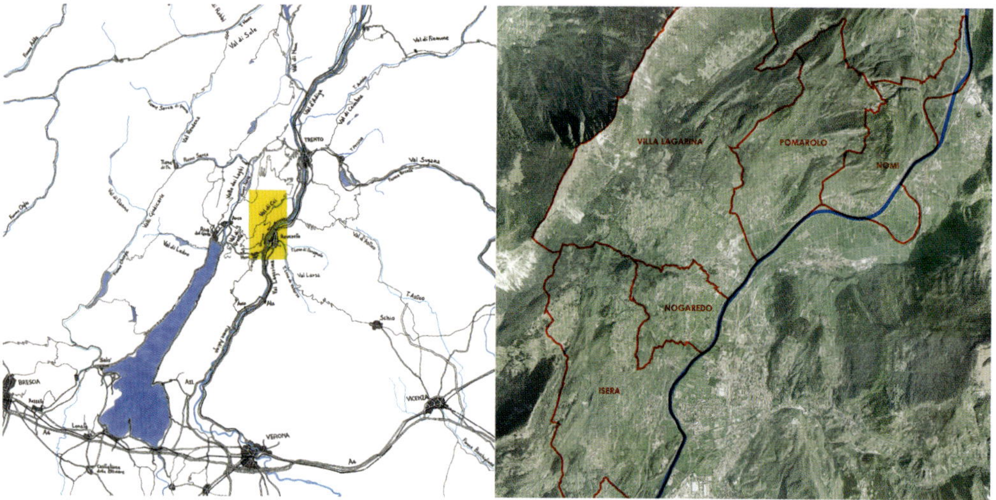

1

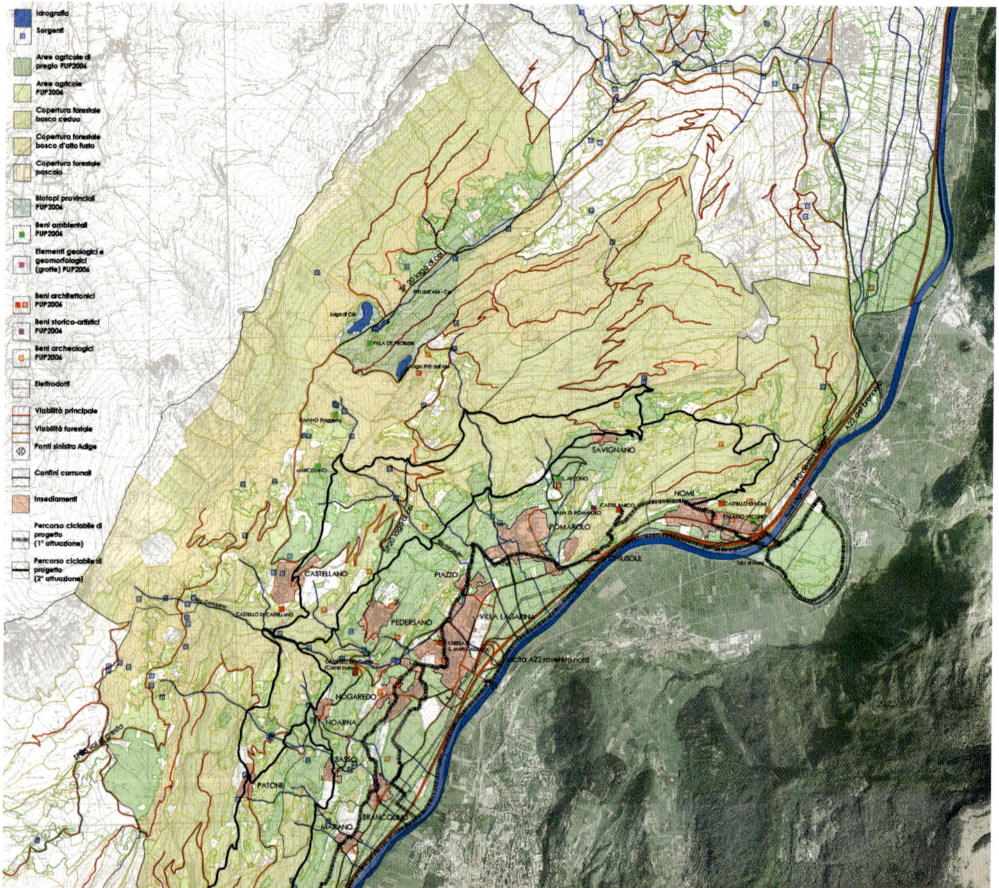

2

Experiences of the design course, Prof. Giovanna Massari, Faculty of Engineering, University of Trento: readings of Vallagarina, project hypothesis for a pedestrian and cycle route.

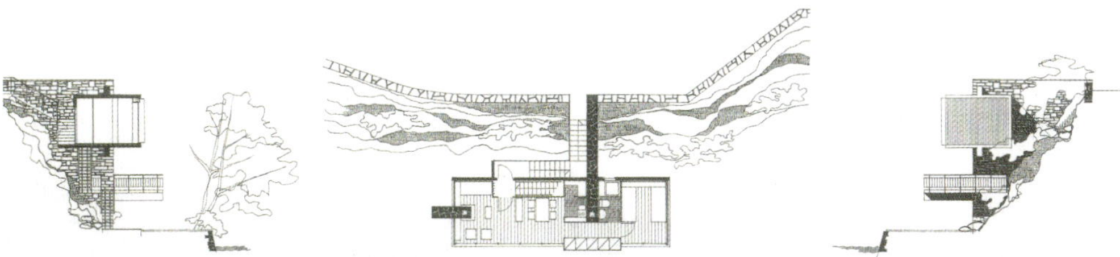

1

2

1. Rino Tami, house in Maroggia 1957
2. Rino Tami, 3 vacation houses 1954. Edited by Domenico Lungo

1

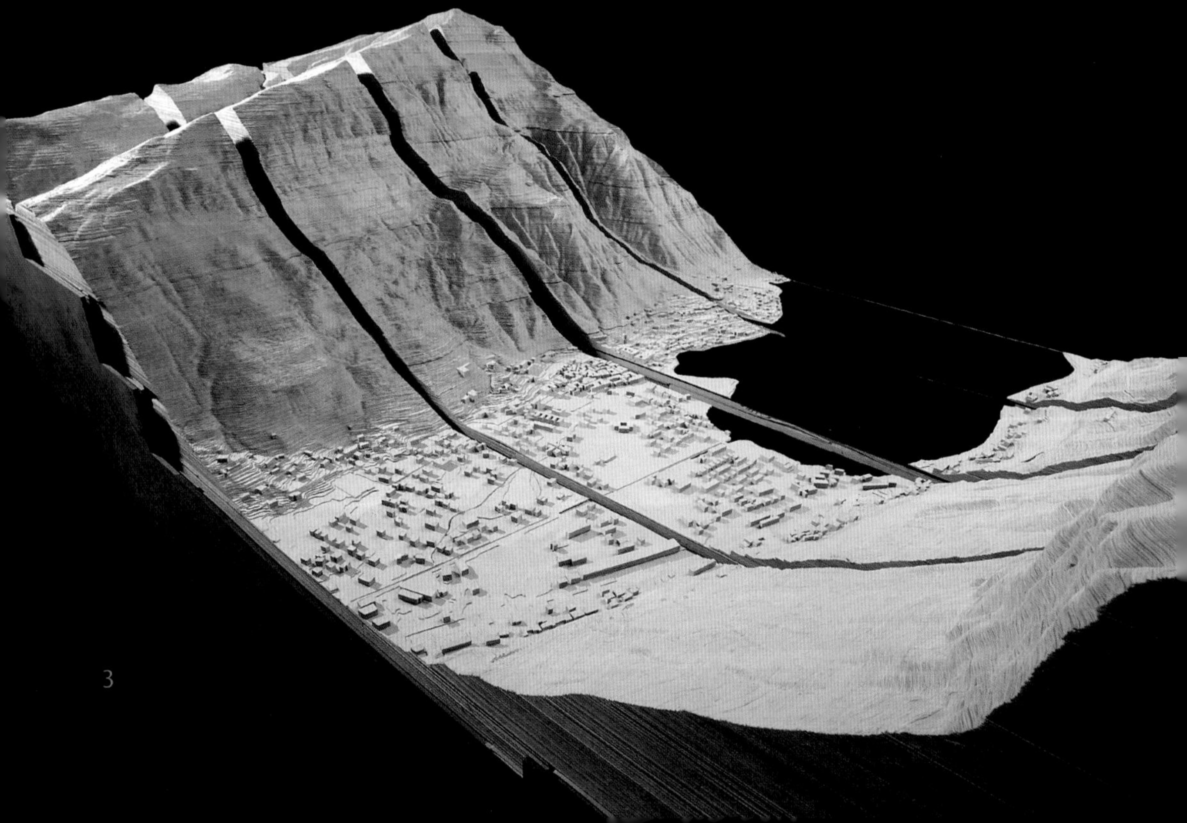

3

2

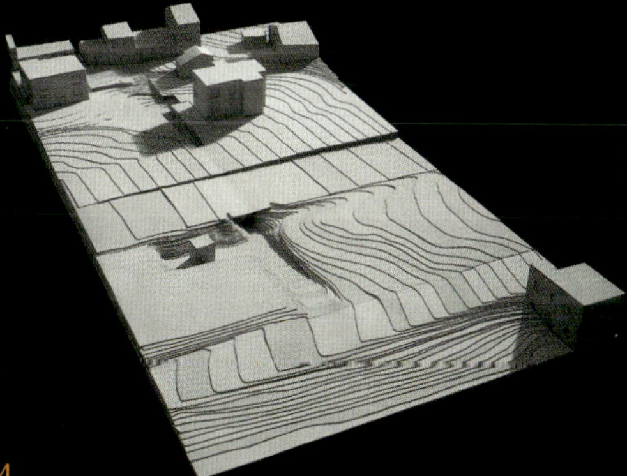

4

5

Academy of Architecture of Mendrisio
1. “From Gotthard to Milan” - The Ticino Canton - Scale model 1: 25000
2. “From Mendrisio to Capolago” - Laveggio Plan - Scale model 1: 5000
3. “A piece of the valley” - Laveggio Plan - Scale model 1: 500
4.-5. “A piece of mountain from Monte San Giorgio” - Plan scale model 1: 500

1

2

Academy of Architecture of Mendrisio
"Space for itself"- housing space project of the Laveggio Plan
1-2. Detailed model scale 1:1000
Opposite page "Space for itself" scale model 1:50. Edited by Domenico Lungo

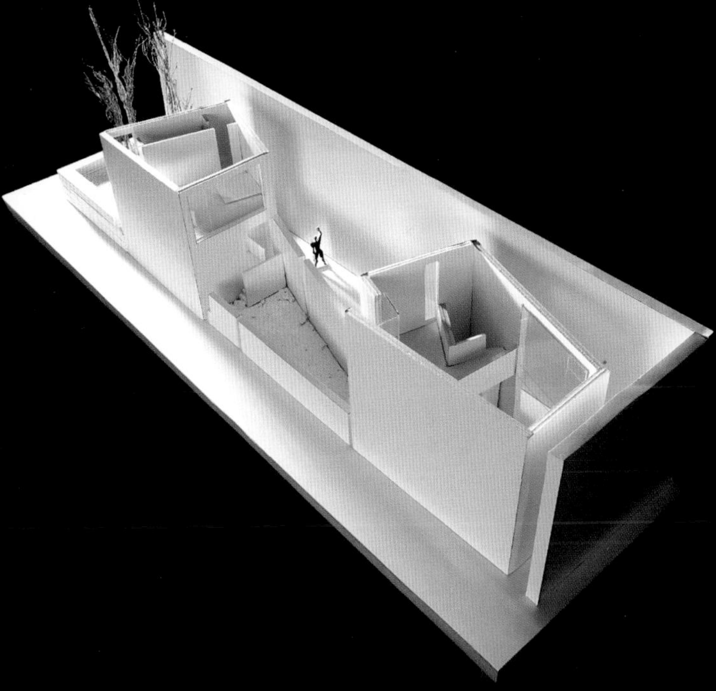
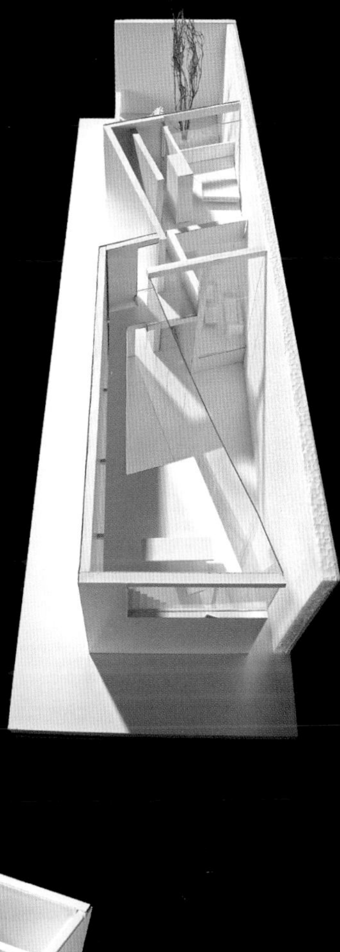
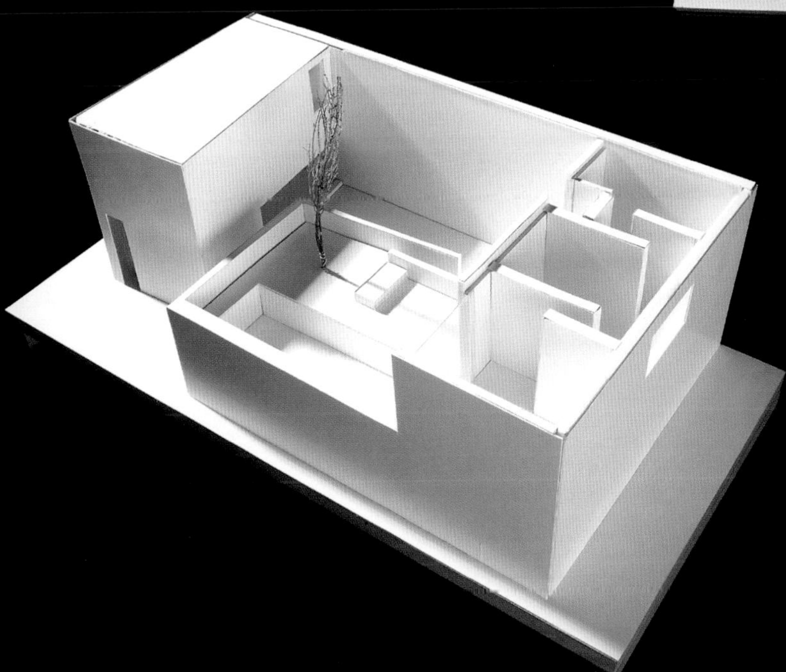

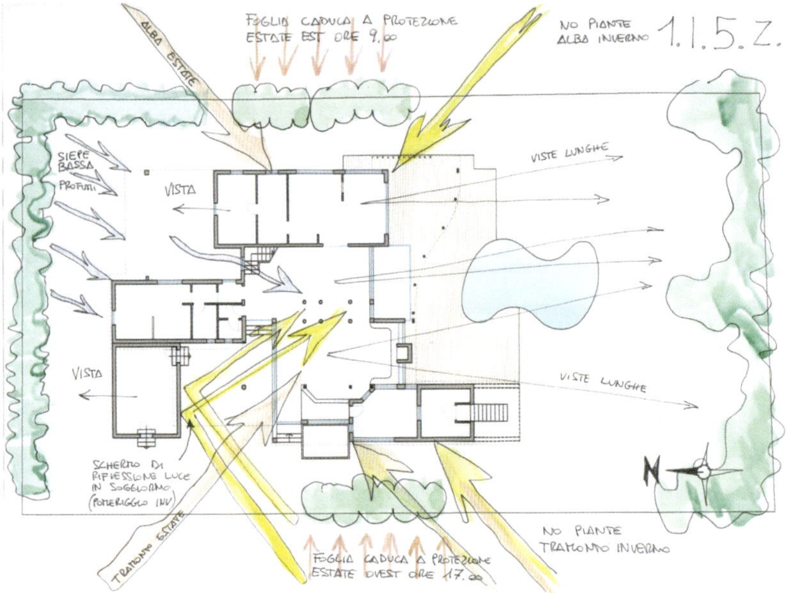
FOGLIA CADUCA A PROTEZIONE
ESTATE EST ORE 9.00
ALBA ESTATE
NO PIANTE
ALBA INVERNO
1.1.5.Z.
SIEPE BASSA
PROFUMI
VISTA
VISTE LUNGHE
VISTA
VISTE LUNGHE
SCHERMO DI
RIFLESSIONE LUCE
IN SOGGIORNO
(POMERIGGIO INV)
TRAMONTO ESTATE
NO PIANTE
TRAMONTO INVERNO
FOGLIA CADUCA A PROTEZIONE
ESTATE OVEST ORE 17.00

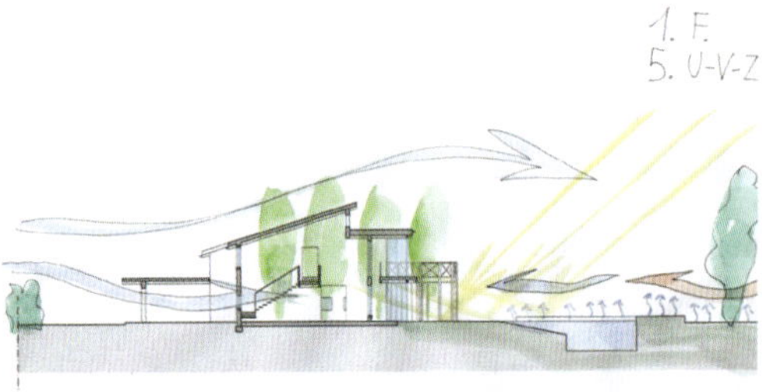
1. F.
5. U-V-Z

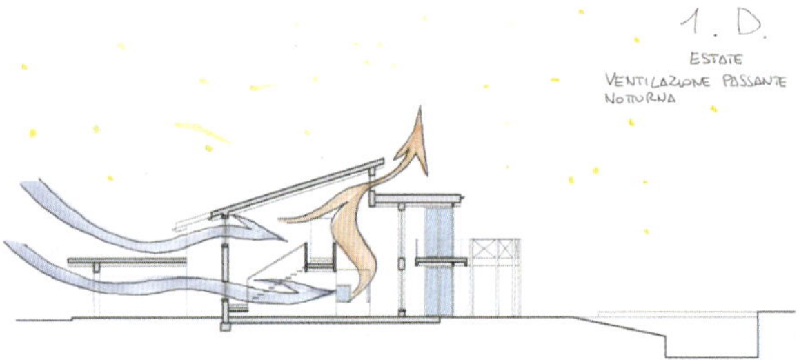
1. D.
ESTATE
VENTILAZIONE PASSANTE
NOTTURNA

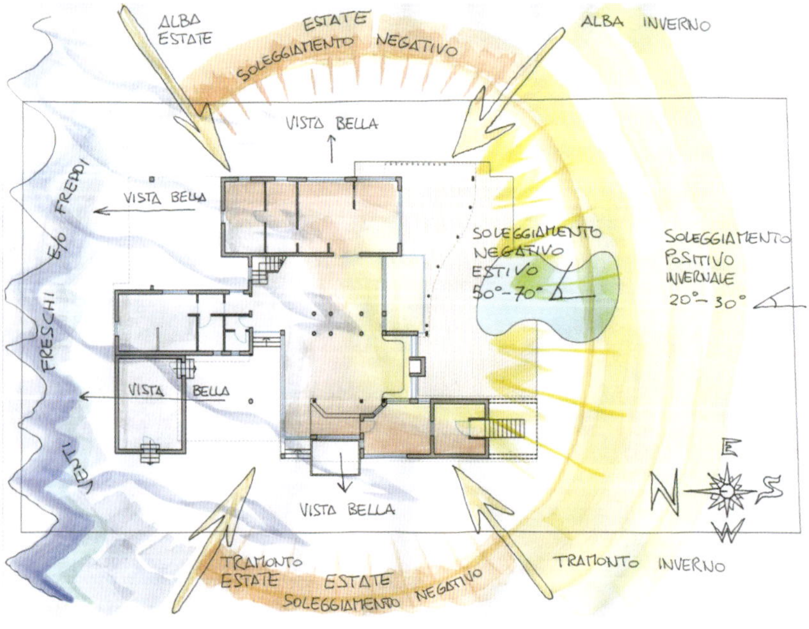
ALBA
ESTATE
ESTATE
SOLEGGIAMENTO NEGATIVO
ALBA INVERNO
VISTA BELLA
VISTA BELLA
SOLEGGIAMENTO
NEGATIVO
ESTIVO
50°-70°
SOLEGGIAMENTO
POSITIVO
INVERNALE
20°-30°
VENTI FRESCHI E/O FREDDI
VISTA BELLA
VISTA BELLA
E
N
S
W
TRAMONTO
ESTATE
ESTATE
SOLEGGIAMENTO NEGATIVO
TRAMONTO INVERNO

University of Trento, Faculty of Engineering, group work coordinated by Prof. Antono Frattari:
Zero Energy House Project, production "The Plus Villas": preliminary sketches of the project
(original sketches from the architect Arnaldo Savorelli)

BRAVE_NEW_ALPS

Design faculty of Bolzano

The new winter

The members of the creative collective ^^^Brave New Alps^^^^^, Bianca Elzenbaumer and Fabio Franz, are orientating their work around the »First Things First Manifesto« by Ken Garland, trying to apply their skills and talents at issues which are highly relevant for society and the natural environment we are living in. In their projects they put a particular focus on the alpine region, trying to reach the local population as well as the guests which every year come to visit the mountains. Their aim is to encourage a more sustainable use of the alpine environment. The project »L'inverno nuovo« (Brave New Winter) is investigating the controversial issue of artificial snow-making as one of the main pillars of today's mass-tourism in the Alps. »L'inverno nuovo« tries to give a critical vision of this practice by giving an exclusive look behind the scenes of the daring staging of winter which is put into place by the tourist industry every year in order to sustain its existence. The title of the project is clearly ironic as it refers to Aldous Huxley's book »Brave New World«. In Huxley's vision of the future social system, all the individuals are artificially forged since their birth, in order to render their role in the system most productive and as unproblematic as possible.

In this sense the connections between the project and the book are twofold: Nowadays, the first time children growing up in the Alps see, touch and taste snow, they are having this experience with man-made snow and not that which is naturally coming from the sky. The artificial snow, the emulation of nature by men is natural for them. Isn't this as well some sort of psychological induction? The beings belonging to Huxley's system, in order to conform to the society, are being induced to see nature as mere sport equipment, thus becoming a consumer while being out in nature. Like this the role of nature as part of the system is absolutely legitimised. Aren't we also experiencing this new relationship towards nature whereby nature is no longer a source of beauty but a catalyst for consumption? »L'inverno nuovo« invites us to ask questions like these and to think about our relationship toward the alpine environment.

www.brave-new-alps.com

1

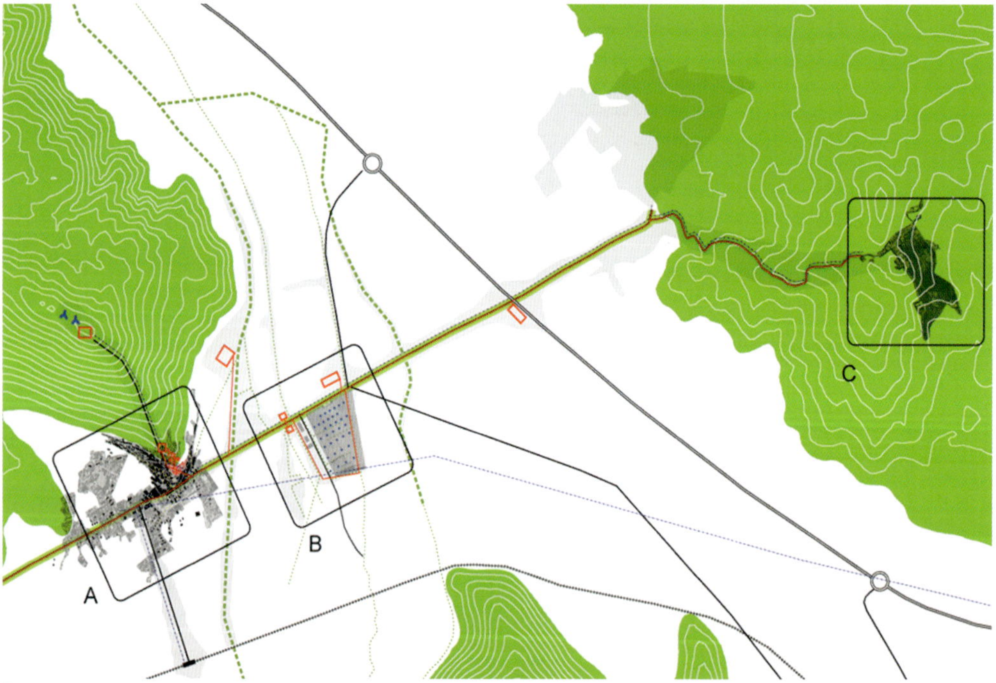

2

Palentini maps (Appennino abruzzese) project for the realization of the Santa Maria della Vittoria site, coordination Prof. Archt. Massimo Angrilli, University of Pescara;
1. photo insert
2. planimetric map of territorial placement

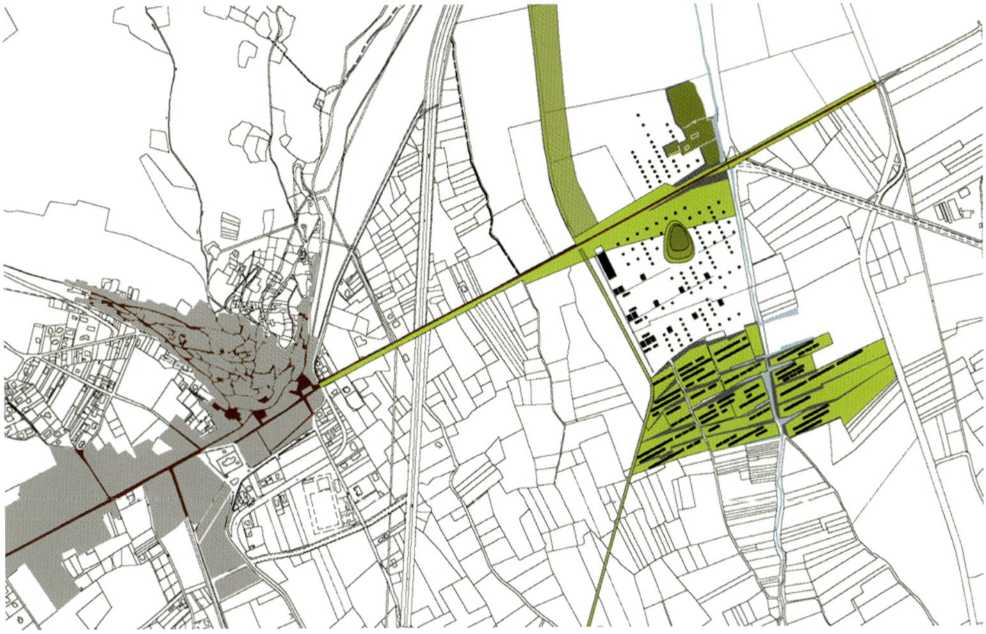

3

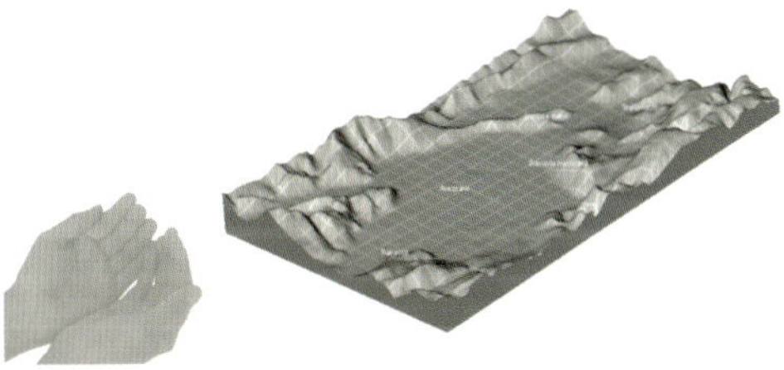

4

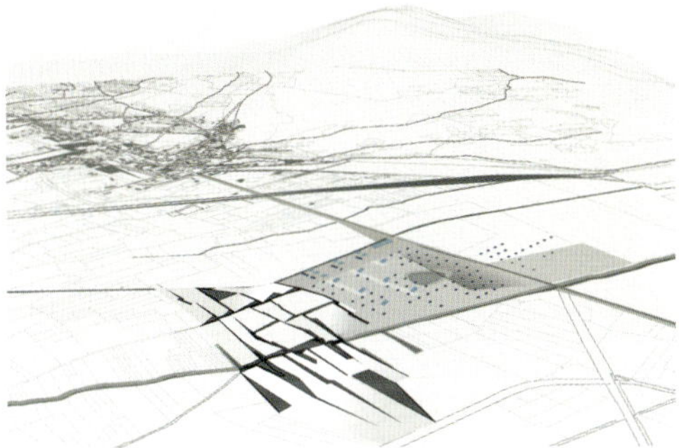

5

6

3. Planimetric map of the photovoltaic energy park project
4. Landscape context as a landscape house
5. General view of the project
6. Multifunction of the ground use. Coexistence between traditional productive uses and technologic innovations

1

2

IUAV Venice

1.2. Ground sculpting: architectural redevelopment - frontal landscape of Lake Arcense
project by Chiara Azzali, thesis, supervisor, Prof. Archt. Renato Bocchi

3

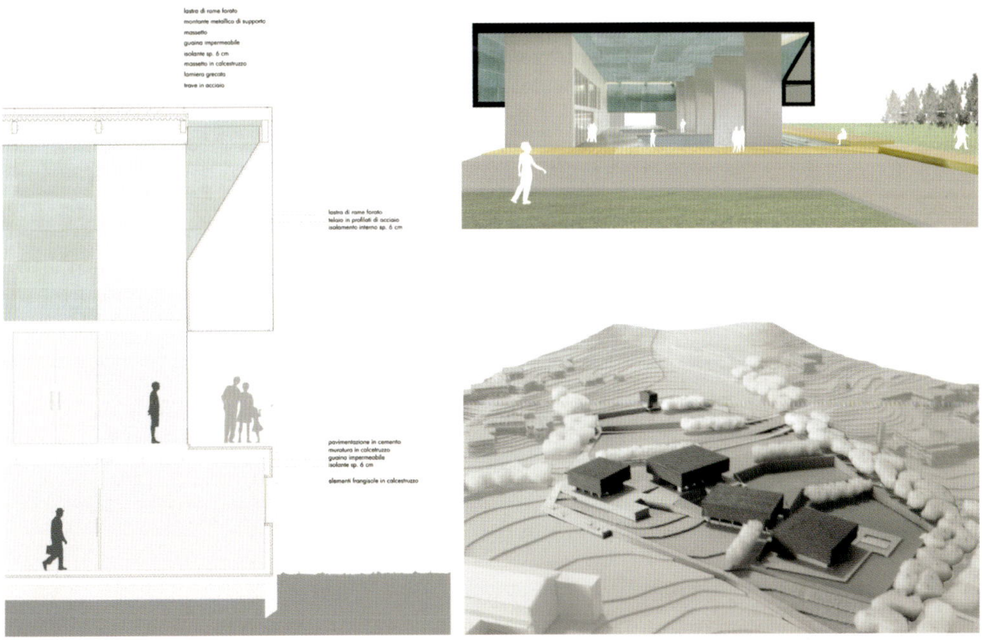

4

IUAV Venice

3.4. The new thermal pools: urban analysis and redevelopment of the public spaces for a new image of the thermal city, project by Pierluigi Peruzzo and Giovanni Roncador, thesis, supervisor, Prof. Archt. Renato Bocchi

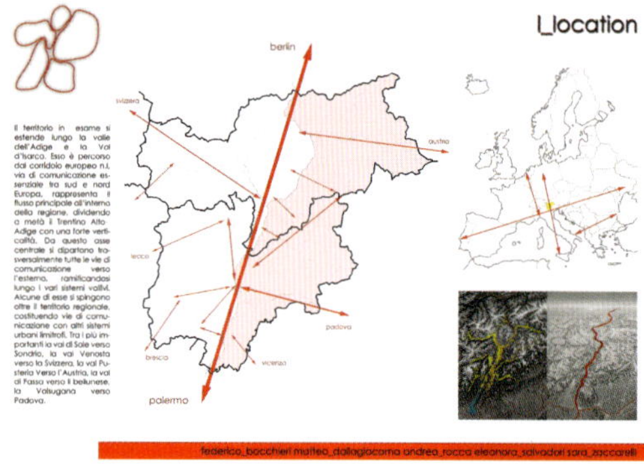

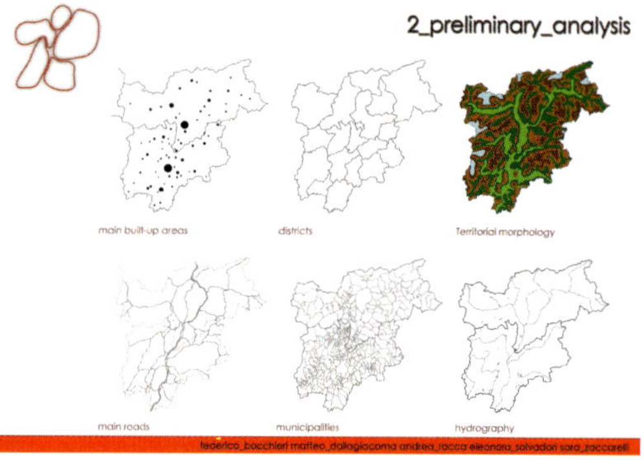

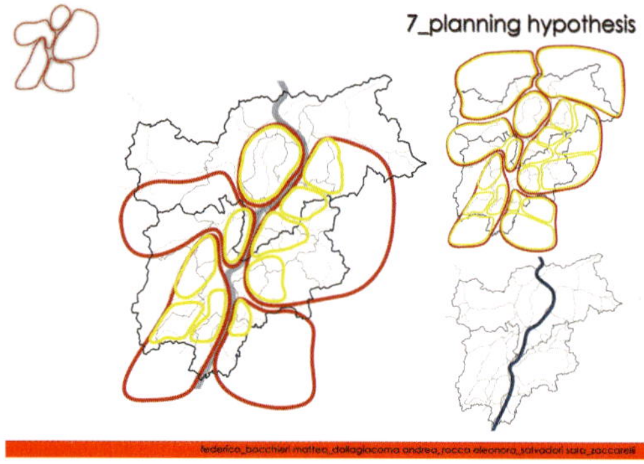

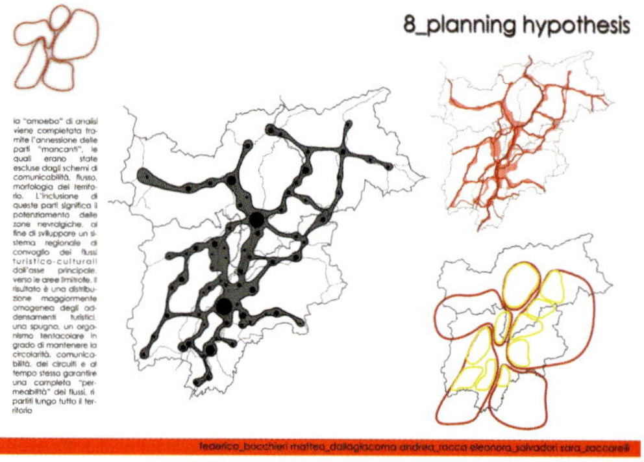

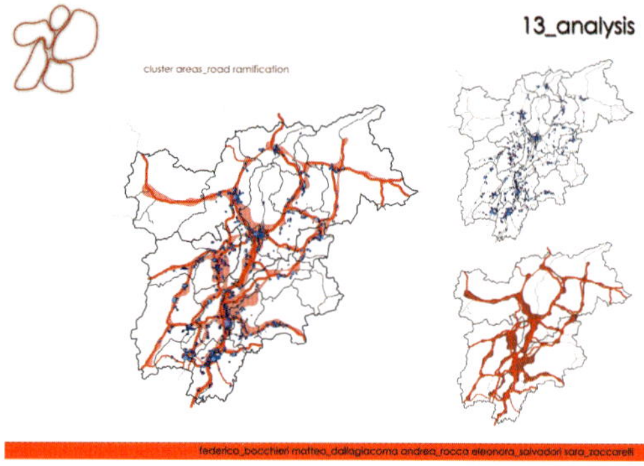

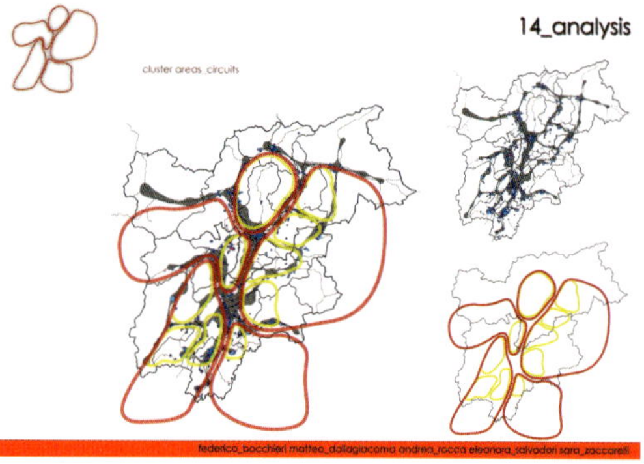

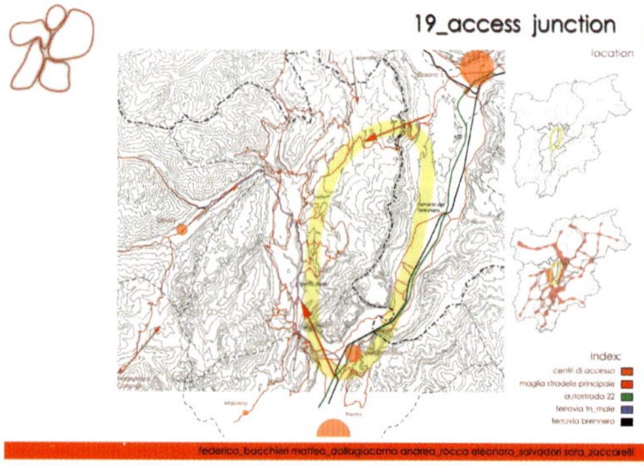

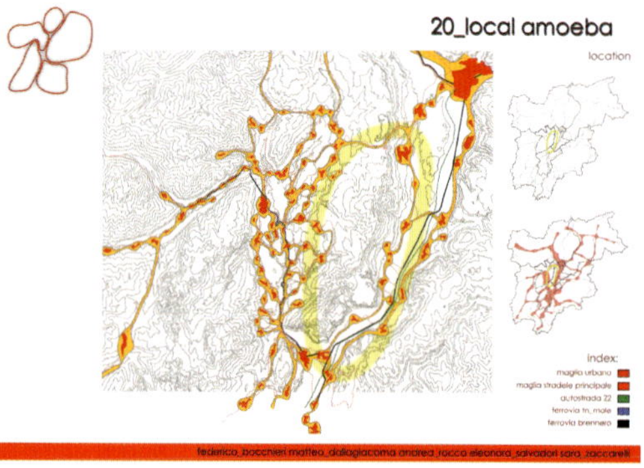

Fourth year urban design course, Prof. Archt. G. Scaglione, University of Trento
"Strategies for the future slow city of the Adige Valley",
Students: Federico Bocchieri, Matteo Dallagiacoma, Andrea Rocca, Sara Zaccarelli, Eleonora Salvadori

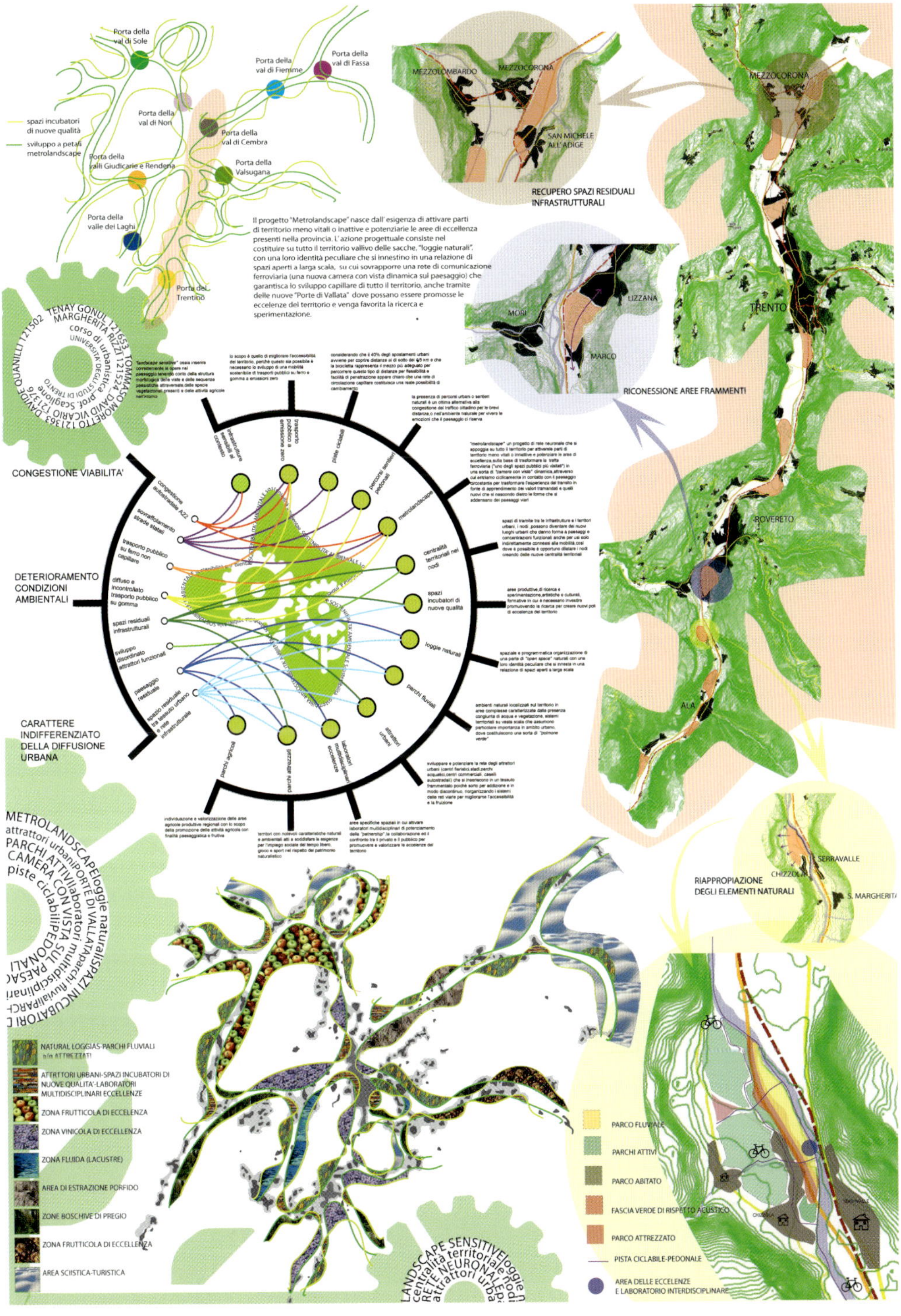

Fourth year urban design course, Prof. Archt. G. Scaglione, University of Trento
"Strategies for the future slow city of the Adige Valley",
Students: Margherita Rizzi, Davide Quanili, David Vicario, Tommaso Moretto, Tenay Gonul

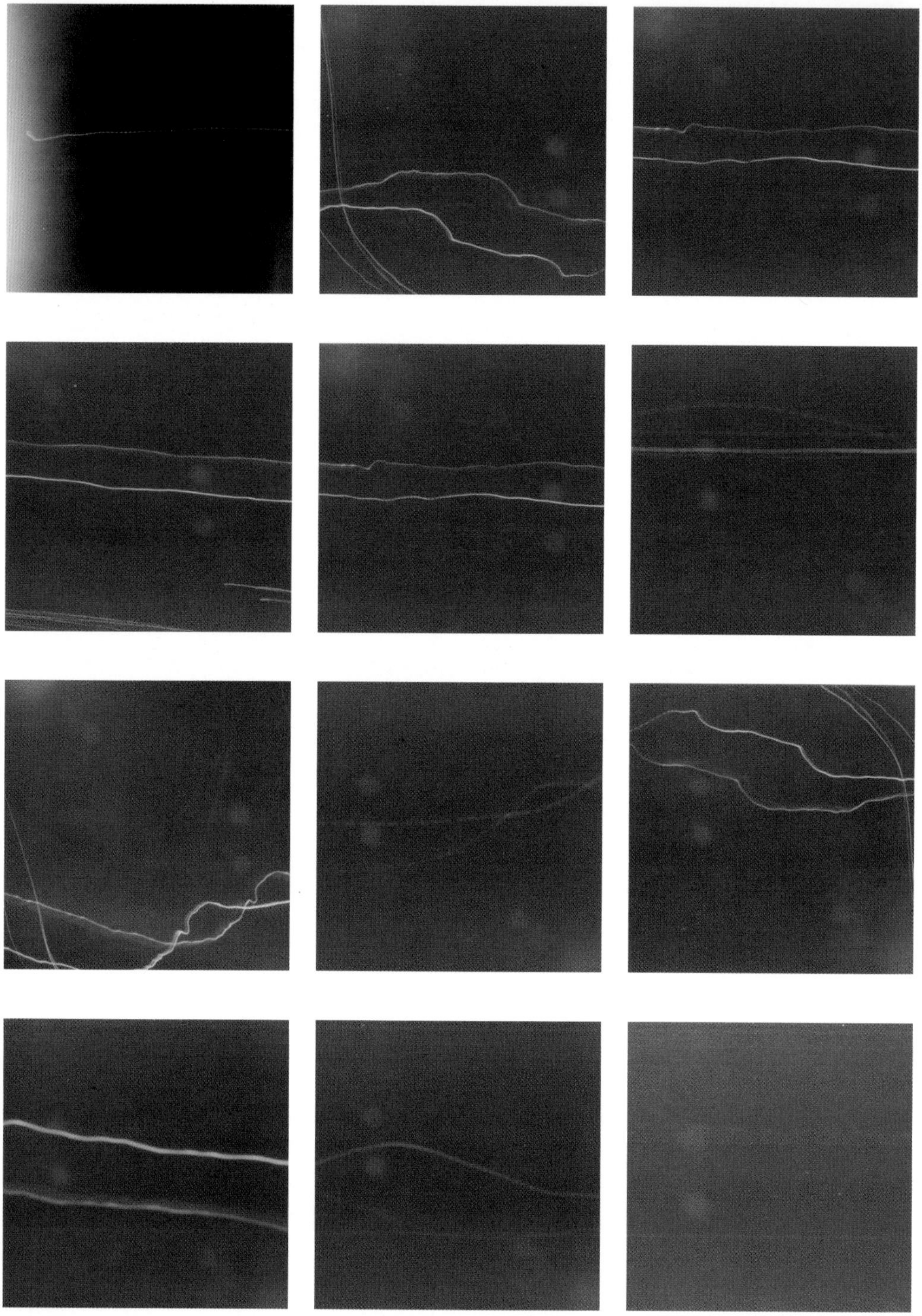

Horizon
There is no single horizon in the alpine landscape. The succession of shifting profiles hints at the presence of infinite variables, implicit between the visible multiple horizon. There is always a new horizon behind the other.

Alexander Pfanzelt
Silhouetten Roadster, 2004
monochrome photographic prints, 49,5 x 49,5 cm

Innsbruck, landscape research and experiences

"It is fascinating how we interpret history: it is the accuracy by which we narrate a fact that determines the way it is apprehended."
Jamie Shovlin, interview with Isabella Panizza in Vogue Italia n.690

The image is a complex one, layers of scales, perceptions and systems collapsing into a view. In the alpine topography, endlessness can only be experienced at the top of a mountain. Below, the landscape is divided into discrete pieces, moulded into places with an identity that precede any sign. Signs are our cultural language, our short-hand and concentrates, stepping stones to meanings and implications, while the landscape only has form, the shape of its substance. An Urlandschaft can be seen when stripping back all layers of information, all objects and additions gathered over time. It is, in fact, almost invisible.

The way we experience the landscape is very much conditioned by our perception, by the context or framework in which we position ourselves. This is not so much a question of physical location, but rather of critical reference to a situation.

Much of the work done at Studio1 engages the complexity of these landscapes, identifying layers, processes and correlations, remixing them as speculative views or likely outcomes.

Stefano de Martino

Studio1 Credits, Studio1/Institut für Gestaltung, Professor S. de Martino
Alexander Pfanzelt, Research Assistant, Faculty of Architecture, University of Innsbruck,
www.uibk.ac.at/gestaltung/studio1/

Markus Bernhart, Alex Del Bello, Klaus Gummerer, Gianluca Pagliara, Martin Schgaguler
Untitled (orange safety mat, rope), 2007 (Karen Lohrmann, visiting faculty)
installation, Innsbruck

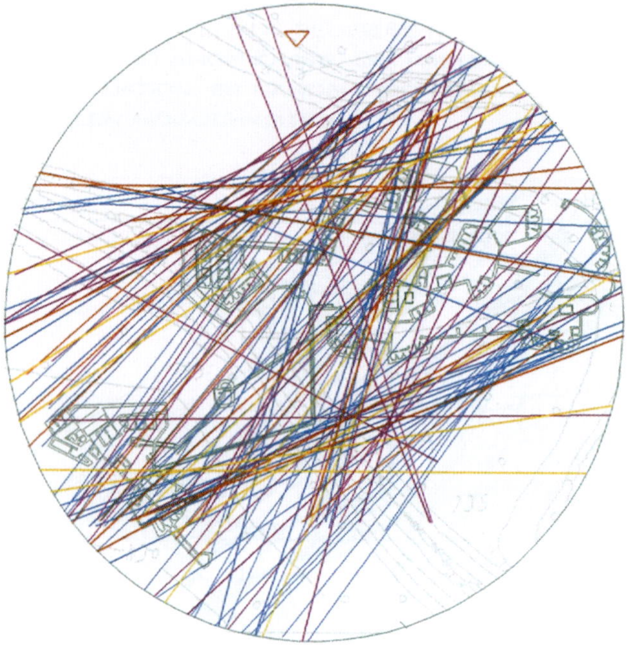

Site/ non-site
The perception of landscape has to be trained during a process of observation, carefully identifying, filtering and assembling phenomena. A precise mapping of streams of information from the broader context reveals the site of Franzensfeste as an interface of virtual and physical phenomena, as a field of convergences lending new possibilities for interaction.

Ursula Unterpertinger
Die Morphologie des Amorphen, 2001

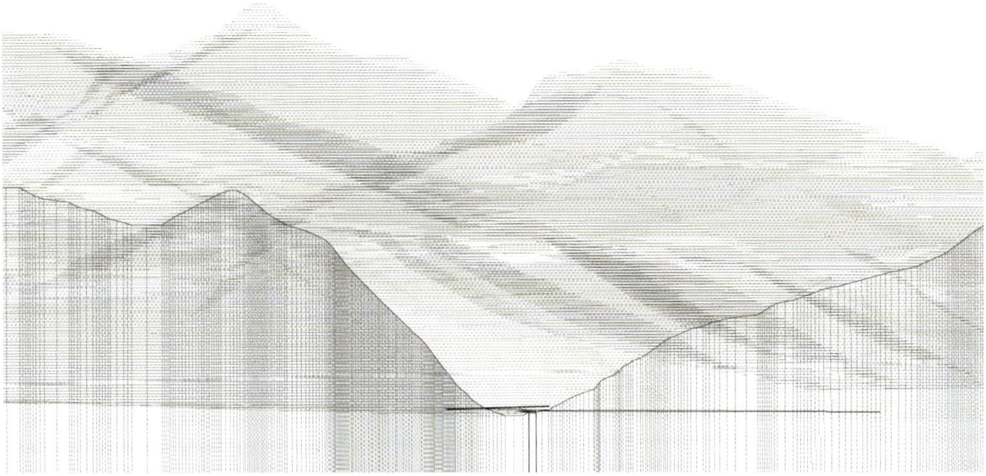

Measurement
Selective representation of the landscape enables the engagement of information otherwise hidden by the complexity of the visual image. Here time-related factors (traveling with different modes of transportation, the movement of tectonic plates) modify our perception of the landscape. Bringing into focus different scales of context and degrees of detail, simultaneous systems of reference are constructed for the same location, each with its own spatial and temporal logic.

Matthias Maier
ca. 3cm - Brennerbad - Wahrnehmungsmaschine einer beschleunigten Landschaft, 2006

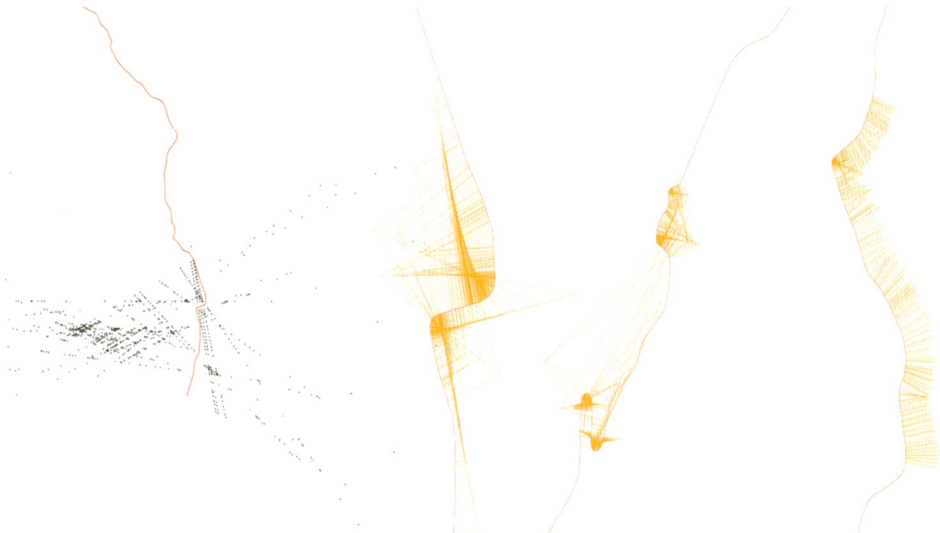

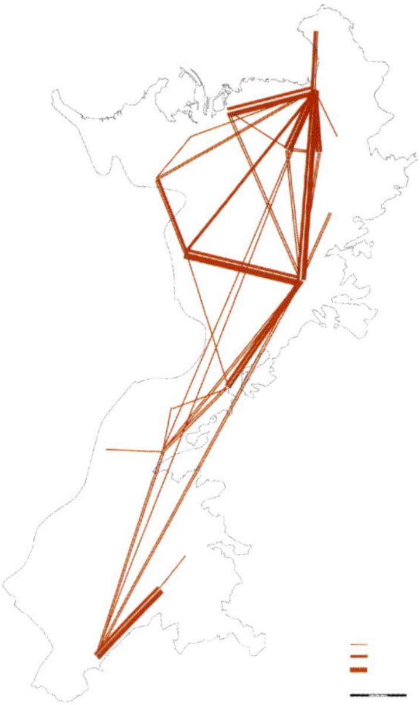

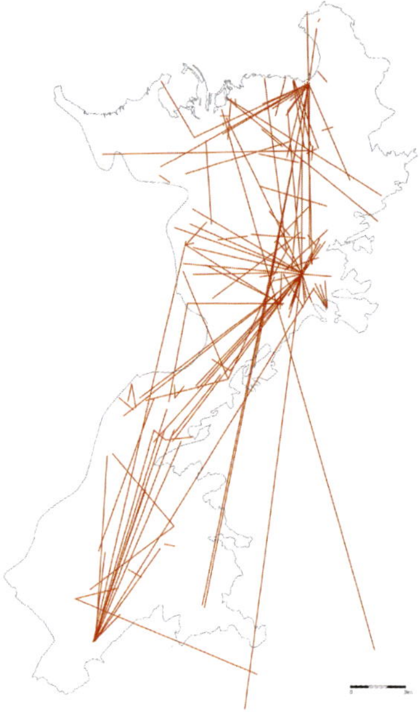

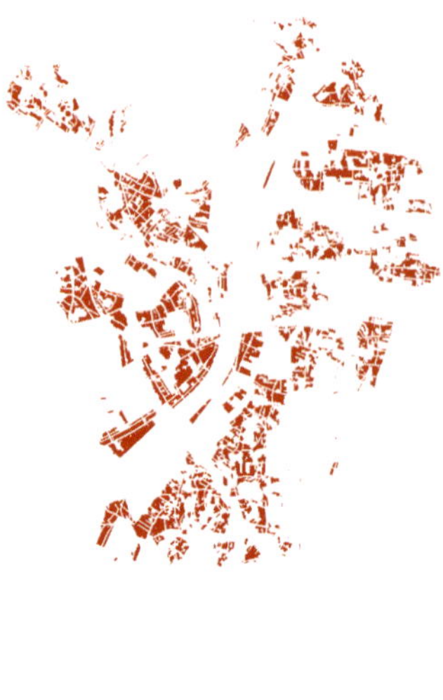

Projection
The incipient development of all land resources for private speculation generates an undifferentiated, continous village determined only by the most resistant topographic features. Layers of traditional and contemporary activities fuse into a conglomerate suburban situation. An ersatz urbanity is created by an incessant flow of traffic between distant points of residual centrality (cinemas, cafes, supermarkets, gas stations, car dealerships). Each inhabitant produces a personal tracklog, or personal network, a virtual locale, with its own densities and borders. This model of blatant inefficiency can only live up to its never-delivered promise by introducing urban spaces as engines for coalescence (of social and cultural spheres) and programmatic diversification. Land can only be an infinite resource in our minds.

Claudia Hammerle
Liminal, 2005

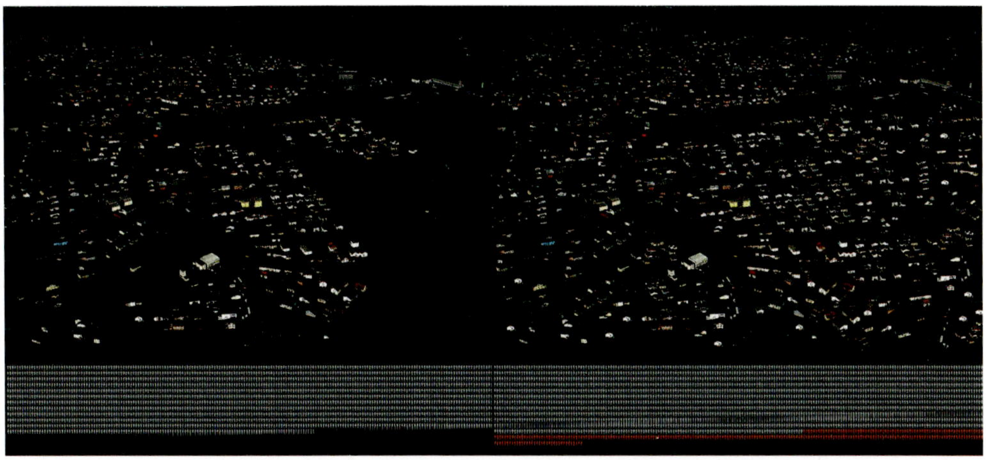

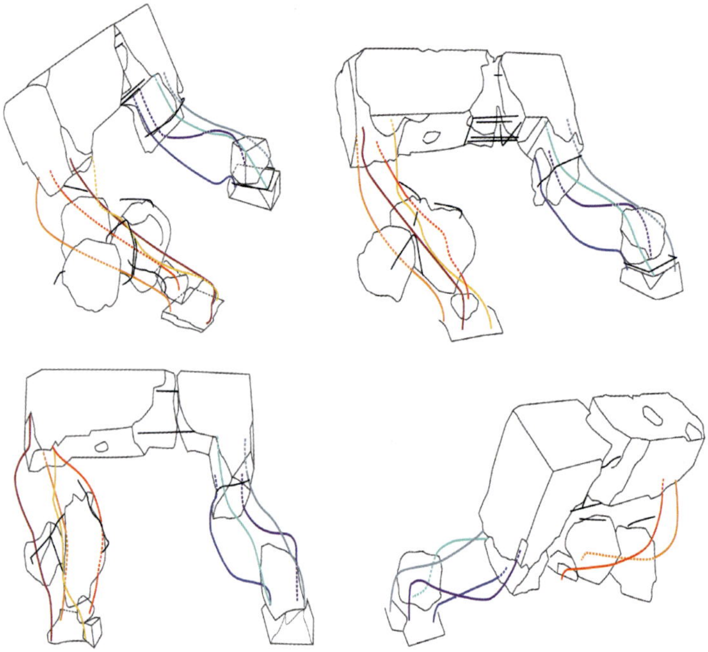

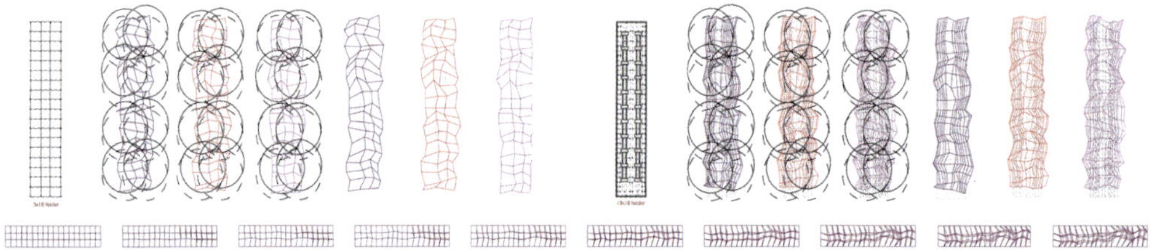

Dependencies

Applying a set of complex actions (identified and analyzed in a sample) to a whole system informs the emergence of a topography. The effect of a local catastrophe on the whole illustrates the dependencies and resonances within a dynamic system. Going well beyond the virtual spatial model, this highlights an ethical aspect in all systems, whether they be environmental, structural or social.

Moritz Keitel
Aufbruch der repetitiven Monotonie - case-study: ex-aluminio Montecatini di Mori, 2007

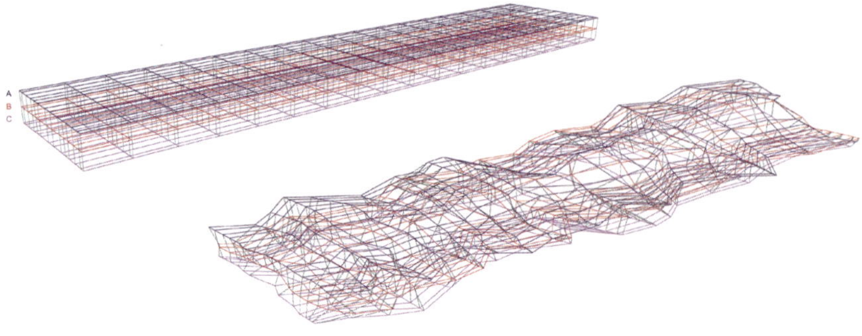

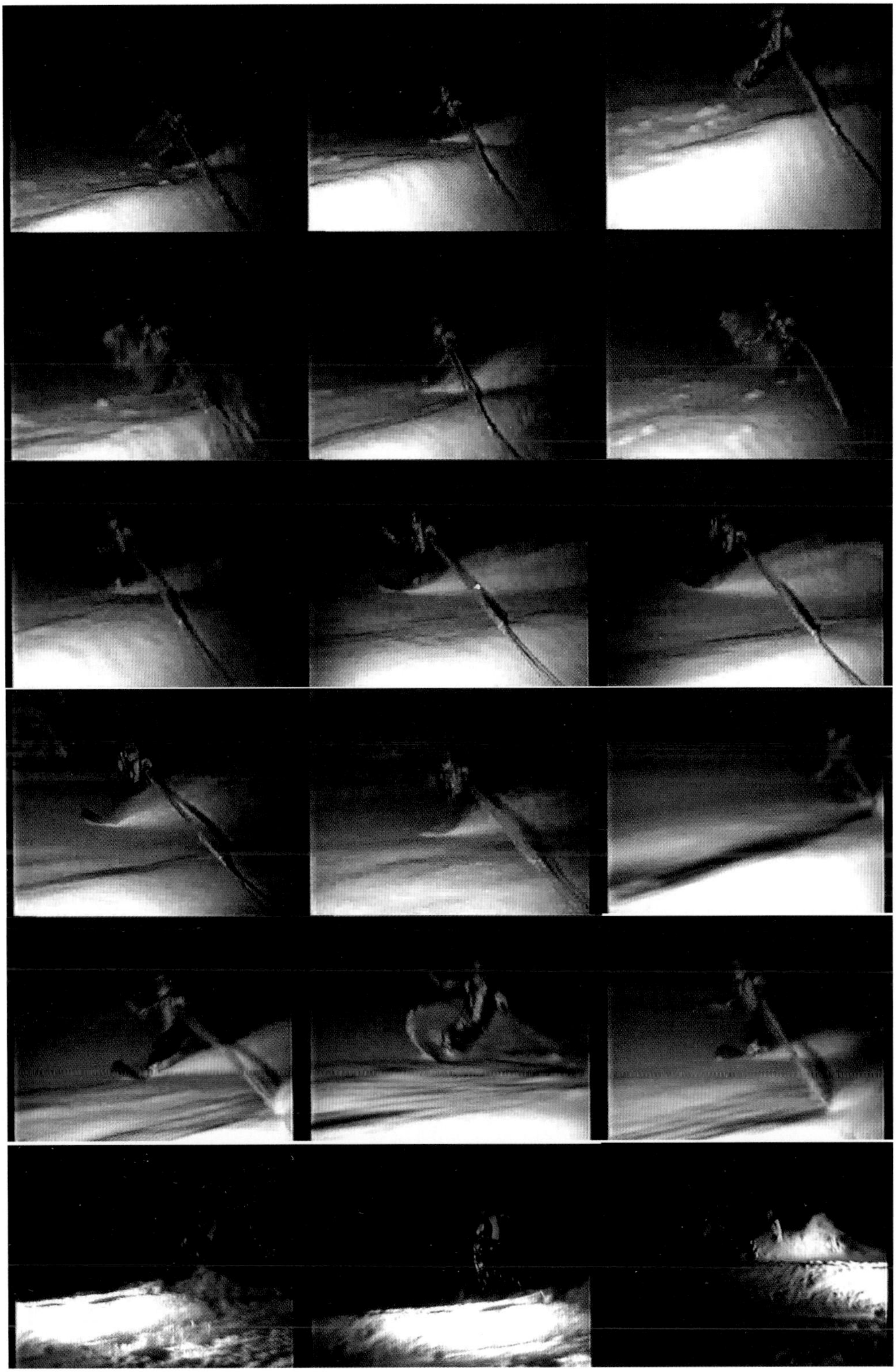

Tom Hillebrand, Gianluca Pagliara, Stephan Rief, Bernhard Wolf
Erdgeist, single-channel video, 14:37, 2000   stills from: video

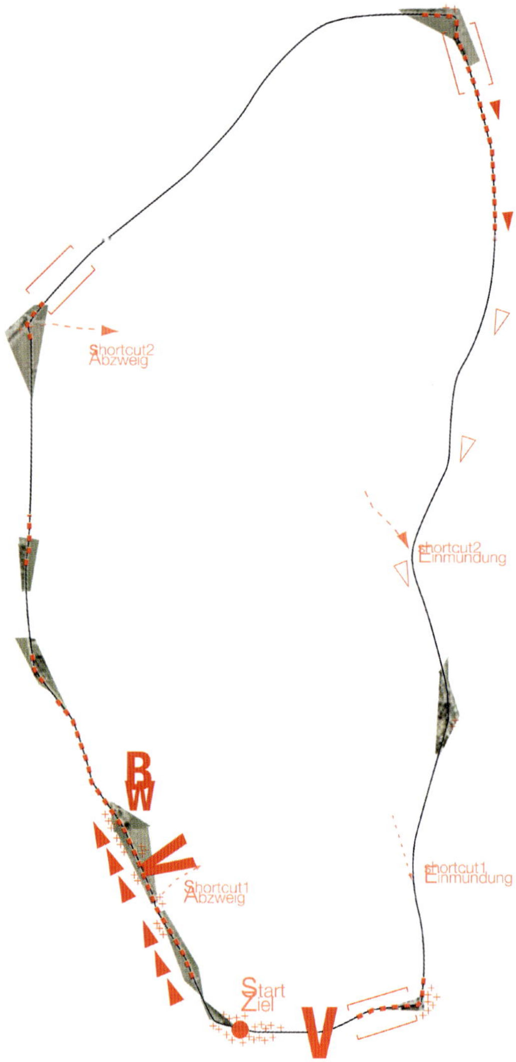
shortcut2
Abzweig
shortcut2
Einmündung
R
W
V
shortcut1
Abzweig
shortcut1
Einmündung
Start
Ziel
V

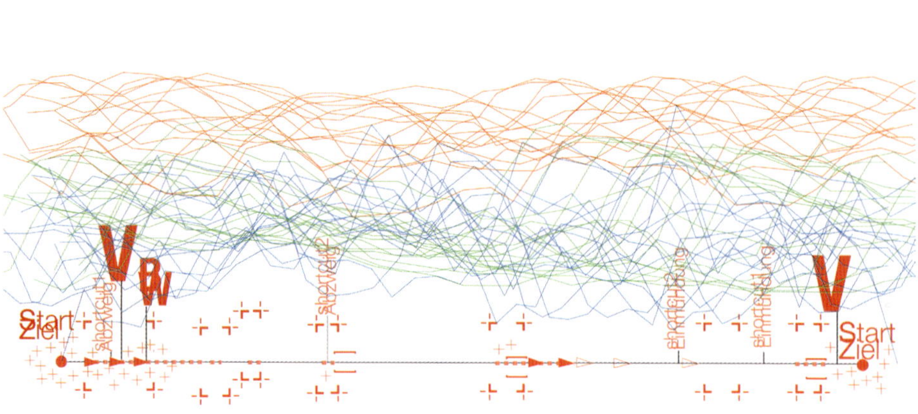
Start
Ziel
V
R
W
V
Start
Ziel

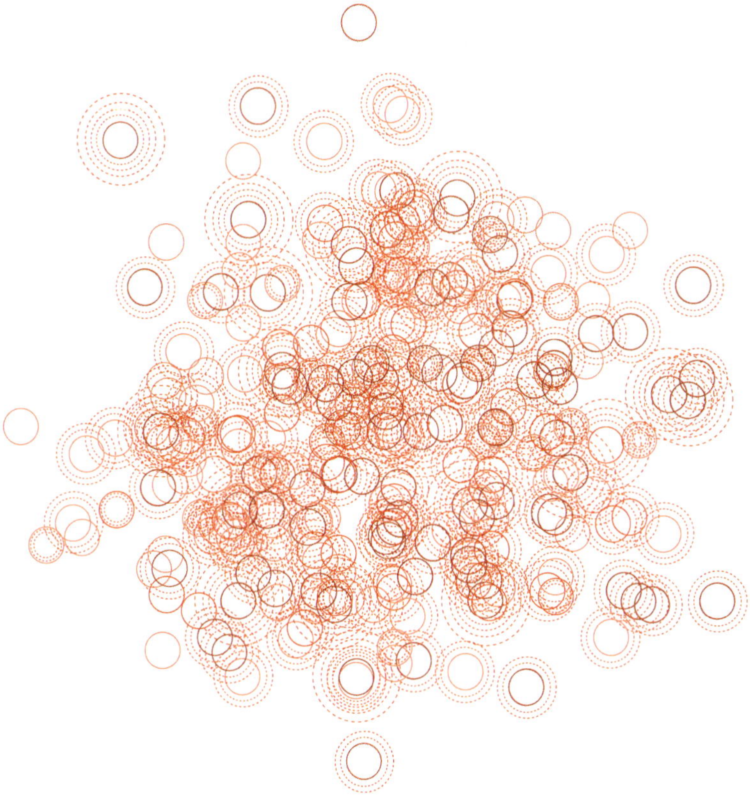

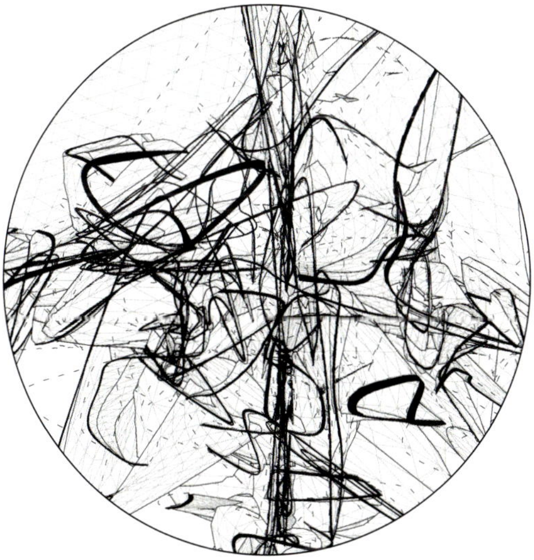

Translation
The cartesian system is not the only means for mapping landscape. Through a qualitative, sequential evaluation of physiological responses, a different continuum is described that is proper to the direct experience of a terrain and its topographical data. Within this the orientation in a carthesian-system ceases to be operative. It is a total whiteout, a new strategy is inevitable.

Alexander Pfanzelt
Nur wer die Form beherrscht darf mit ihr spielen,
2006

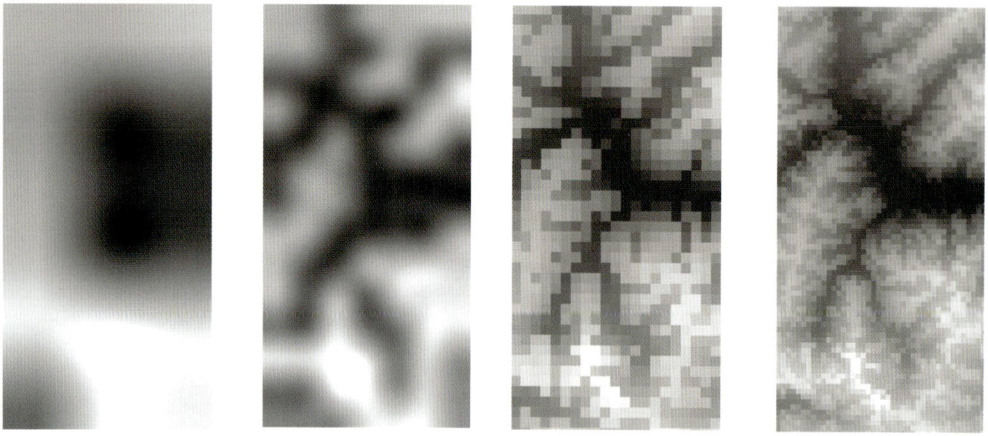

Uncertainty

A geographical survey soon reveals its limitations, particularly when applied to a topography as extreme as that of the Alps. At best it can be an approximation of a landscape, describing a limited set of factors and locations. Zooming into the terrain reveals exponential degrees of detail, from rough massings to specific places, but the nature of it remains elusive. A reading of the territory that shift modality from topographic to temporal parameters enables the formulation of seasonal, rather than permanent, cadastral interventions, that exploit this uncertainty as a means to diversification and contextualization.

Christoph Gapp
von ALP über VIN nach SUL zu ALP und wieder zurück, 2002

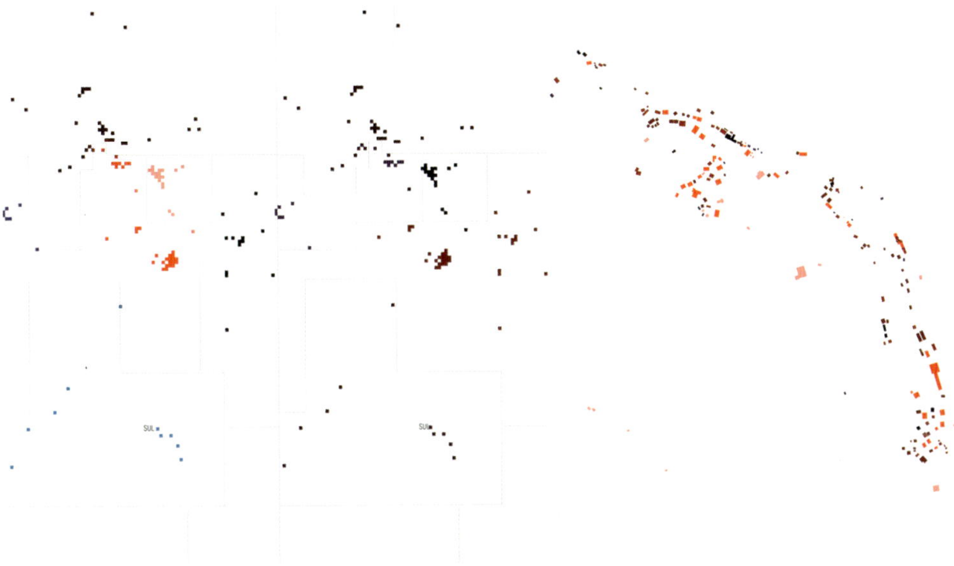
SUL
SUL

winter
frühling
sommer

Katja Pargger
Rendezvous mit Bluatschink, 2008 (Reinhard Honold, visiting faculty)
pinhole-camera photographs, 140 x 99 mm

Architectures and alpine projects

alpi.tecture®

To construct in the alpine area means to confront the topic of uneven terrain. The backgrounds, composed of imposing elevation, they are the emerging territories that roll into the valleys in a sequence of slopes and plateaus articulated by natural stubs and a network of settlements. The context assumes a declination that oversees beyond it place of transformation: the traditional constructed figures are enriched by the relation with the third dimension, surpassing the urban scale to project itself in the landscape. The thresholds of these phenomenons linked to the dwelling in this territory are wider and broadened to the clear understanding of the third dimension. Matteo Thun defines in this sense the coverage of the buildings as "fifth façade". An always more physically superior point of view exists, which has the power to decipher the complex fabric of interelations between settlements and natural systems in the alpine area. The natural elements become systematich components of the context, in which operating through the project and the same relation between architectural handwork and territory acquires new declinations. To live in the alpine territory means to live in the landscape, and due to this, we procede to organize the space in a cluster of values strongly interrelated by an economic scale, meant as the whole of actions finalized by the management of the often scarce resources, to the scale of affection of the identifying features. The relation between handwork and territory, between architecture and context, between living and landscape in the alpine region, is strongly oriented towards a dual examination for which architecture's traditional hyerarchies are becoming more liquid. To build in the alpine area demands a non linear approach and capable of approving a sistematic conception in the defining of single project strategies. The alpine mountain, to dwell it, from the modern movement is already a significant occasion of disciplinary construction of the architecture: the various paths that architeture follows, both mounted or along the ridges of the Alps, contribute to the introduction of the project's philosophy the context, element of architectural significance. The panoptic solution of the company town recreative by FIAT at Sestriere, the abacus for a new alpine architecture by Gio' Ponti, made from buildings strongly oriented towards measuring themselves with the elements of nature, the hotel and cableway projects of Franz Baumann or Carlo Mollino incorporate the landscape in the architecture, they make it an element of measure regarding the project according to the methodological guidelines that go from the panoramic dimension to the real construction of the landscape. For a long time, the configuratioin of the natural elements fluctuate in the interpretation of their role from the pure perceptive or trivially panoramic scale to the assumption of morphological conditions. The towers of Bonadè-Bottino (1930) are the landmarks that still identify the location of Sestriere today, even though their efficency on the landscape is measured above all to being a stage rather than configurating new morphology. The station of Nordkettenbahn of Innsbruck designed by Baumann in 1928 chooses to be part of the mountain range, to transform the rocky spurs into a built volume. Zaha Hadid's intervention in 2007, the renovation of the cableways, mantains the same philosophy, creating a delicate roof, which reminds us of thawed ice inside glaciers, arranged in outward curved incisions of the rocky terrain. The renovation project of the mountain hut in the Furka Pass in Switzerland, "Furka-Blick" of OMA intensifies the panoramic threshold of the landscape, playing with figural elements inspired by the bellows of the antique camera, tranforming the main openings into frames. The projects of Group8, a Swiss studio, which in the multiple approaches is paradigmatic in architecture, it seem to oscilate between both levels of possible action (different residential building collect the formal and material elements of traditionally constructing in the alpine area while others intend to become landscape), introducing a third level inferring the landscape in the building, in continuity with the general reflection of the relation between nature and human settlment that has connoted the architectural debate. The creations of Matteo Thun express an action oriented towards the trascendence of the landscape in the building. The acknowledgement of the role of the sloped section in the project construction is evident in the main hotels, planned and completed in the last few years. The morphological elements of the territory are adopted in the configuration of the volumes in the dual role of living and experimenting the landscape. The wineries of Alberto Cecchetto make the affirmation about the roof façades significant of the volumes built in the valleys. The study of the planimetric restores a sequence of signs that originate from the binding of territorial forms, enriching and unaffecting the array of patterns that from the uninterrupted slopes of the valley of the Adige, encounter privileged perceptions. Some of the projects presented in the ALPS Biennial course offer a horizon of disciplinary development that go beyond architecture or landscape. Showing a course of disciplinary hybridization between landscape and architecture that goes beyond the consolidated subjects of architecture or landscape planning: they rather go towards the definition of a disciplinary statute of something that can be attempted to define scaping.tecture or for the specific alpine territory can be designated alpi.tettura ®.

Thomas, M. Demetz, Phd Student, University of Genoa

Valerio Olgiati, Switzerland
Atelier Bardill in Scharans

The Atelierhouse Bardill replaces an old barn in the protected centre of the village Scharans. The building permission was granted by the local authorities only under the condition that the new building would have exactly the same volume as the old barn.
The client, Linard Bardill, who lives in a house a very short walking distance away from the site, needed only one single space, a room to work in. This working space occupies not even a third of the stipulated volume. The rest of it constitutes a courtyard that is monumentalized by a huge round opening to the sky. This is where the house expresses greatness and clearness in contrast to the arbitrary geometry of its external appearance and to the small-scale environment of the village.
office Valerio Olgiati /2007

Atelier Bardill, Scharans, Switzerland
object: private atelier - one working space
location: Scharans, Switzerland; client: Linard Bardill, musician + poet
architect: Valerio Olgiati, prof. dipl. architect ETH/SIA, Via Nova, 7017 Flims
Tel. +41 81 650 33 11, Fax +41 81 650 33 12, mail@olgiati.net
collaborators: Nathan Ghiringhelli (project manager office Olgiati), Nikolai Müller, Mario Beeli
construction supervisor: Linard Bardill
structural engineer: Patrick Gartmann, partner of Conzett, Bronzini, Gartmann AG, Chur
materials: red in-situ concrete, steel, copper
begin of planning: 2002
begin of construction: July 2006
end of construction: August 2007
volume: 665 m3
area: atelier space: 70 m2
garage, storage, technic: 65 m2
courtyard: 150 m2
technical information: heated by solar energy, tabs, controled air ventilation system
please mention: Atelier Bardill is open for the public on Fridays between 1 pm and 5 pm
copyright pictures + plans: archiv olgiati, Domleschg, Javier Miguel Verme

On the previous and following pages,
Images of the Atelier Bardill in Scharans,
Valerio Olgiati

Matteo Thun, Alto Adige, Switzerland
Architecture in the Alps

Vigilius Mountain Resort - Alto Adige

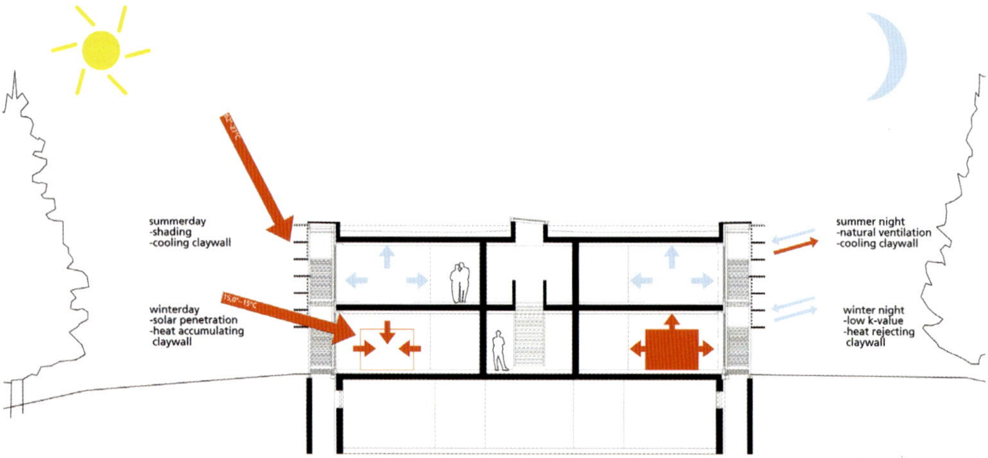

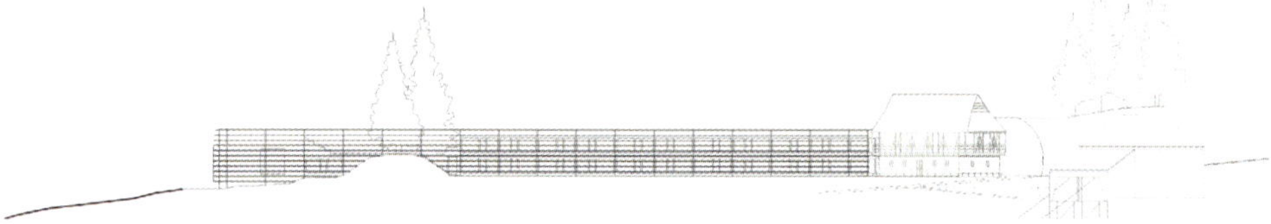

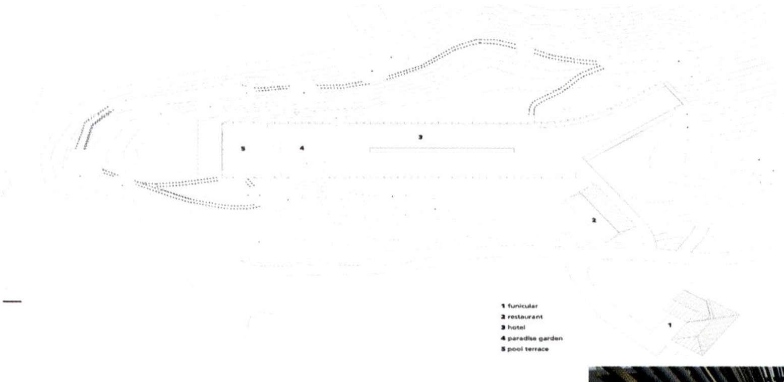

Matteo Thun, Resort La Pergola - Alto Adige

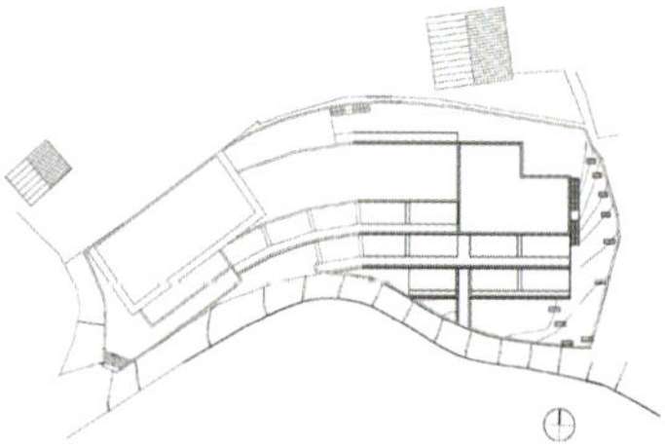

THERME MERAN
TERME MERANO

Matteo Thun, Terme di Merano - Alto Adige

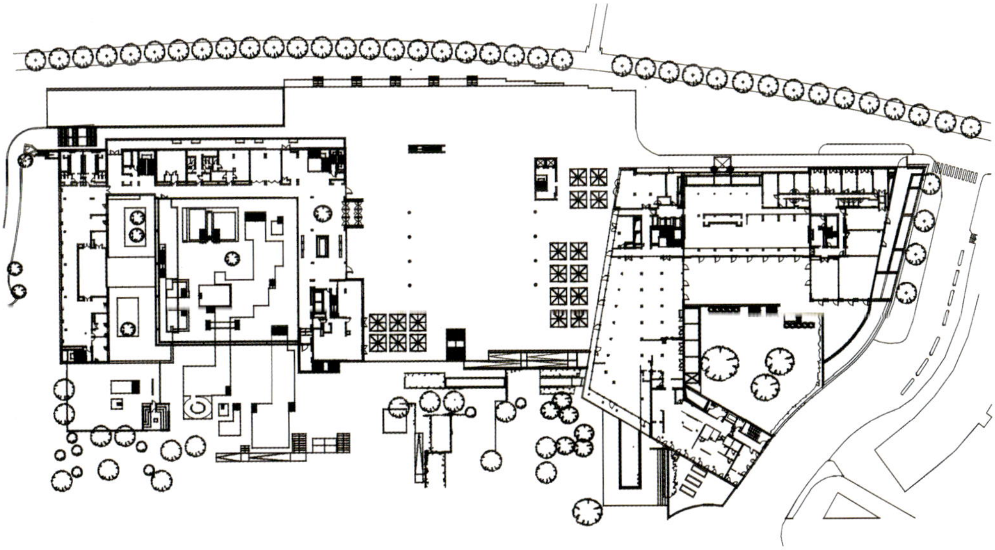

Opposite: external view
Above: internal view, pool and jacuzzi
Transparency and perpetuity within the interior and exterior of the building of the Merano hot springs, generate a sensation of physical and spatial well-being, even among the relationship between the building and the surrounding landscape.

Matteo Thun, Vertical Village Zermat - Svizzera

Matteo Thun, Panorama Residence - Austria

Alberto Cecchetto, Trentino

Landscape in a bottle
Cittadella del Vino, Mezzocorona

The Cittadella del Vino in Mezzocorona, with its cellars for wine storage and bottling, offices, shop, auditorium and display space is the largest wine-making complex in Europe.
Occupying 12 hectares, its 500-meter long frontage creates a glass and aluminium embankment that runs through the Adige River Valley. The project, devoid of any monumental rhetoric, demonstrates how it is possible to construct a large industrial complex that is in symbiosis with its surrounding landscape.
Built in three phases, at a total cost of 84.400.000 Euro, the citadel is not only a site for the production and sale of wine, but also a programme for contemporary architecture.
An industrial area, which once violated and polluted the environment, can be transformed into a site that is in harmony with the surrounding territory and landscape. A mono-functional building for a specialised activity can become a building complex where the activities of production are joined with those of free-time, exhibits, cultural events and conferences. A new, complex urban reality.
A qualitative architectural project, capable of receiving numerous awards and mentions and being presented in international architectural exhibits can attract interest and consensus and be completed at industrial prices.

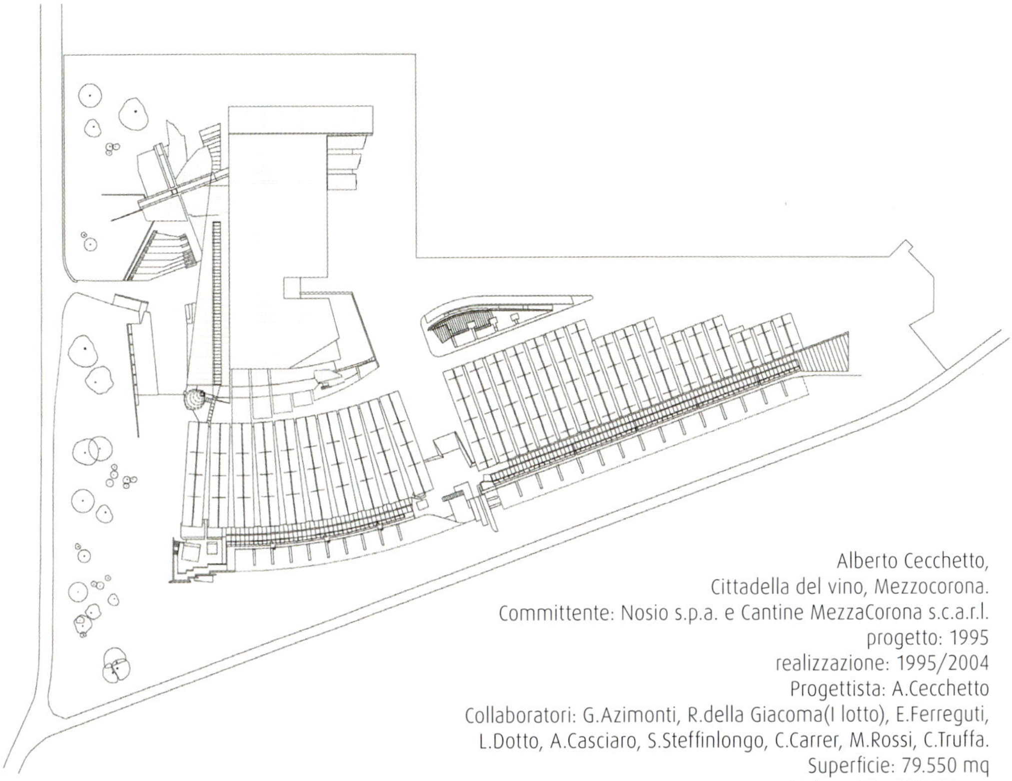

Alberto Cecchetto,
Cittadella del vino, Mezzocorona.
Committente: Nosio s.p.a. e Cantine MezzaCorona s.c.a.r.l.
progetto: 1995
realizzazione: 1995/2004
Progettista: A.Cecchetto
Collaboratori: G.Azimonti, R.della Giacoma(I lotto), E.Ferreguti,
L.Dotto, A.Casciaro, S.Steffinlongo, C.Carrer, M.Rossi, C.Truffa.
Superficie: 79.550 mq
Volumetria: 814.100 mc

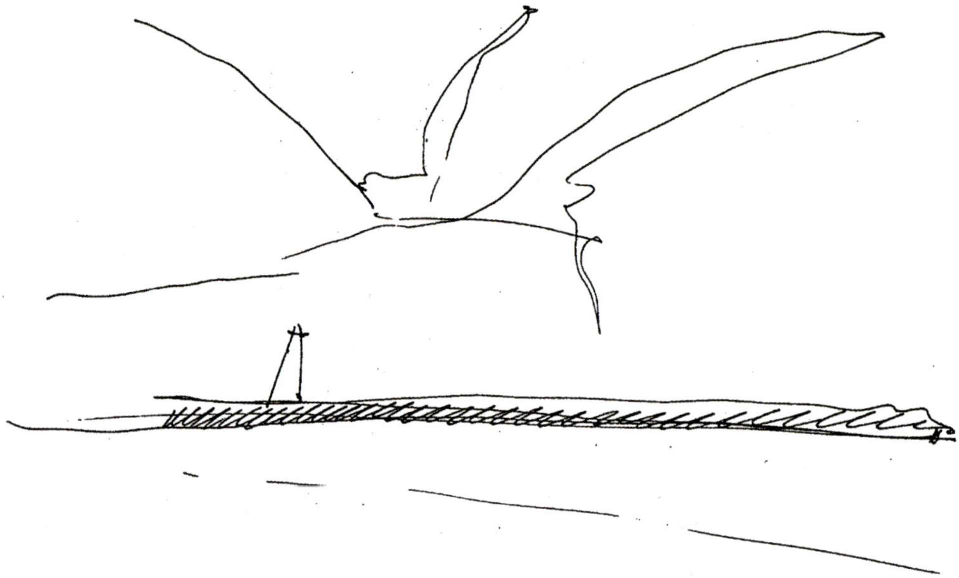

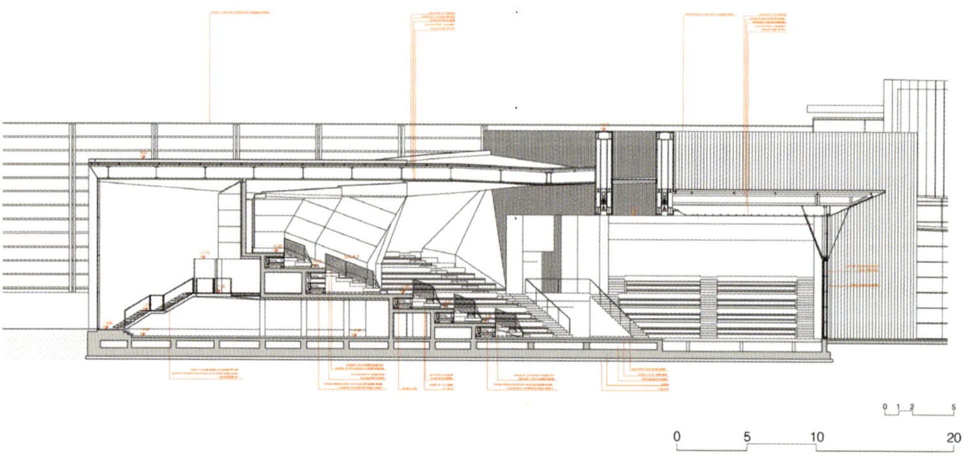
0 1 2 5
0 5 10 20

A virtual blade in the park
Cultural Centre and Auditorium, Arco

At the edge of the historical centre, parks, public facilities and 19th-century buildings immersed in nature testify to the creation of Arco, the city of well-being. Of particular note are two Liberty style villas, with a beautiful private garden. Abandoned for years, they are now home to the city's new cultural and social centre. The project assumes the natural system as the matrix of the site. The new auditorium is conceived of as part of the park. An artificial hill covers the 500-seat auditorium and is surmounted by a blade of glass, a path through the museum, and a the connections to the new social centre, located in the two villas. Images and films are projected on the glazed surfaces of the blade in order to communicate and dialogue with the citizens who use the park. The new auditorium will become a virtual backdrop that completes and valorises the city's park.

Centro culturale e auditorium, Arco.
Committente: iniziative Urbane spa
Progetto:2005/2007
Progetto: A. Cecchetto
Collaboratori:G. Azimonti, E. Friselle, S. Antonello, A. Grossi, F. Gambarotto.
Superficie totale: 3.000mq. superficie Auditorium: 1.200mq. Superficie Edifici Ristrutturati: 1.800mq.
Capienza Auditorium: 450 persone

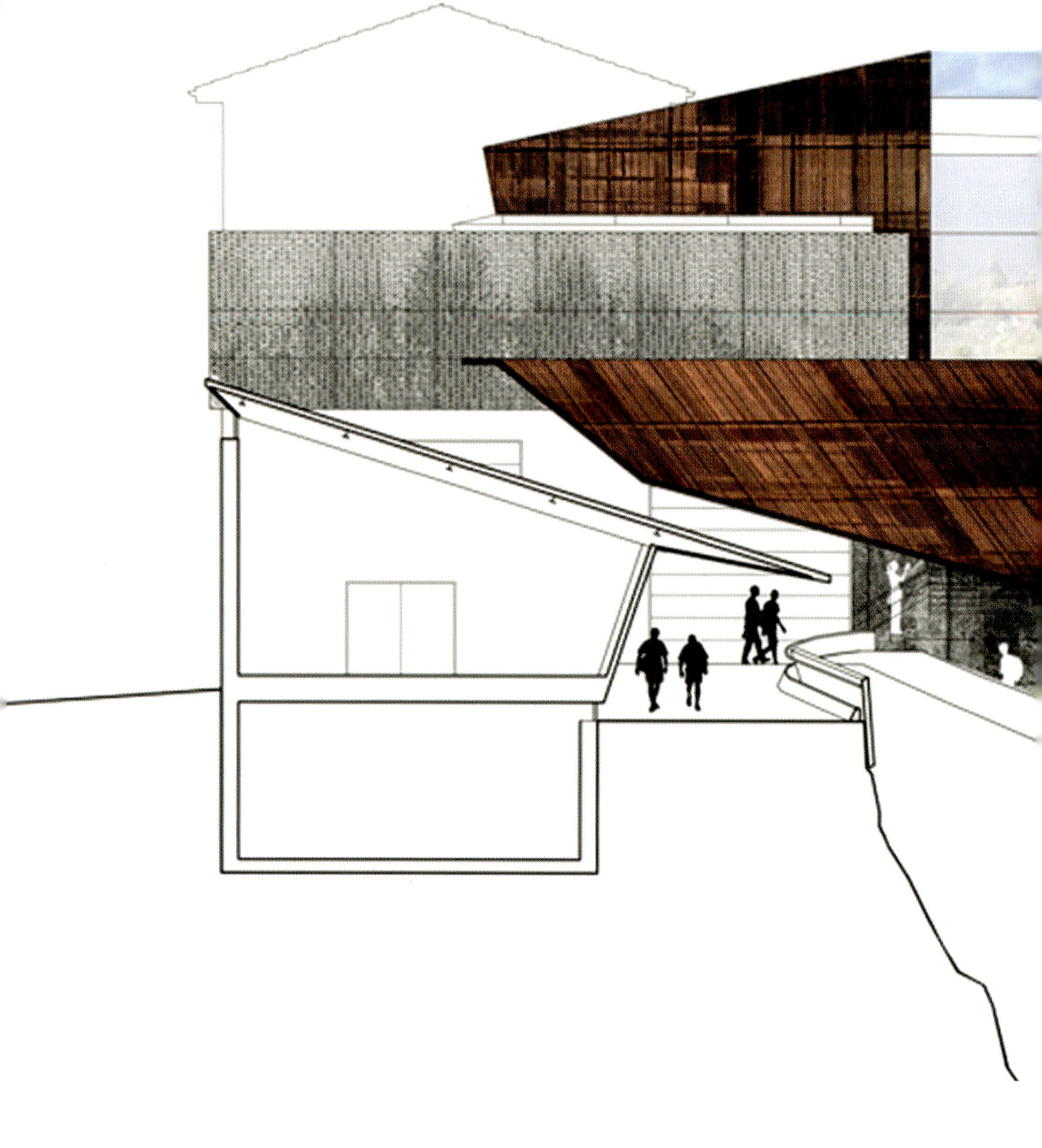

A green copper hill
Cantine Serre, Miane

A hilly landscape encloses vines of highly quality prosecco grapes. We were asked to design a large, new winery to be located at the top of the hill, dominating a landscape of great beauty. The project uses the existing contour lines, the form of the hill and the variable slope of the hillsides as a compositional matrix for the new building. The work area, with its large steel reservoirs, the storage area, the warehouse, the visitor's path, the tasting area and all of the other areas that make up the winery are enclosed by large "green copper" sails, creating a new "artificial ridge" that substitutes the existing one.

Cantina Serre, Miane
Committente: Azienda Serre
Progetto: 2004-2006
Progetto: Alberto Cecchetto
Collaboratori:
G. Azimonti, E. Friselle, A. Grossi
Superficie: 3.700 mq

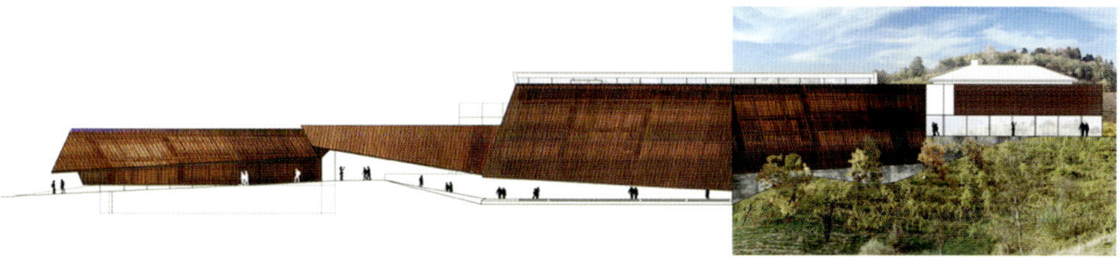

Arturo Montanelli, Lecco
Dwelling the alpine lake landscape

Stone house, Fiumelatte area, Varenna (LC)

The idea of creating a compact architecture comes from a double objective: on one hand the respect for the environment restraining the building's connection to the ground, and on the other hand the respect for the panoramic views of the lake, not disturbing them.
The perfect shapes and morphology of the architecture with their simple and linear geometry, are harmonically inserted into a flourishing natural context thanks to the use and combination of different materials, such as the local stone, wood, steel, glass all put together and mixed to obtain the right balance of colours and perceptions.
The glass gutter that runs along the perimeter of the house becomes an element of lightness and unity. The emptiness of the shapes is interrupted by transparent cuts on each side, which allow the landscape to be a virtual part of the built space, so that a never-ending reciprocal exchange can be created between the architectural and the natural reality. This exchange is evident even in the continuum of the materials such as the stone and chestnut wood covering on the floor which is the same inside and outside.
We can define it as an organic and rational architecture at the same time, appearing as a type of sustainable building concept, assuming its significance by existing in that place in harmony with its context.

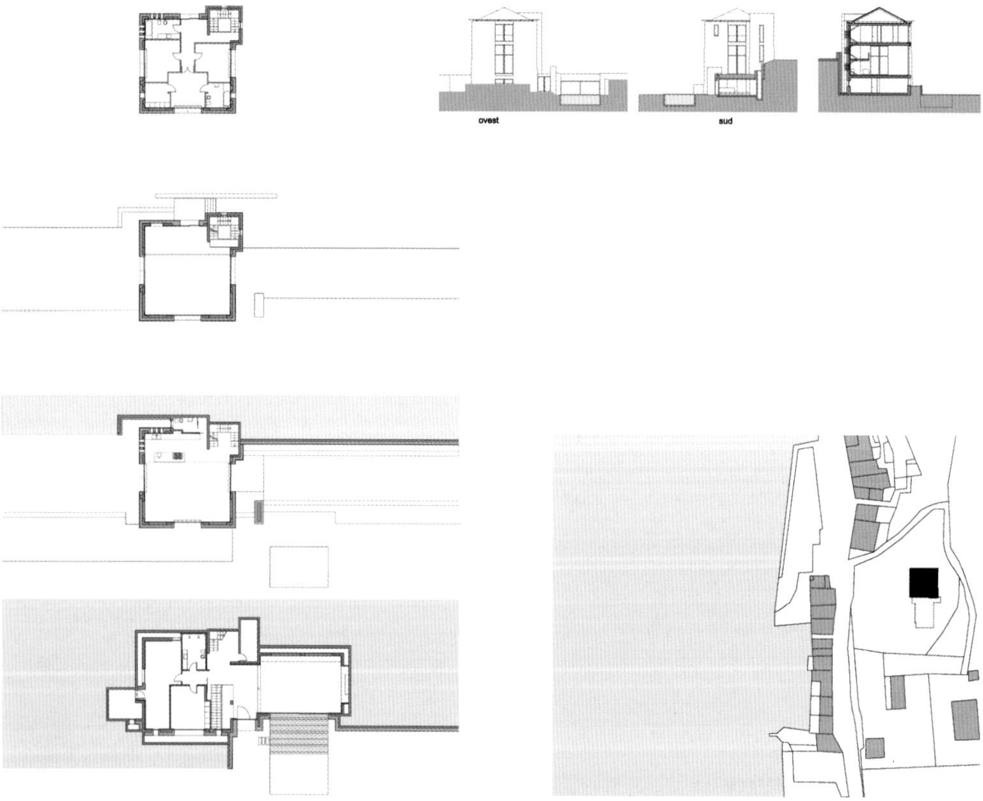

above: planimetry, plans and sections
opposite: external view - photo, Alberto Muciaccia

Internal view of the house, project by Arturo Montanelli - photo, Toni Meneguzzo

Residence Park "Sant'Andrea", Menaggio (CO)

The "Parco Sant'Andrea" is completely integrated in the landscape thanks to a morphological composition which foresees, due to the volumes, an elongated development parallel to the existing terraces, exploited as ideal plans for the positioning of the living units.

This kind of plan organization together with the prevailing horizontal lines that characterise the buildings, give the lakefront an homogeneous and precise appearance.

Glass and steel are included into the natural environment due to the objective of integrating the vegetation with the whole project. Thanks to the choice of creating roof-gardens and flat green roofs, the different volumes of the living units vanish in the global view of the hill so that an eco-friendly purpose is better pursued.

Above, opposite and following page: external views, project by Arturo Montanelli - photo, Matteo Imbriani

Group 8, Ginevra
As found, the context

Among the world's vast array of natural elements, mountainous landscapes have persistently inhabited the imagination of humanity and thus heavily influenced our endeavors. As architecture on the skin of the earth, mountains exert their force by both creating rungs on the ladder of the land and by forming labyrinthine clefts, both of which have become imbedded in our projects – they serve us by carving the matter of the earth so that it can be in greater contact with the environment, and thus more easily used as a substrate. This constant dialogue incorporated in our constructions aim to associate it within it's respective landscapes, the notion of contour and of integrating the architectural object into its location is essential to us. The location entrenches, dissolves and camouflages the constructions in a local context, as well as literally linking them into the globe.
We have always been fascinated with the elements situated outside the world of architecture, which produces a will to integrate them into our design. It can be done freely – the subject is out there, everywhere, already built. Projects conceptualized in this matter give birth to unsigned, anonymous accents to their backdrop. When we evoke the notion of "enlarging the landscape", an abstract architectural form encompassing an "integrated landscape" can also become a reality. Projects using environmental context to define the form of an architectural object result in constructions seamlessly embedded in their surroundings.
This strategy produces architectural objects that we can qualify as "picturesque". People tend to reserve this classical term for objects represented in artwork, but for us it underlines the belief that architecture and the landscape irrevocably inscribe their names upon each other. The uniqueness of these architectural designs resides in the fact that each embraces its environment, while at the same time they share a collective identity because all are adopted from elements found across the globe: vegetation, geological formations and contours in the landscape.

group8
associates architects
Geneva, Switzerland

Team

Principals
Laurent Ammeter Architect ETS
Adrien Besson Architect EPFL-SIA, ing. civil ETS
Tarramo Broennimann Architect IAUG-SIA
François de Marignac Architect EPFL
Manuel Der Hagopian Architect IAUG-AGA
Grégoire Du Pasquier Architect EPFL-SIA-AGA
Oscar Frisk Architect EPFL-ETS-SIA
Christophe Pidoux Architect EPFL
Daniel Zamarbide Architect IAUG-SIA

Associates
Christian Giussoni Architect EPFL
Grégoire Thomas Architect IAUG, ETS

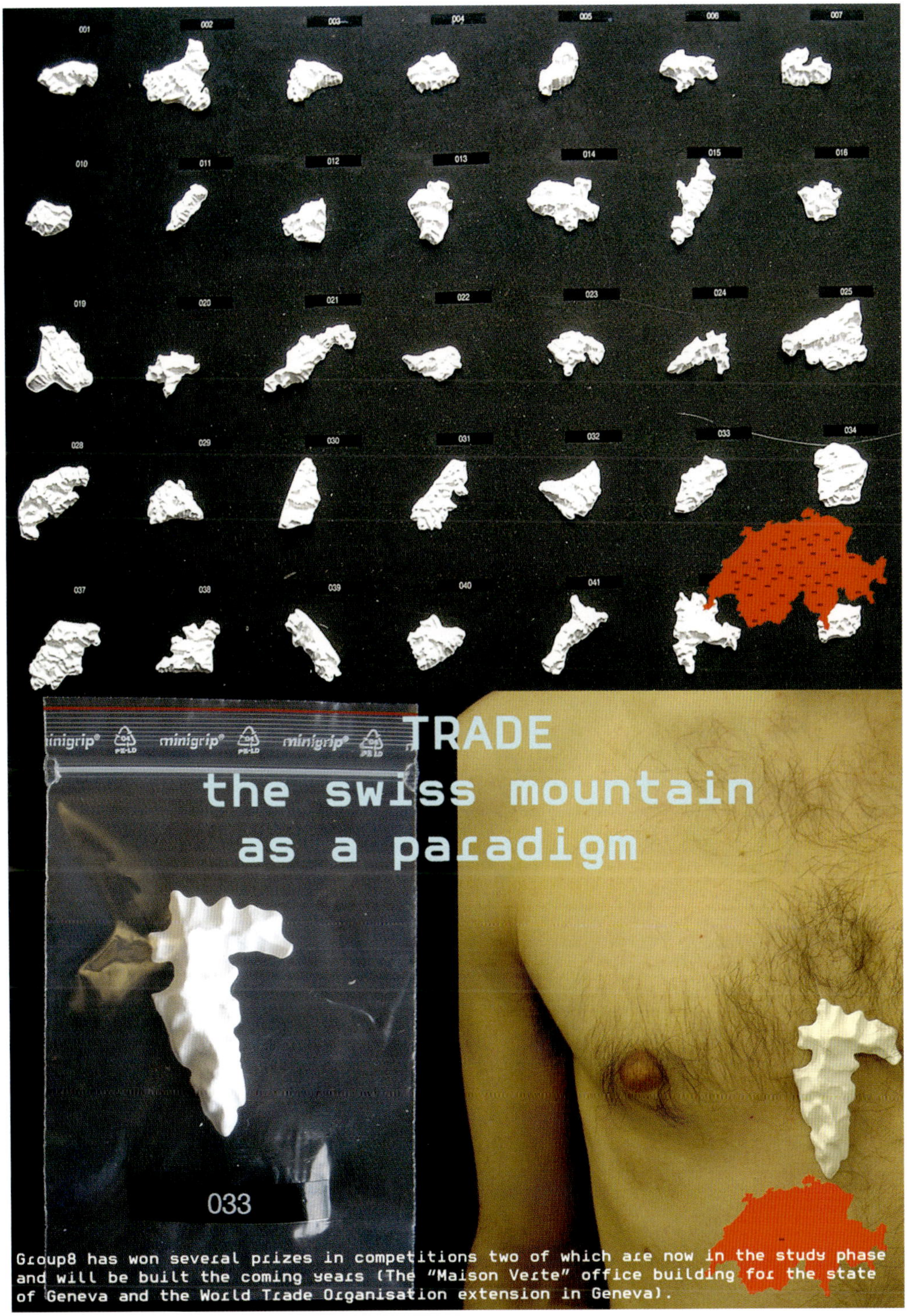

From top, an interpretation of the Swiss territory

Group8:
Villa quarter in Andermatt

Location:
Andermatt, Uri; Competition with preselection, project qualified for developpement.
Client: Orascom, Samih Sawiris
Project team:
Laurent Ammeter, Christophe Pidoux, Daniel Zamarbide, Bérengère Tobler, Thomas Sponti, Jérémy Palingle
Partner:
Guscetti & Tournier (ingeneering)
2007

Group8:
Villa quarter in Andermatt

Location:
Andermatt, Uri; Competition with preselection, project qualified for developpement.
Client: Orascom, Samih Sawiris
Project team:
Laurent Ammeter, Christophe Pidoux, Daniel Zamarbide, Bérengère Tobler, Thomas Sponti, Jérémy Palingle
Partner:
Guscetti & Tournier (ingeneering)
2007

Group8:
Swiss pavillon for the Shanghai International exposition 2010;

Location: Shanghai, Chine; 2 round competitio-2nd price. Client: Présence Suisse
Project team:
Adrien Besson, Christophe Pidoux, François de Marignac, Daniel Zamarbide, Grégoire Thomas (associated), Thomas Sponti
Partner:
Guscetti & Tournier (ingeneering)
Christian Haller (géomantic studies)
NORM, Manuel Krebs, Dimitri Brüni, Zürich (Graphic identity)
Hager AG, Zürich (Landscape architect)
2006-2007

Group8, 3 Houses complex
Location:
Crans-Près-Céligny (VD)
Project team:
Chistophe Pidoux
François De Marignac
Gregoire Du Pasquier
Gabriel Du Pasquier
Christian Giussoni
2006-2008

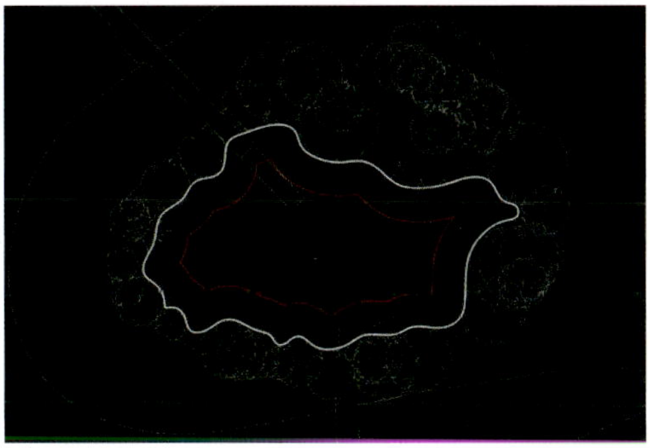

Birdcage for exotic birds in a public garden
Location:
Bois de la Bâtie, Geneve
Type of commission:
public
Client:
Ville de Genève
Project team:
Daniel Zamarbide
Grégoire Du Pasquier
Thomas Sponti
Partner:
Guscetti & Tournier,(ingeneering) Genève
2007-2008

Ebv-Estudio Barozzi-Veiga, Alto Adige
Identity and landscape

The identity of a place is always expressed through images, atmospheres and forms, that through memories we manage to recognize like fundamental elements of the place itself. Searching for those elements can reflect an architecture able to embed into the site, able to dissolve the border between the building and the site in a way that this architecture could transmit the simplicity of being in the place. Searching for those particular elements is what defines the project. Further than a simple relationship with tradition, the project looks for a different hidden geometry, that allows locating the project on the threshold of architecture and place.

Extension of Savoy School, Merano (Italia)
The presented project moves up from the research of a tonal consonance with the existent architecture, investigating this relationship with the Savoy building through the interpretation of its composing elements: mass and surface. The new mass is defined by the alignments, in plan as well as in section, with Savoy, while the surfaces are composed in a search for continuity with the façades of the existent building.
In this way, the project depends volumetrically from Savoy, establishing a tension between the two monolithic masses. The full-height glass surfaces mark punctual views of the surroundings, while externally are distributed uniformly and treated in a way that stresses the reflections. This gives to the building an isotropous aspect, like in the case of Savoy, and offers an image of an abstract, dark and noble volume that dissolves in the nature.

School, kindergarten and visitors centre, Funes (Italy)
The research for the bilateral relationship between the building and its surroundings, the artificial and the natural, brings the project to a confrontation with the landscape while a dialog is established.
On a project level this restless research expresses itself through a form able to rest in equilibrium between an abstract tension towards the landscape and the rigid nature of the insertion in the immediate environment. In this way, the project advances towards Odle mountains, in an attempt to confront them, by establishing a relationship where the scale does not work as a system of reference but through superior and abstract geometry that allows to form three emerging elements, that as iconic stones are standing and establish a dialog with the monumentality of the landscape.

Extension of the Congress Center, Davos (Switzerland)
The organic form of the presented project emerges from the wavy lines of the park and reflects the independence of its use, aiming to integrate itself into the nature and to be a new representative building.
The fluent transition from the roof to the facade accents the pureness and simplicity of the geometry of the building from all perspectives.The façade is made of metal and creates a contrast with the colors of the park. It reflects the light as a mountain lake and raises the building up from the surrounding area.
The extension amplifies not only the existing congress center, but also marks a new limit for the park, rising as a monolith in the natural landscape.

Barozzi-Veiga:
Top, two images of the Visitor Center in Funes

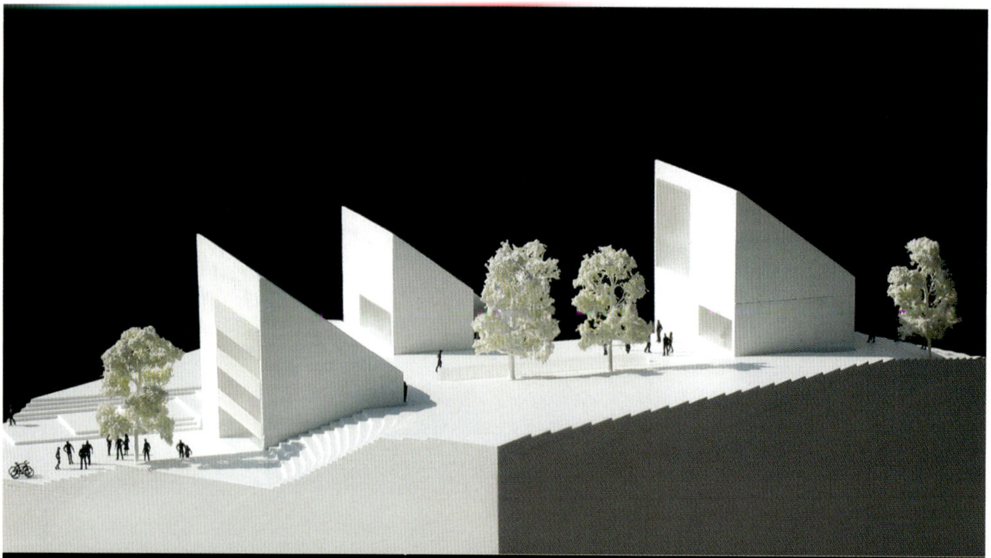

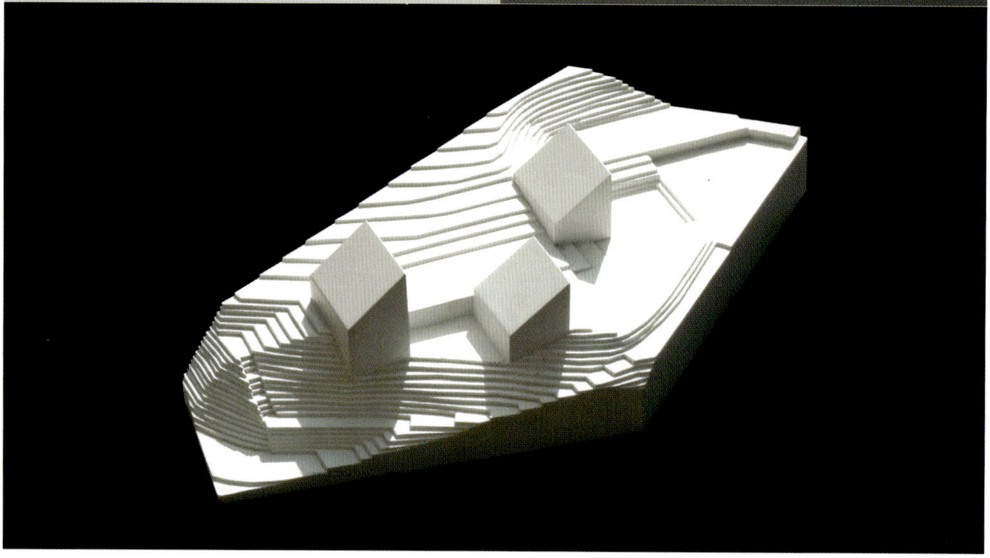

SCHNITT AA' 1:250
+13.30
+10.25
+6.85
+6.20
+5.80
+3.20
+0.00
A
A'

+15.25
SCHNITT BB' 1:250
+8.60
+6.20
+3.20
+0.00
B
B'

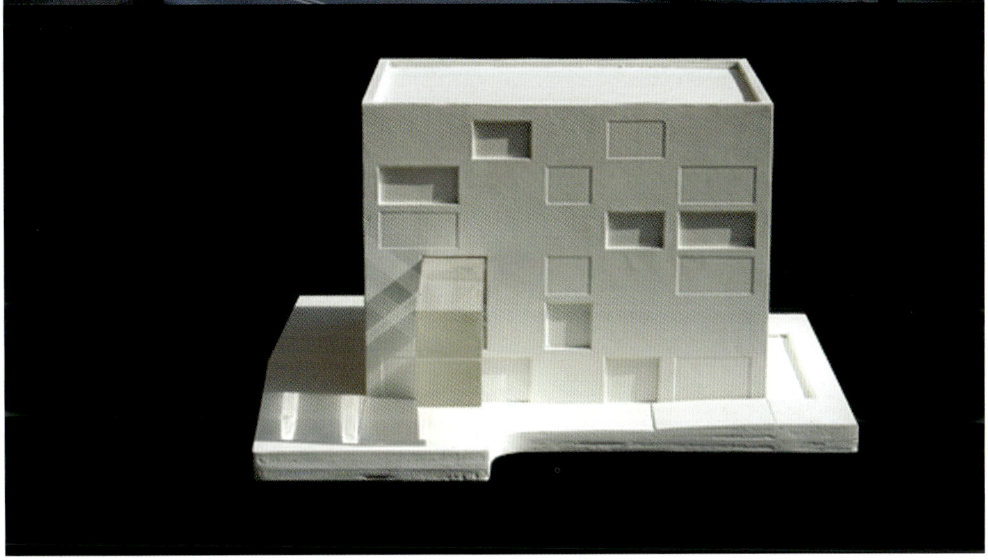

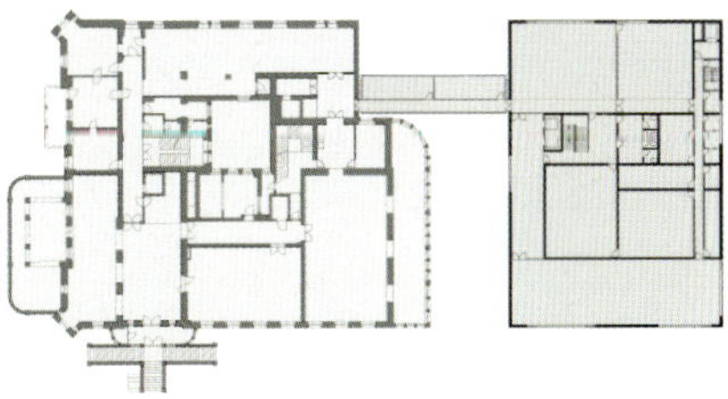

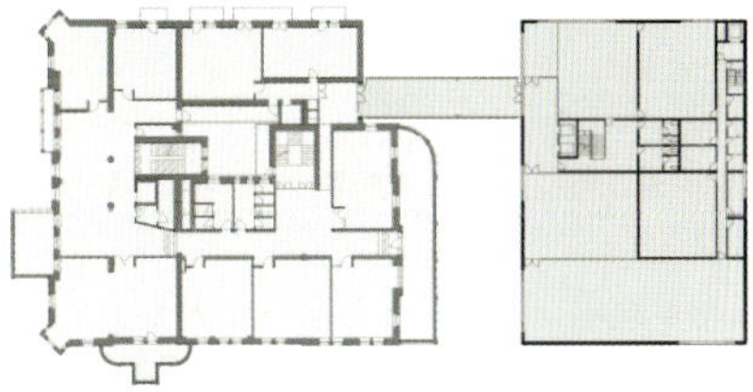

Barozzi-Veiga:
Opposite, other different views and designs of the Visitor Center in Funes;
On this page, extension of the Savoy School in Merano

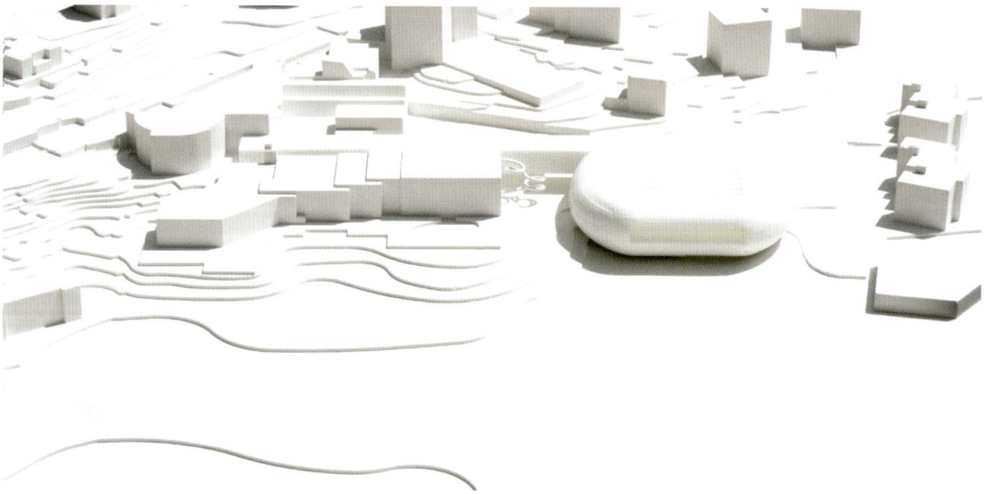

Barozzi-Veiga:
Extension of the Congress Center in Davos, Switzerland, ideas competition

Karoline Seywald, Klagenfurt
Cappella Sant'Anna

In 2006 I was given the contract to plan a chapel in the Lesachtal – situated on the Guggenberg, 1405 meters above sea level - by a builder-owner collective of three mountain farming families.

The point of departure

The Lesachtal – a high valley nestled between the Karnischen Alpen (Carnic Alps) and the Lienzer Dolomiten (Dolomite Alps) – has received several awards, e.g. an award for 'Landscape of the Year' by the International Friends of Nature in 1995. In fact, the characteristic cultural landscape can still be found in large sections, as a result of climatic and topographic factors, and above all, because of the use of very labour intensive traditional forms of cultivation. Up until the 1960's subsistence agriculture was still being practised. Man and nature were symbiotically connected and were directly dependent on each other. Rapid structural changes in both agriculture and society also led to changes in the landscape; watermills disappearing, the woods claiming back formally cultivated areas, the bio-diversity of the mountain meadows is on the decrease and numerous pseudo Tyrolean-style-architecture still exist.

Nevertheless, important impulses can be drawn from traditional knowledge, e.g. the practice of not taking more from nature than it can reproduce, thus endangering the following years' harvests; or the construction of energy-efficient and space-saving buildings, leaving more areas for cultivation. A sustainable and more careful use of natural space is also reflected in the concept of "green tourism", which has been practised by the commune since the 1980's; which means, no ski-lifts and cable cars, and the assurance of establishing a socially acceptable ratio of guest-beds to the local population, in other words, no hotel monstrosities.

Clearly, the manifestation of the valley has never been static. Every generation has modified the traditional rules, while natural phenomena have also contributed to the change process. But these processes have left their marks; a cultivated landscape gradually evolves through the sedimentation of history and provides identity to the people living in it.

(Excerpt taken from the presentation of the project)

Karoline Seywald, cappella dedicata a Sant'Anna.

The German word for church - " Kirche" - comes from the Greek word 'ekklesia', which includes not only the actual building, but also the congregation. This definition also correlates with the concept of carrying out the project as a collaborative one; a project for the community through the community.

In July 2007 the new St. Anna Chapel on the Guggenberg was inaugurated. The fundamental concept was to carry out the construction of a church as a collaborative project. As the entire village took part in the building of the church, a construction of solid plaster and a timber rafter roof were chosen. The Larch timber was felled in the surrounding woods of the Guggenberg, the marble used for the floor and the altar came from Gummern in Upper Carinthia.

Riegler & Riewe
Innsbruck Main Railway Station

The existing main railway station was completely removed and constructed anew some 6 m further east. In moving it, the narrow station forecourt (Südtiroler Platz) was widened – to the benefit of functional facilities on the forecourt. The main functions and transport areas of the new station concourse are now in the basement. Due to this, there is now direct access to the tunnels connecting the platforms and to the underground car park built under Südtiroler Platz. Owing to the lowered main area, there is now a view of the platforms from Südtiroler Platz; thus the station, which stands alone, and the happenings in it have been placed in the context of the city structure. There is access to the station concourse from Südtiroler Platz by way of the ground floor and from the underground car park by way of the basement. It is clearly arranged and light. Generously sized escalators carry users and visitors to the ÖBB (Austrian railways) service facilities, such as the travel centre and waiting area in the basement. The frescos by Max Weiler were removed by restorers, stored during building work, and repositioned in a prominent place in the new concourse. A business zone on two levels has been built joining the station concourse and laid out in the form of a mall; eating facilities have also been established in the mall. The upper storeys adjacent to the station concourse are reserved for the ÖBB and are being used as offices. The entire station building is enveloped in a concrete lattice structure with lines of casement windows. The concrete is a brown-red colour. The access areas are weather protected by a surrounding canopy. An almost unique opportunity was taken in Innsbruck to build an entire station completely from scratch; something that will definitely contribute to boosting the city's image. The happenings on the platforms can be seen from the city side, and at the same time the station is effective as an urban space. The station, which lies in a transitional space, is transparent but not dematerialised; open and yet space-occupying at the same time. It creates spatial sequences and also combines them. The station has been designed as an independent building in the context of the city. Due to this positioning, the historic clock tower to the south is in alignment. Its concise design allows it to articulate its independence over the much higher building developments bordering on the station forecourt. The building is 180 m long and 12.5 m high; the actual interior of the station concourse measures 104 m x 11 m. Making the level 4.5 m deeper allowed the station concourse to be designed to a height of 15.5 m. Essential station facilities are on the lower level, and at the same time the newly built underground car park under the station forecourt is connected to the platforms by means of underground access ways. By making the level of the concourse deeper, the aimed at transparency could be achieved and guaranteed, since this enabled construction of buildings on the level of the square to be avoided. The conciseness shown by the draft refers not only to the outer design but also to the interior, and especially to the station concourse itself. Clarity and unambiguousness in transport management as well as the impressive daylight ambience support desired customer satisfaction, which should not least contribute to improving the image of the ÖBB.

ÖBB

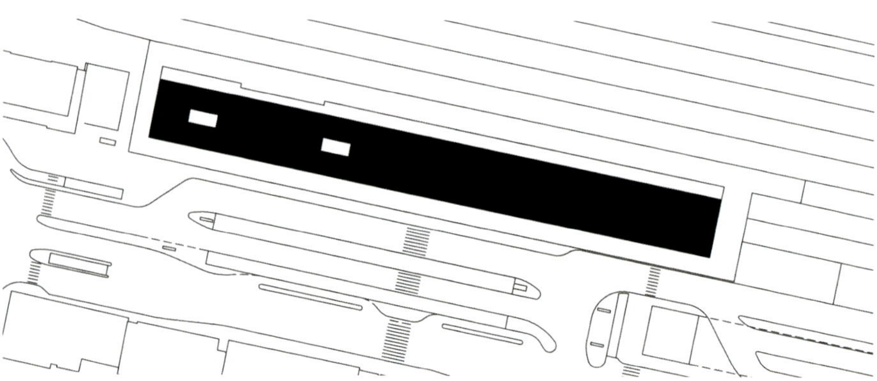

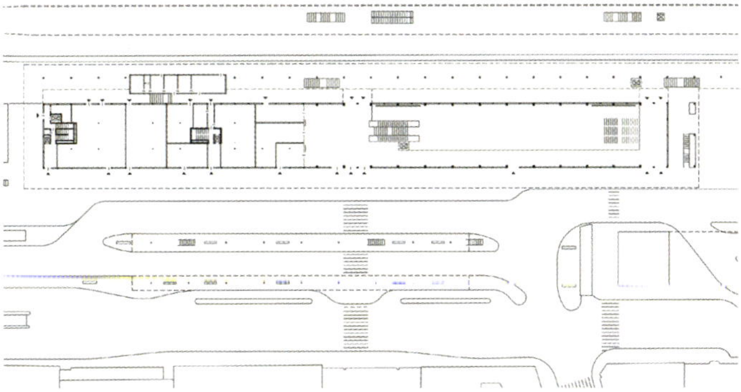

Riegler & Riewe:
view of the train shelter of
the Innsbruck Station

Paolo L. Burgi, Switzerland
The art of creating landscape

Cardada (Locarno, CH; project 1995-1999; completion 1999-2000).
This landscape intervention originates contextually at the renovation of the cableway that connects Orselina a Cardada, a location above Locarno, and constitutes a very particular declination of the infrastructure-landscape relation. It is an operation that enables the infrastructure to become a real opportunity to "renovate" the mountain, both in terms of project and in terms of definition. The landscape is infact redeveloped in its most profound cultural aspect, including all the historic horizons of the place, and at the same time interpreted by a contemporary sensibility that can remove that consumed and decorative image that derives from an experience distracted by the places. But the new cableway is not the only infrastructure of this place: a series of small and significant operations diffused in the landscape constute the real "bone structure" of the renovation of the entire zone, creating new points of interest and incite the attention towards the natural particularities of Cardada. A flying bridge of steel and titanium zinc, suspended over the panorama of Lake Maggiore (landscape promontory) and a cement disc, that "sections" the rocks of Cimetta's peak at 1670 m. of altitude (geologic observatory), constitute the coming episodes of this extensive task, sensible and innovative, that treats the entire mountain with the same attention that is usually only given to the urban centers.

Loredana Ponticelli Trento
In "New Infrastructure for New Landscapes", Skira publisher, Milan

On this page and the following, images of the observatory at Cardada, Switzerland, project by Paolo L. Burgi

Architecture in the Alps, a short overwiev

by Luca Zecchin

Sopra:
Romegialli Gianmatteo, Morbegno Roberto, Casa alpina delle guide, Valmasino, Italia, 1999
nella pagina a lato, in senso orario:
Ruch Hans-Jîrg, Spirig Toni, interno del Rifugio Tschierva, Engadina, Svizzera, 2003
veduta esterna del Rifugio Tschierva, Engadina
Luger & Maul, Bagni di Attaersee, Lago di Attersee, Austria, 2002

On the previous page, clockwise from top:
Zaha Hadid, Bergisel Ski Jump, Austria
Wissounig Dietger, nursing home, Steinfeld-Carinzia-Austria, 2005
Dietrich Untertrifaller, Bielerhîhe Hotel, Silvretta, Austria, 1992
Baserga Mozzetti Architects, expansion of the Rifugio Michela, Alpe Motterascio, Valle di Blenio, Switzerland, 2006
Zumthor Peter, Terme di Vals, Vals, Switzerland, 1996

From top:
Castelletti Marco, bathhouse, Lake Segrino, Eupilio, Como, Italy, 2004
Dietrich Untertrifaller, Hotel Wellness Congress Center, St. Anton am Arlberg, Austria, 2001

Ross Lovegrove
Alpine Capsula
Piz La Ila, Alta Val Badia (Bolzano)

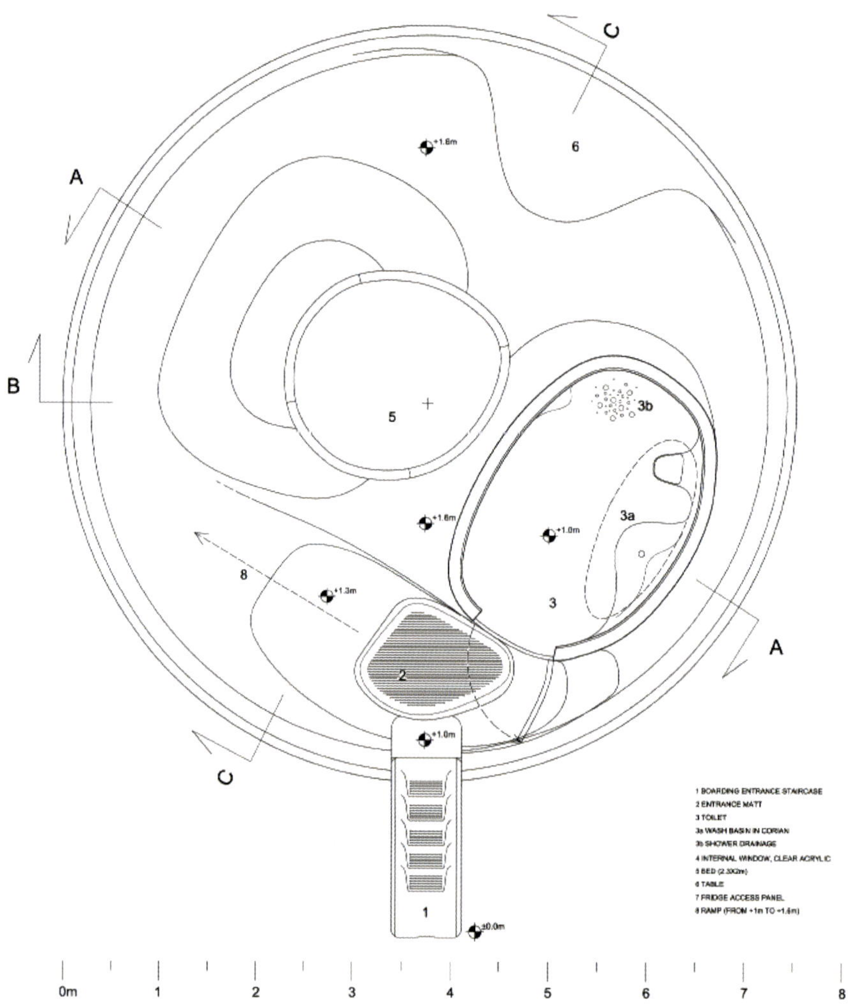

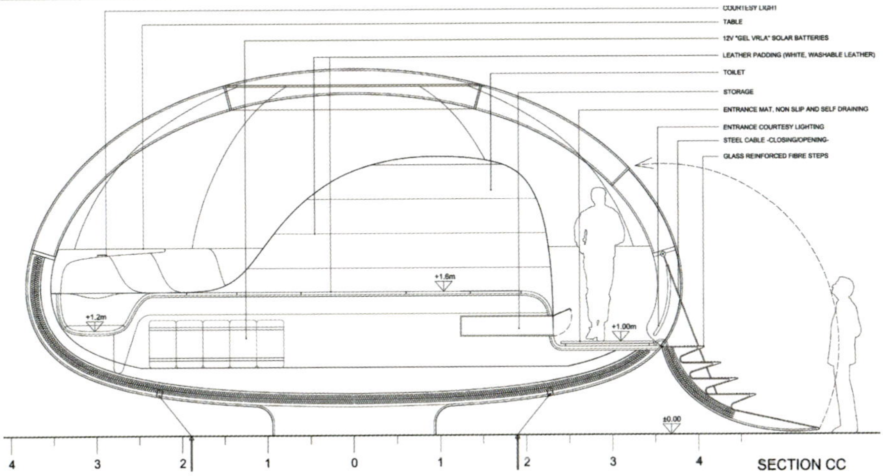

ALPINE CAPSULE STATEMENT

The Alpine capsula defines a new architetcural condition, off grid and harmonic with the nature. It expands the potential of modern life, its comforts its tecnhological connect and its vision, away form cities and into the realm of landscape and "Open Space".Open Space/open Mind"; the realization that being out in nature but super connected to cultural portals and the information age connected to cultural portals and the information age can bring you both health and Imagination to people in a very sensual way.The capsule is in fact a sanctuary of peace and tranquility, a placet o think and wonder in awe of the changing nature of nature...Its colours its textures...the experiences of day and night seasons and the infinity of the cosmos. The projects is a prototype for a new way of living off grid even as a temporary experience, a new ambition for the 21ST Century that can be implanted in so many environments. Its tests principles of dematerialization, invisibility, visibility, and life support systems imported from space but blended with terresrial comforts. Made from advanced techonolgies that support the magic of a pure water droplet that landed as a spaceship, form another world to help us feel and breath in another condition the beauty of expansive space and intellectually tranquility.
Ross Lovegrove....2008

Dati di progetto-luogo: Piz La Ila, 2100m, Alta Badia, Italy
Cliente: Moritz Craffonara-Club Moritzino, Piz la Ila, Alta Badia, Italy www.Moritzino.It
design/concept: Ross Lovegrove Studio

ALPINE CAPSULE/EXTERIOR

The concept proposal for Alpine Capsule follows two synergistic design directions: the Capsule and the Power-Plants, as remote devices providing renewable energy to the Capsule itself. The Alpine Capsule is in principle a compact, self-sufficient living unit, defined by an external envelope containing an internal "soft" landscape, technical components,
such as solar batteries, water tanks and a bathroom

ALPINE CAPSULE/INTERIOR

The Alpine Capsule wants to offer a new approach to experience the Dolomites while connecting with nature in such a fashion that no other architecture can offer at the moment. The interior needs to support this vision and approach to nature, creating a space which is intimate and yet permeable to the outside environment. Inside the capsule, a wellbeing space is generated where contemplation and mediation are enhanced by the physicality and tactility of the space and materials. The Capsule provides a high standard of accommodation for two people, defining two main areas: living/sleeping/contemplation and a separate bathroom, with exceptional views over the mountains.

ALPINE CAPSULE/INTERIOR

Nigth and day wiev of the bathroom

Credits

comunication for the first edition ALPS

BIENNALE ALPS-BIENNALE DEI PAESAGGI ALPINI E MONTANI- GIUGNO 2008- PROMOSSA DA:

UNIVERSITÀ DEGLI STUDI DI TRENTO

FACOLTA' DI INGEGNERIA
CORSO DI LAUREA EDILE-ARCHITETTURA

CON IL SUPPORTO

PROVINCIA AUTONOMA DI TRENTO
ASSESSORATO URBANISTICA

COMUNE DI TRENTO

COMUNE DI ROVERETO

PARTNER

PROVINCIA AUTONOMA DI BOLZANO
RIPARTIZIONE PAESAGGIO

CassaCentraleBanca
Credito Cooperativo del Nord Est

COMUNE DI BORGO VALSUGANA

COMUNE DI RIVA DEL GARDA

E LA COLLABORAZIONE DI

casaCittà

Ordine degli Architetti Pianificatori Paesaggisti e Conservatori

Ordine degli Ingegneri della provincia di Trento

CIPRA

EIM Ente Italiano Montagna

MaR

FILMWORK

List

ALPS Alpine Landscapes Projects Sustainability
Promoted by: Università degli Studi di Trento Facoltà di Ingegneria/Corso di Laurea Ingegneria Edile Architettura, con il sostegno e la collaborazione della Provincia Autonoma di Trento, Assessorato Urbanistica e dei comuni di: Trento, Rovereto, Riva del Garda, Borgo Valsugana, la partecipazione di rappresentanti di: Provincia Autonoma di Bolzano, Regione Autonoma del Friuli V.G., Regione Autonoma Val d'Aosta, Regione Veneto, Regione Lombardia, Regione Piemonte, Regione Liguria, EIMEnte Italiano Montagna/CIPRA, e di docenti e ricercatori delle Università: Libera Università di Bolzano, Facoltà di Architettura-Venezia, Facoltà di Architettura-Trieste, Facoltà di Architettura-Genova, Facoltà di Architettura-Sassari, Facoltà di Architet tura-Pescara, Politecnico di Torino, Fundacion Politecnica de Catalugna/Barcellona, EPF-Losanna, Università Alpe Adria, Facoltà di Architettura-Innsbruck; Ordine degli Architetti PPC di Trento, Ordine degli Architetti PPC di Bolzano, Ordine degli Ingegneri di Trento;
SIU-Società Italiana Urbanisti; INU Trentino-Alto Adige
With the collaboration: MARTMuseo d'Arte Moderna e Contem poranea di Rovereto e del Trentino.
Trento-Rovereto: 20/21 giugno 2008

Scientific Board and Committment:
Marco Tubino, Preside Facoltà Ingegneria, Giorgio Cacciague rra, Presidente Corso di Laurea Edile Architettura, Corrado Diamantini, Presidente Corso di Laurea Ing. Ambiente e Te rritorio, Pino Scaglione, Professore di Progettazione Urbana, Mauro Gilmozzi, Assessore all'Urbanistica Provincia A. di Trento, Alberto Pacher, Sindaco di Trento, Guglielmo Valduga, Sindaco di Rovereto, Claudio Molinari, Sindaco di Riva del Garda, Laura Froner, Sindaco di Borgo Valsugana, Alessandro Andreatta, Assessore all'Urbanistica Comune di Trento, Mauri zio Tomazzoni, Assessore all'Urbanistica Comune di Rovereto, Gabriella Belli, direttrice Mart.

Organization:
Corso di Laurea Ingegneria Edile-Architettura/Facoltà di In gegneria, Università di Trento; TALL/Trentino Advanced Land scape Lab; collaborazione per l'organizzazione e gli eventi editoriali, la comunicazione: List/Laboratorio Internazionale Editoriale/Barcellona-Trento

Scientific direction and curator: Prof. Arch. Pino Scaglione

Relations, matters and exhibition web site:
Arch. Thomas Demetz, Arch. Alessandro Franceschini.

Thanks to:
dott.ssa Elisabetta Nones, ufficio Stampa Università di Trento, Dott. Fabio Scalet, Dott. P.Giorgio Mattei, Arch. Furio Sembianti, Provincia Autonoma di Trento, componenti ufficio del PUP, Assessorato Urbanistica, PAT; Arch. Roland Della Giacoma, Provincia Autonoma di Bolzano, Ripartizione Paesag gio; Gabriella Belli, Flavia Fossa Margutti, Clementina Rizzi, Claudio Merz, MART;Arch. Marco Malossini, Rubner, Josef Innerhofer, Studio Thun, Studio Olgiati, Studio EBV, Studio Montanelli, Group8, Studio Burgi, Studio Lovegrove, Andrea Morgante, Riegler&Riewe, Karoine Seywald, tutti i docenti delle Università partecipanti, la Film Work e il regista Andrea Andreotti, Alberto Clementi, Alberto Cecchetto,Franco Fari nelli, Manuel Gausa, Mosè Ricci, Matteo Thun, Greta Brugnoli, Laura Cantarella, Massimiliano Scaglione e Simone Iovacchini, e tutti coloro che hanno contribuito alla riuscita della Biennale e del presente volume. Un ringraziamento particolare al Prof. Giorgio Cacciaguerra, Presidente del Corso di Ingegneria Edile-Architettura

Publishing by
LISt Laboratorio
Internazionale Editoriale
Barcelona (Spain)
www.listlab.eu
www.momboo.net
(in Italy: Trento-Roma)
Production

Actar D
Roca i Batlle 2
E-08023 Barcelona
T +34 93 417 4993
F +34 93 418 6707
office@actar-d.com
www.actar-d.com
Sales Promotion and International Distribution

Edited and coordinated by:
Pino Scaglione

Editorial Collaboration:
Alessandro Franceschini
(Section plan and program)
Thomas Demetz
(Architecture and alpine projects)

Graphic Design
Simone Iovacchini

Art Direction
Massimiliano Scaglione

Translations
Paz Gutierrez, e autori dei testi

ISBN 978-88-95623-27-6

Printed and bound
In the European Union, 2009
Printing: - Printer Trento

Printed with the contribution by:
Provincia Autonoma di Trento, Assessorato Urbanistica; Comune di Rovereto;

List is an editorial workshop, set in Barcelona, works on the contemporary issues. List not only publishes, but also researches, proposes, endeawour, promotes, produces, creates networks

cover: Alpine Capsula, Ross Lovegrove